Dedication

This book is dedicated to the memory of my beloved mother, Inez, and to all souls with a creative inner child, an adventuresome spirit, and the desire to create.

About the Author

Doug Sahlin is an author, digital artist and Web site designer living in Central Florida. He is the author of Carrara 1 Bible and Carrara 1 For Dummies. He has developed and written an on-line Flash 4 course and is an on-line Flash 4 tutor for Digital-Think. Doug's articles and tutorials have appeared in numerous national publications and Internet sites devoted to 3D and Web graphics.

Contents

Flash 5

Virtual Classroom

Doug Sahlin

Osborne/**McGraw-Hill**

Berkeley   New York   St. Louis   San Francisco
Auckland   Bogota   Hamburg   London   Madrid
Mexico City   Milan   Montreal   New Delhi
Panama City   Paris   Sao Paulo   Singapore
Sydney   Tokyo   Toronto

Osborne/**McGraw-Hill**
2600 Tenth Street
Berkeley, California 94710
U.S.A.

For information on translations or book distributors outside the U.S.A., or to arrange bulk purchase discounts for sales promotions, premiums, or fund-raisers, please contact Osborne/McGraw-Hill at the above address.

Flash 5 Virtual Classroom

Brainsville.com™
The better way to learn.™

1234567890 QPD QPD 01987654321
Book p/n 0-07-213099-7 and CD p/n 0-07-213100-4
parts of
ISBN 0-07-213115-2

Publisher: Brandon A. Nordin

Vice President & Associate Publisher: Scott Rogers

Editorial Director: Roger Stewart

Acquisitions Coordinator: Cindy Wathen

Project Manager: David Nash

Project Editor: Steve Johnson of Perspection, Inc.

Production Editor: Tracy Teyler of Perspection, Inc.

Technical Editor: Den Laurent

Copy Editor: Elise Bishop

Proofreader: Melinda Lankford

Indexer: Michael Brackney of Savage Indexing

Series Design: Katie Chester, Tracy Teyler

Cover Design: Ted Holladay

This book was composed with QuarkXPress™

2 Creating Graphic Objects

3 Modifying Graphic Objects

v

4 Creating Complex Graphic Objects

5 Importing Non-Flash Graphics

contents

6 Creating Reusable Graphic Symbols

7 Working With Layers

8 Creating Frame-By-Frame Animations

9 Animating Objects With Tweening

10 Creating Complex Animations

11 Creating Buttons

12 Creating Interactive Movies

13 Adding Sound to Flash Movies

14 Introduction to ActionScript

15 Publishing Your Flash Production

Acknowledgments

This book was a great deal of fun to write, thanks to the team effort that went into it. Kudos to Roger Stewart for coming up with an excellent concept, the Virtual Classroom, a revolutionary new way to present complicated information. Special thanks to Cindy Wathen for greasing the wheels and making sure the pages got to the right people at the right time. Hats off to the lovely and talented Den Laurent, Tech Editor extraordinaire. Her insightful comments helped keep me on track.

I'd also like to thank the Flash 5 team at Macromedia, first for creating an excellent product, and second for the support and information they provided during the creation of this book.

I'd like to thank Copy Editor Elise Bishop for manicuring my text into its finished form and being old enough to remember "Revolution Number 9" by the Beatles.

I'd be remiss if I didn't mention two very creative gentlemen, Bob Cowart and Daniel Newman, the brains behind Brainsville and the creative force behind the Virtual Classroom CD-ROM that accompanies this book. It was a great pleasure getting to know and work with them while filming the lessons for the CD-ROM. Special thanks to Elaine for providing the necessary materials to make me more presentable for the camera.

And last but not least, I'd like to thank the most important people in my life: my family, friends, and mentors.

Introduction

About the Flash 5 Virtual Classroom

Welcome to a new book, a new series, and an exciting new way to learn computer software. The Flash 5 Virtual Classroom differs from conventional computer books in the way the material is presented. Throughout the book, you will learn how to use Flash 5 by reading concise chapters with oversized graphics that explain how to use the software to create entertaining and visually compelling Web sites. In addition, this book comes with over an hour of Virtual Classroom lessons in which I show you how to create several finished products using the various Flash tools. The lessons aren't static slides that you click through one at a time; they're video lessons of the software in action. In one screen, you will be able to view the Flash interface, watching the action unfold as I select tools to create objects and menu commands to modify and animate them. In the other screen, you will see my smiling face, narrating the action as the lesson progresses.

My goal is to instruct each lesson as if I were showing a friend how to use Flash. Occasionally, you will notice that I look down from the camera. This was necessary to synchronize my narration with the unfolding action on my computer screen, the same action that you will see when you view each lesson. The videos were great fun to film, and I hope you will find them beneficial. I will close this section by saying I am an author and a Web site designer, not an actor. If I appear awkward at times, it's just a case of stage fright.

About Flash

Flash is the acknowledged leader in graphic software programs for Web developers who need to create visually compelling, highly interactive Web sites. Major corporations such as Ford Motor Company, Xerox, Nike, and Sprint have created Flash-based Web sites to showcase their wares and services.

The Flash Player is included with most major operating systems and is easily added to most Web browsers as a plug-in. There is a huge Internet audience with Flash-enabled browsers, which has increased the demand for Flash content on new and existing Web sites. Savvy Web designers realize Flash design capability is a must if they are to lure lucrative Web design contracts.

What's New in Flash 5

Flash 5 is a major upgrade. With Flash 5, you have sophisticated drawing tools that allow you to create items more easily, faster, and with a better degree of control than ever before. One exciting addition is the Pen tool, which gives you point-by-point control when creating vector graphics. The interface has also been changed to enhance productivity. New to Flash 5 are panels, which replace the Inspectors from previous versions of Flash. You have better control over your color selections with the Mixer and Fill panels. Also new to Flash 5 is support for the MP3 sound format.

In addition to more tools, you get more actions. In fact, the new Actions panel has so many actions that they are subdivided into groups. Experienced programmers will feel like a kid in a candy store when they peruse the new actions available in Flash. To keep track of everything in a complicated Flash production, you have the Movie Explorer, which breaks all of the elements of a Flash movie into outline form.

How to Get the Most from This Book

If you are a newcomer to Flash, I suggest that you read this book from cover to cover in linear fashion, starting with the basics in Chapter 1. If, however, you are a Flash veteran, feel free to skip around and read the material that you need to get up and running quickly with the new version of Flash. Within the book, you will find icons that present tips, notes, warnings, and useful information. There is a See Also icon that will lead you to other parts of the book containing pertinent information about the topic presented. The CD-ROM icon is your link to the Virtual Classroom CD-ROM. Whenever you see the icon, feel free to set the book down and learn by watching.

At times in the text, the style of certain Flash elements may differ slightly from the style found in the program's tooltips, for example references to names of buttons, icons, or actions. This was done for reader clarity so that the button's or icon's description wouldn't be confusing when it was presented out of context.

How to Get the Most from the Virtual Classroom CD-ROM

Each lesson is presented in RealPlayer format. Included on the CD-ROM is a version of the RealPlayer. The RealPlayer has controls that you can use to fast forward, rewind, pause, or stop the lesson, just like the VCR in your living room.

Where applicable, each Virtual Classroom lesson comes complete with the source file for the completed project. If your computer is powerful enough to multi-task, you should have Flash up and running with the source file loaded while you are viewing the lessons. You can then stop the video lesson at any time and refer to the source file to reinforce your learning. In lieu of the source file, create a new Flash document and follow along.

About the CD

The CD-ROM that comes with this book features supplementary lessons in which the author demonstrates key concepts that will help you more quickly develop proficiency in using the Flash 5 software. These unique Virtual Classroom modules combine two channels of video, allowing you to see the author speak while he uses PowerPoint slides and animated screen captures to illustrate the concepts.

 The stylized CD-ROM icon that appears in the text of the book is your cue to insert the Virtual Classroom CD to view a tutorial.

Please read the following directions carefully to ensure that the lessons play as smoothly as possible.

System Requirements

Exact system requirements are hard to specify (see below, in the Troubleshooting section for the reason why), but the ballpark minimum system requirements are as follows:

PC approximate minimum requirements
Windows 95/98/Me/NT/2000
233 MHz Pentium II
64M RAM
8X CD-ROM drive
speakers or headphones

Mac approximate minimum requirements
System 8 or greater
Real Player 8
64M Ram
PowerPC
8X CD-ROM drive
speakers or headphones

It has been noted that the Virtual Classroom presentation may slow down or freeze up on GigaHertz processors. We do not have a solution for this problem at the time of printing.

Getting Started

The enclosed CD-ROM is optimized to run under version 8 of RealPlayer from Real Networks. It will run with either Windows 95/98/Me/NT/2000 or on an Apple Macintosh. You must have RealPlayer 8 Basic or higher on your computer to run the Virtual Classroom lessons. Previous versions of RealPlayer will not work. If you don't already have RealPlayer 8 installed on your computer, you must install it, either by downloading it from the Internet at www.real.com, or by running the RealPlayer 8 Basic Setup program from the Virtual Classroom CD-ROM. RealPlayer Basic is a free download. Do not confuse it with RealPlayer Plus or Real Jukebox. RealPlayer 8 Plus will work, but the Basic version is free, whereas the RealPlayer 8 Plus is not.

To install RealPlayer 8 Basic for a PC, from the CD-ROM:

1. Insert the CD-ROM in the drive.
2. Open Windows Explorer from the Start menu or by holding down the Windows key while pressing the letter E. Alternatively, double-click My Computer on the Windows desktop to browse the contents of the CD-ROM.
3. Right-click the CD-ROM icon and select Open to view the contents of the CD-ROM.
4. Double-click the Real Player folder, and then double-click the proper sub-folder for your computer (Windows or Mac).
5. Double-click the installation program for your computer (rp8-rn8a-setup for Windows).
6. Follow the setup instructions on screen.

To install RealPlayer 8 Basic for a Mac, from the CD-ROM:

1. Insert the CD-ROM in the drive.
2. Open the drive's folder and run RM8A Installer.
3. Follow on-screen instructions for installing Real Player.

Running on Windows 95/98/Me/NT/2000

Once RealPlayer 8 Basic is installed on your computer, the Virtual Classroom program will start automatically when you insert the CD-ROM into the drive if the auto-start feature is enabled on your computer. When the opening screen appears, you may start the lessons by clicking on the cover of the book or on the word "HERE."

about the cd

If the Virtual Classroom does not start automatically, your system may not be set up to automatically detect CDs. If you don't care about the auto-start setting for your CD-ROM, and don't mind the manual approach, you can start the lessons manually, this way:

1. Insert the CD-ROM.
2. Double-click the My Computer icon on your Windows desktop (or use Windows Explorer) to view the contents of the CD-ROM .
3. Right click to Open the CD-ROM folder.
4. Double-click the jmenucd icon in the folder.
5. Follow instructions on the opening screen to start.

To set your CD-ROM drive to automatically detect CDs and start up the lessons automatically, you can make the following changes to your Windows operating system settings:

1. Choose Settings, Control Panel, and click the System icon.
2. Click the Device Manager tab in the System Properties dialog box.
3. Double-click the Disk drives icon and locate your CD-ROM drive.
4. Double-click the CD-ROM drive icon and then click the Settings tab in the CD-ROM Properties dialog box. Make sure the "Auto insert notification box" is checked. This specifies that Windows will be notified when you insert a compact disc into the drive.

Running on Mac OS

Once RealPlayer 8 Basic is installed on your computer, the Virtual Classroom can be run this way:

1. Open the CD-ROM folder.
2. Double-click on file ClickHereToStart icon. (Alternatively, you can click the Index.html icon and then click on the book image, or open the Real Player and from the Real Player window, open the ClickHereToStart file).

Viewing the Virtual Classroom Lessons

Regardless of how you launch the lessons, the RealPlayer window should open within a few seconds and the Virtual Classroom introduction should begin playing. Please listen through the introduction for an explanation of how the lessons work. (If you don't hear any sound, check your speakers and read the troubleshooting section below.) To view subsequent lessons, click the links in the lower left region of the RealPlayer window. You may view the lessons in any order you wish, but switching is not immediate. When you click a link, be patient and allow the new videos to load. This usually takes about 5 seconds, even on a fast computer.

The Real Player will completely fill a screen that is running at 800x600 resolution. (This is the minimum resolution required to play the lessons). For screens with higher resolution, you can adjust the position of the player on screen as you like.

If you are online, you can click on the Brainsville.com logo under the index marks to jump directly to the Brainsville.com web site (www.brainsville.com) for information about the additional hour of instructional material that is available from Brainsville.com.

Troubleshooting and Optimizing Performance

If you have followed the instructions above and the Virtual Classroom program will not work at all, you may have a defective drive or possibly a defective CD. Be sure the CD is inserted properly in the drive. Test the drive with other CDs, to see if they run.

Your Virtual Classroom CD-ROM employs cutting-edge technologies, requiring that your computer be pretty fast to run the lessons smoothly. Each lesson actually runs two videos at the same time-one for the instructor's image and one for the animated screenshots. Each video stream is being decompressed and rendered on the fly as you watch. Many variables determine a computer's video performance. CPU speed, internal bus speed, amount of RAM, CD-ROM drive transfer rate, video display performance, CD-ROM cache settings, and other variables will determine how well the lessons will play. You'll need at least a Pentium II-class computer running in excess of 300Mhz for best performance.

Here are some troubleshooting tips that may help optimize the performance of the Virtual Classroom CD-ROM:

Close other programs and screen savers For best performance, make sure you are not running other programs in the background while viewing the Virtual Classroom CD-ROM. Rendering the video on your screen takes a lot of computing power, and background programs such as automatic email checking, web-site updating, or Active Desktop applets (such as scrolling stock tickers) can tax the CPU to the point of slowing the videos. You should turn off screen savers, or set them to not start up until 30 minutes or so of non-use. Otherwise, the screen saver could begin while you are viewing a lesson.

Copy the files to the hard disk to speed up performance The CD-ROM drive will whir quite a bit when running the lessons from the CD. If your CD-ROM drive is a bit slow, it's possible the instructor's lips will be out of synch with his voice, as is often the case with Web-based videos. The video might freeze or slow down occasionally, though the audio will typically keep going along just fine. If you don't like the CD constantly whirring, or you are annoyed by out-of-synch video, you may be able to solve either or both problems by copying the CD-ROM's contents to

about the cd

your hard disk and running the lessons from there. To do so:

1. Using My Computer or Explorer, check to see that you have at least 650M free space on the target hard disk.

2. Create a new folder on your hard disk (the name doesn't matter) and copy all the contents of the CD-ROM to the new folder (you must preserve the subfolder names and folder organization as it is on the CD-ROM).

3. Once this is done, you can start the program by opening the new folder and double-clicking on the file **jmenucd** (for Windows users, or the **ClickHereToStart** file (for Mac users). This will automatically start the lessons and run them from the hard disk.

Adjust the screen color depth to speed up performance Synchronization problems can also be caused by running your screen with too great a color depth. Lowering the color depth to 16 bit color makes a world of difference with many computers, laptops included. Rarely do people need 24-bit or 32-bit color for their work anyway, and it makes scrolling your screen (in any program) that much slower when running in those higher color depths. To adjust your color settings:

Windows:

1. Right click on the desktop and choose Properties.

2. Click the Settings tab.

3. In the Colors section, open the drop-down list box and choose a lower setting. If you are currently running at 24-bit (True Color) color, for example, try 16-bit (High Color). Don't use 256 colors, since video will appear very funky if you do, and you'll be prompted by Real Player to increase the color depth anyway.

4. Click OK. With most computers these days, you don't have to restart the computer after making this change.

> **TIP** (Windows users) For convenience, you can create a shortcut to the jmenu.exe file and place it on your desktop. You will then be able to start the program by clicking on the shortcut.

Mac:

1. Open the Apple Menu and choose Control Panels.

2. Click on Monitors

3. A panel opens indicating your type of display.

4. On that panel click the button that says Monitor.

5. In the color depth box click the Color button and choose the number of colors—256, thousands, or millions. You'll want to choose thousands.

RealPlayer should run more smoothly now, since your computer's CPU doesn't have to work as hard to paint the video pictures on your screen.

Real Player hangs at the beginning If RealPlayer opens up in a small window and just seems to hang, wait a moment (perhaps 15 seconds), and it will sometimes start up. If not, you may have to restart the computer to get RealPlayer to start properly again.

The screen movie in a lesson hangs If the author continues to talk, but the accompanying animated screen shots of Flash seem to be stuck, just click on the lesson index in the lower left region of the RealPlayer window and wait a few seconds. The specific lesson should begin playing again. If this doesn't help, close the RealPlayer window, and restart the Virtual Classroom CD. If this happens again, try restarting your computer and starting then restart the CD.

Real Player hangs or crashes and Windows shuts it down RealPlayer from time to time may hang or not perform properly. In some cases, Windows will terminate the RealPlayer, and report that the player has gone awry. This appears to be a RealPlayer problem, and has been noted most often with Windows 2000. We haven't been able to determine the cause for this, but it's often solved by rebooting the computer and starting the lessons again. Copying the CD-ROM files to the hard disk may help. If that doesn't help, try uninstalling RealPlayer and reinstalling it or contacting Real Networks via their web site www.real.com .

For additional technical support or replacement of a defective CD, call Hudson Software at (800) 217-0059. Real Networks is not affiliated with Osborne/McGraw-Hill or Brainsville.com and does not provide support for the Virtual Classroom modules.

Fun Outtakes

If you need a break and want to have some fun, open the CD folder in Explorer or the Mac finder and double-click the file on the CD called outtakes.rm. You'll see some wacky stuff that didn't make it into the lessons!

Getting to Know Flash 5

When you launch Flash 5 for the first time, you may be tempted to dive right in and start creating objects for a movie, especially if you have used Flash before. While the fundamental program is the same, Flash 5 offers many new features that enhance usability and make it possible to speed up your workflow and to create movies more easily than ever before. This chapter provides an overview of how Flash works and how the various components of the interface work together to create the finished product. This chapter also gives you a solid foundation to build on when the Flash tools and components are presented in greater detail in upcoming chapters.

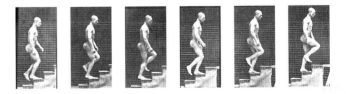

Flash Concepts

Flash began as a vector-based program that was capable of creating impressive animations for the Internet. As the program evolved, it became capable of creating full-fledged interactive Web sites with sophisticated animation and sound. Today, Flash is the recognized leader for creating compelling, high impact, low bandwidth content for the Internet at a fraction of the file size used by other media.

During a typical Flash project, you create objects on the Stage using the drawing tools, or you import objects created in other programs. To animate these objects, you change one or more of their parameters in keyframes along the Timeline. In most animations, you need to add layers to organize the various components of your production. To create an interactive movie, you add buttons and actions. You preview your movie using the Controller, a tool that functions like the remote for your VCR. After fine-tuning the animation in the authoring environment, you publish it as a .swf (pronounced Swiff) file for use on the Internet or in another format for use as part of a multi-media presentation.

Understanding Bitmap and Vector Graphics

Before you begin creating content for your productions, you need to understand the characteristics of bitmap and vector graphics. Flash's native graphic format is vector-based. Vector objects are comprised of paths, which form curves, lines, and shapes. These paths may be filled with a solid color or gradient, or they may be left unfilled to create an outline. Flash and other vector drawing programs draw vector graphics using mathematical formulas that enable them to maintain crisp detail when they are enlarged. Vector graphics are small in file size.

Bitmap graphics are comprised of pixels, dots of color that are assembled to create the final image. Bitmap graphics are resolution dependent. When a bitmap image is changed to a different size or resolution in Flash or an image-editing program, pixels must be redrawn, which inevitably results in image distortion. As a rule, bitmap images create larger files than vector graphics, with the exception of vector graphics with large areas of complex gradient fills.

When initially planning a Flash project, you need to consider which graphics format to use. If you plan to show the finished movie on the Internet, you want to keep bitmap images to an absolute minimum. If, however, you are creating the movie for a client in the fashion business, for example, bitmaps images may be the only way to accurately portray your client's wares. In this case, you can break the site into several different movies, linking them together with ActionScript. This technique will be covered in a Virtual Classroom CD-ROM lesson.

Introducing Symbols and Instances

Symbols are reusable images, animations, or buttons. When you convert a graphic object into a symbol, it is stored in the document Library. You can use a symbol an ywhere within a movie. An occurrence of a symbol is known as an instance. You can modify many parameters of an instance, such as size, tint, and opacity. However, the symbol's basic shape remains constant with every instance.

The judicious use of symbols greatly reduces the file size of a movie. No matter how often you use a symbol in a movie, once the movie is published, the Flash player needs to download a symbol only once and then redraw it wherever an instance of it occurs along the Timeline. Symbols also reduce editing time. When you edit a symbol, Flash updates all instances of it to reflect the change.

Creating a Flash Document

When you initially launch Flash, the program creates a blank document with the default movie size and background color. However, sometimes you will need to create a new document.

 To learn more about the Flash interface, watch The Flash Interface lesson on the Virtual Classroom CD-ROM.

To Create a NEW DOCUMENT

1 Choose New from the File menu.

2 Flash creates a new document.

To Open AND EDIT AN EXISTING FILE

1 Choose Open from the File menu. The Open dialog box appears.

2 Locate the desired file, and then click Open. The file opens along with the elements that you used to create it.

To Save a DOCUMENT

1 Choose Save from the File menu. The Save As dialog box appears.

2 Select a folder to save the file in.

3 Enter a name for the file in the File Name field, and then click Save.

TIP You can save a Flash document as an .fla file for future editing.

Configuring the Flash Movie

The default size for a Flash movie is 550 pixels by 400 pixels on a white background. If this size is too small or too large for your production, you can modify the default settings by using the Modify Menu command.

To Configure A FLASH MOVIE

1 Choose Movie from the Modify menu. The Movie Properties dialog box appears, as shown in Figure 1-1.

2 In the Frame Rate field, enter the desired frame rate.

3 Choose one of the following dimension options:

To specify the Stage size in pixels, enter the desired Width and Height in the Dimensions field. The minimum Stage size is 18 pixels by 18 pixels; the maximum is 2880 pixels by 2880 pixels.

To match the Stage size to the contents, click Match Contents. Flash configures the Stage with an equal border around the contents on all sides.

Click Match Printer to set the Stage size to the maximum available print area. This area is equal to the paper size minus the current margin as defined in the Page Setup dialog box (Windows) or the Print Margins dialog box (Macintosh).

4 Click the color swatch in the Background Color field. The cursor becomes an eye-dropper, and a color palette appears, as shown in Figure 1-2. Drag to select the desired color, and then release the mouse button to apply it.

continues

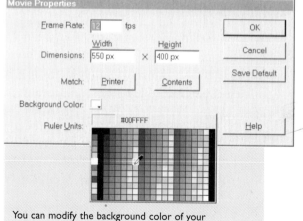

FIGURE 1-1

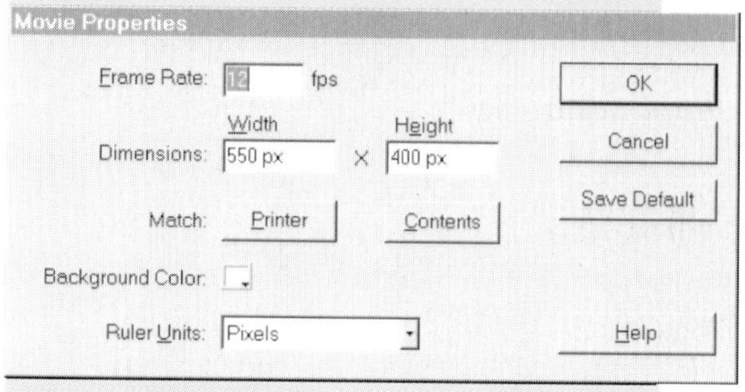

The Movie Properties dialog box lets you modify a movie's parameters.

FIGURE 1-2

You can modify the background color of your movie by selecting a color from the color palette.

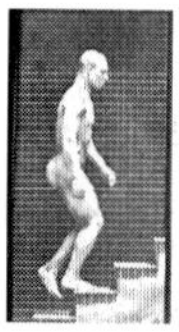

continued

5 Click the arrow to the right of the Ruler Units field. Choose a unit of measure drop from the drop-down menu.

6 Click OK to apply the new settings.

n°te A higher frame rate will ensure smoother motion, but will create a larger file size. Frame rates will be covered in detail in Chapter 8.

Using Rulers

Rulers are another useful visual aid. You can use them to place objects and to create and set up guidelines.

To Turn ON RULERS

Select Rulers from the View menu. A vertical ruler and a horizontal ruler appear at the left and top corners of the main window in the unit of measure that you specified with the Modify Movie command.

Modifying the Grid

Flash provides a grid that is useful for aligning objects. You can configure the grid to the color and dimensions of your choice. By default, the grid is turned off.

To Enable THE GRID AND ADJUST ITS SETTINGS

1 Choose Grid from the View menu, and then choose Edit. The Grid dialog box appears, as shown in Figure 1-3.

2 To set the grid color, click the swatch in the Color field to open the color palette. Click a swatch in the palette to select a color, and then release the mouse button to apply it.

3 Click the Show Grid box to make the grid visible.

4 To turn on snapping to grid points, click the Snap to Grid box. With this option enabled, objects are attracted to grid intersections as you move them across the Stage.

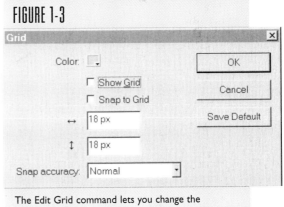

FIGURE 1-3

The Edit Grid command lets you change the properties of the grid.

continues

continued

5 Click the arrow to the right of the Snap Accuracy field, and then select an option from the drop-down menu. This setting determines how close an object must be to a grid line before it snaps to it. The actual distance varies, depending upon the grid spacing. Unless you have created a very wide grid, stay with the default setting of Normal.

Exploring the Workspace

The Flash workspace, as shown in Figure 1-4, consists of a large rectangular area called the Stage, which is bordered on the top by the Timeline. It may help you to visualize the Flash Stage as a movie set with you as the director. You direct where on the Stage to place the objects that you create, and you put them into motion using the Timeline. In its default layout, four floating panels appear on the right side of the workspace. You use panels to modify the parameters of elements in your movie. Each panel is comprised of tabs that, when clicked, open up a different set of commands or options. To the left of the Stage is a floating Toolbox. You use the Toolbox tools to create objects, select objects, modify objects, and change the view of the Stage.

FIGURE 1-4

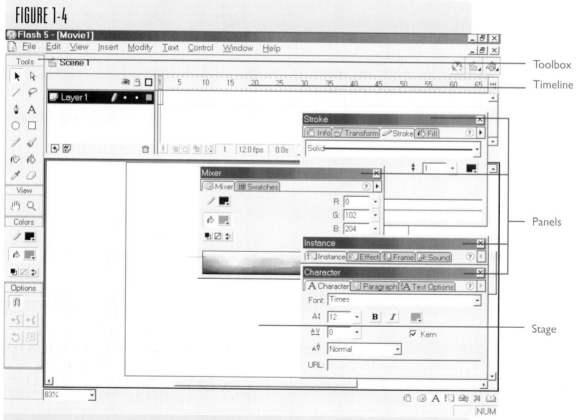

The workspace consists of four major areas: the Stage, the Timeline, the Panels, and the Toolbox.

chapter 1: getting to know Flash 5

Introducing the Timeline

The Timeline appears in the large window directly above the Stage. The major components of the Timeline, shown in Figure 1-5, are frames, layers, and the playhead. You organize the content of a movie in frames and layers. You animate objects in your movie by changing their attributes along the Timeline. You create major changes in keyframes. When you drag the playhead across a keyframe, action occurs. Each layer has its own Timeline and is noted in a column on the left side of the Timeline window. At the top of the window is the Timeline Header, which indicates individual frame numbers. You can navigate the Timeline by clicking the playhead and dragging it to the desired frame. The Timeline Status Display, located at the bottom of the Timeline, indicates the current position of the playhead, the selected frame rate, and the elapsed time to the current frame.

FIGURE 1-5

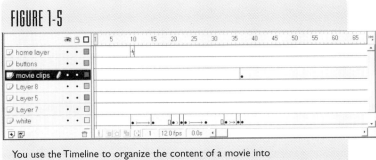

You use the Timeline to organize the content of a movie into layers and frames.

Using the Controller

You can preview the movie in the authoring environment by dragging the playhead along the Timeline. You can generate a more accurate preview of the movie by using the Controller, as shown in Figure 1-6. The buttons on the Controller are as follows: Stop, Rewind, Step Back, Play, Step Forward, Go To End.

FIGURE 1-6

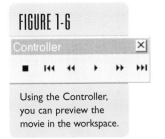

Using the Controller, you can preview the movie in the workspace.

TIP To play the animation, press Enter or Return; to step backward one frame at a time press <; and press > to step forward one frame at a time.

Introducing the Toolbars (Windows Only)

The Flash workspace has three toolbars: Main, Status, and Controller.

To Show OR HIDE A TOOLBAR

1 Choose Toolbars on the Windows menu.

2 Choose one of the following:

Main: This is the standard toolbar with shortcuts for various menu commands, such as Open, Save, Print, etc.

Status: This toolbar is displayed at the bottom-right corner of the work-space and contains information about the status of the Num Lock and Caps Lock keys. Displayed at the lower-left corner is information about the selected menu command or tool.

Controller: You use the Controller to preview the movie in the authoring environment.

Introducing the Toolbox

The Toolbox contains tools that you use to create, color, select, and modify objects, as well as change the view of the Stage. Figure 1-7 shows the Toolbox, which is divided into four sections:

Tools: This section contains drawing, painting, and selection tools.

View: This section contains tools to pan and to change the view of the Stage.

Colors: This section contains tools to modify an object's stroke and fill colors.

Options: This section displays modifiers for a selected tool. A tool's modifiers control how a tool performs; for example, the Brush tool has modifiers for brush size and style. If a selected tool has no modifiers, the Options section is blank.

FIGURE 1-7

The Toolbox lets you create and modify objects, as well as change the view of the Stage.

To Select A TOOL

 Click the desired tool. If the tool has modifiers, they are displayed in the Options section. Alternately, press the tool's keyboard shortcut.

see a⌐so For more information on using the Drawing tools, refer to Chapter 2. For more information on using the Selection tools and the Color section, refer to Chapter 3.

Introducing Layers

Layers are used to organize content in a movie. Layers can be compared to thin sheets of acetate stacked on top of the stage. As you create and edit objects on one layer, objects on other layers are not affected. Objects drawn on a layer will eclipse all underlying objects on lower layers. In traditional graphics programs, you use layers to organize artwork. In Flash, you also use layers to segregate other items in your production, such as sound, animations, and actions. When you are creating complex movies, layers are an invaluable tool. You can create as many layers as you need; the only limiting factor is your computer's memory. Layers do not increase movie file sizes. Layers can be locked, hidden, and displayed as outlines. In addition, you can organize the hierarchy of layers. Refer to Figure 1-5 for an example of layers in action. For more information on layers, refer to Chapter 7.

Using Flash Panels

Floating panels are handy devices for editing elements in a movie. Depending upon the panel that you select, you can edit objects, colors, text objects, frames, instances, or scenes. Panels are arranged in groups of like commands or actions, and you can customize panels to suit your needs. Figure 1-8 shows all of the panels arranged in the workspace.

To Open A PANEL

 Choose Panels from the Window menu, and then select the desired panel from the submenu. To access an individual panel in a group, click its tab.

To Close A PANEL, DO ONE OF THE FOLLOWING:

■ ....Click the Close button in the panel's upper-right corner (Windows) or upper-left corner (Macintosh).

■ ....Choose Panel from the Window menu, and then select the desired panel from the list.

■ ....Right-click (Windows) or Control-click (Macintosh) the panel's tab, and then choose Close Panel from the context menu.

FIGURE 1-8

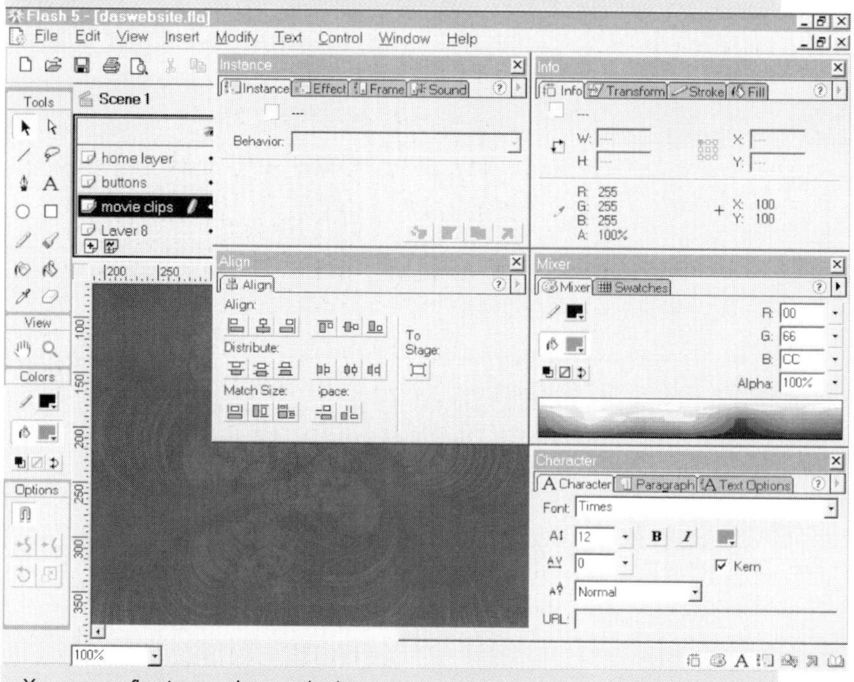

You can use floating panels to apply changes
and edit elements in a movie.

Working with Panels

Panels can be arranged to suit your working habits.

To Arrange THE PANEL LAYOUT TO SUIT YOUR WORKING NEEDS, YOU CAN:

■........Move a panel by clicking its title and dragging it to a new position.

■........Remove a panel from its group by clicking its tab and dragging it beyond the group's window.

■........Dock a panel by dragging it to the bottom or side of another panel.

■........Collapse a panel to its title bar and tab by double-clicking its title.

■........Collapse a panel (Macintosh only) to its title bar and tab by clicking the collapse box at the right end of its title bar.

■........Resize a panel by dragging its lower-right corner (Windows) or by dragging the size box at its lower-right corner (Macintosh).

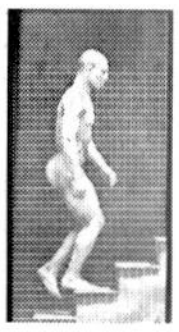

chapter 1: getting to know Flash 5

Using Panel Options

If a panel has available options, the triangle to the right of the last tab is black. If a panel has no options, the triangle is dimmed. To access the panel's options, click the triangle. Figure 1-9 shows a panel with its Option menu displayed.

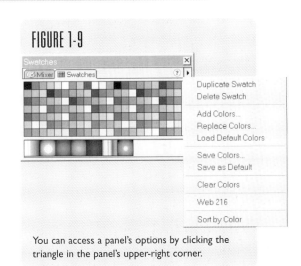

FIGURE 1-9

You can access a panel's options by clicking the triangle in the panel's upper-right corner.

Grouping Panels

After you gain experience with Flash, you will find yourself using certain panels more than others. To group a frequently used panel within another panel group, click the panel's tab and then drag and drop it onto a tab in another group.

To Create A CUSTOM PANEL SET

1 Create groups of the panels.

2 Position the groups in the workspace to suit your working habits. Collapse and dock groups as needed.

3 Choose Save Panel Layout from the Window menu. The Save Panel Layout dialog box appears.

4 Enter a name for the layout in the Name field, and then click OK.

TIP To delete a custom layout, open the Flash 5 folder on your hard drive. Open the Panel Sets folder. Select and delete the desired layout.

To Select A SAVED PANEL LAYOUT

1 Choose Panel Sets from the Window menu.

2 Select the desired set from the submenu. To return panels to their default layout, select Default Layout.

Using the Flash Launcher Bar

Conveniently located in the lower-right corner of the workspace is the Launcher bar, shown in Figure 1-10. You use the Launcher bar to start any of these applications: Info panel, Mixer panel, Character panel, Instance panel, Movie Explorer, Object Actions panel, or the document Library. To launch an application from the Launcher bar, you click its button.

FIGURE 1-10

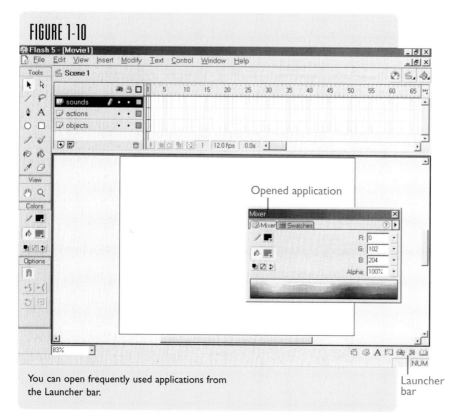

Opened application

You can open frequently used applications from the Launcher bar.

Launcher bar

Using the Flash Document Library

Earlier in the chapter, you learned the importance of symbols. After you convert a graphic object to a symbol, Flash stores the symbol in the document's Library. Imported objects, such as bitmaps and sounds, are also stored within the document Library. The Library lets you organize the elements used within your movie, a feature that is useful when you are dealing with a large production. A typical document Library is shown in Figure 1-11.

FIGURE 1-11

Preview window

Options menu icon

Sort Selected Column

Create New Symbol

Add Folder

Delete Symbol

Name	Kind	Use Count	Linkage	Date Modified
buttons	Folder			
images	Folder			
0	Graphic	-		Sunday, July 09, 2000 3:46:14 PM
1	Graphic	-		Sunday, July 09, 2000 3:46:21 PM
about head	Graphic	-		Tuesday, July 11, 2000 1:52:46 PM
background	Graphic	-		Saturday, July 08, 2000 4:31:19 PM
background.png	Bitmap	-		Sunday, July 02, 2000 5:21:44 PM
contact	Graphic	-		Thursday, July 13, 2000 8:22:00 PM
contact 1	Graphic	-		Tuesday, July 11, 2000 6:46:00 PM
contact 2	Graphic	-		Tuesday, July 11, 2000 6:43:51 PM
contact 3	Graphic	-		Tuesday, July 11, 2000 6:44:41 PM
das designs	Graphic	-		Thursday, July 13, 2000 9:21:26 AM
das designs logo	Graphic	-		Saturday, July 08, 2000 10:28:38 PM
filled circle	Graphic	-		Saturday, July 08, 2000 5:20:41 PM
filled circle 2	Graphic	-		Tuesday, July 11, 2000 1:46:44 PM
hammer	Graphic	-		Wednesday, July 12, 2000 9:19:37 PM
hollow circle	Graphic	-		Tuesday, July 11, 2000 1:47:05 PM

78 items

Options

The document Library stores all symbols and objects used in the scene.

The Library in Figure 1-11 is displayed in Wide State so that you can see all of its features. Notice that the window is split into two sections. The top section displays a preview of the selected item; the bottom section lists folders and Library items. If the selected item is a movie clip, button, or sound, a Stop button and a Play button appear to the right of the symbol in the preview window. You press the Play button to preview the item as it will appear in the movie.

To use a Library item, click the item in either section of the Library window, and then drag it onto the Stage. Flash adds the item to the currently selected layer.

Changing the Size of the Library Window

When you initially open the Library, it is displayed in Narrow State mode.

To Change THE SIZE OF THE LIBRARY WINDOW, DO ONE OF THE FOLLOWING:

■ ......Click the Wide State button to expand the window.

■ ......Click the Narrow State button to display only the Name column.

■ ......Drag the lower-right corner to resize the window.

TIP To change the width of a Library column, position the cursor between two columns, and then drag to resize.

13

Using the Library Options Menu

The Library has its own Options menu, as shown in Figure 1-12. To reveal the menu, click the Options button in the upper-right corner of the Library window.

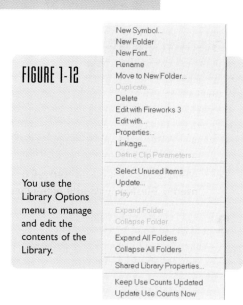

FIGURE 1-12

You use the Library Options menu to manage and edit the contents of the Library.

New Symbol...
New Folder
New Font...
Rename
Move to New Folder...
Duplicate
Delete
Edit with Fireworks 3
Edit with...
Properties...
Linkage...
Define Clip Parameters...

Select Unused Items
Update...
Play

Expand Folder
Collapse Folder

Expand All Folders
Collapse All Folders

Shared Library Properties...

Keep Use Counts Updated
Update Use Counts Now

Using Library Folders

As your expertise in Flash grows, so will the size of your movies, which inevitably means that you will end up with some very large document Libraries. Fortunately, you can organize Library items in folders. Whenever you create a new symbol or import an item into a movie, it is stored in the currently selected folder. If no folder is selected when you create a symbol, Flash adds the item at the root of the Library.

Using Library Folders

To	Do
Open or close a folder	Double-click it. Alternately, choose Expand Folder or Collapse Folder from the Options menu.
Create a folder	Choose New Folder from the Library Options menu, or click the New Folder button at the bottom of the Library window.
Name a folder	While the default name is still highlighted, enter a new name.
Rename an existing folder	Double-click its name. While the current name is highlighted, enter a new name. Alternately, you can right-click (Windows) or Control-click (Macintosh) the folder, and then choose Rename from the context menu.
Delete a folder	Select it, and then click the Delete button at the bottom of the Library window. Alternately, choose Delete from the Options menu.
Move items between folders	Select the item(s), and then drag and drop it into the desired folder.

Maintaining the Library

If you experiment with a lot of different items in a movie, you may end up with many unused Library items. Unused files make navigating the Library more difficult and also bloat the size of the published movie. When working on a complex project, keep the Library in good order by deleting unused items.

To Delete UNUSED ITEMS

1 Choose Select Unused Items from the Options menu. Flash selects and highlights all unused items.

2 Click the Delete button at the bottom of the Library window. Alternately, choose Delete from the Options menu.

> **TIP** Double-click the icon to the left of a Library symbol's name to immediately enter symbol-editing mode.

Editing Library Items

You can edit any Library item directly in Flash or use an external editor.

To Edit A LIBRARY ITEM CREATED IN FLASH

1 Select the desired item from the Library.

2 Choose Edit from the Options menu.

3 The Library item opens up in symbol-editing mode.

> **note** If the selected symbol cannot be edited with an external editor, the Edit With command is grayed out.

To Edit A LIBRARY ITEM IN AN EXTERNAL EDITOR

1 Click the desired item in the Library to select it.

2 Choose Edit With from the Options menu. The Select External Editor dialog box appears.

3 Locate the appropriate program for editing the item, and then click Open. The selected item opens in the external editor.

4 Edit the item, and then save it in the external editor.

continues

continued

5 Exit the external editor.

6 Flash updates the Library item to reflect the edits that you made in the external editor.

Updating Imported Files in the Library

You can update imported Library items that are edited in an external editor not launched from within Flash without importing the files again.

To Update AN IMPORTED FILE

1 Select the imported file in the Library. Hold down the Shift key, and then click additional files to add them to the selection.

2 Choose Update from the Options menu.

3 The Update Media dialog box appears, as shown in Figure 1-13. The number of files that need updating is noted at the bottom of the dialog box.

4 Click Update.

5 Click Close.

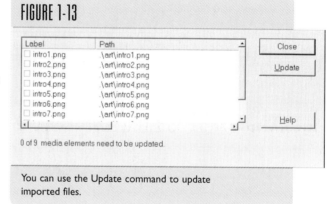

FIGURE 1-13

Label	Path
intro1.png	.\art\intro1.png
intro2.png	.\art\intro2.png
intro3.png	.\art\intro3.png
intro4.png	.\art\intro4.png
intro5.png	.\art\intro5.png
intro6.png	.\art\intro6.png
intro7.png	.\art\intro7.png

Close
Update
Help

0 of 9 media elements need to be updated.

You can use the Update command to update imported files.

Using the Common Libraries

Common libraries are preset libraries included with Flash that contain items such as buttons, symbols, and sounds.

To Use AN ITEM FROM A COMMON LIBRARY IN A MOVIE

1 Choose Common Libraries from the Window menu, and then choose the desired library from the submenu.

2 Drag the desired item from the common library into the document Library. Alternately, you can drag the item from the common library onto the Stage.

Creating a Custom Library

You can also create your common library of items. For example, if you repeatedly use the same buttons, sounds, or symbols in your work, creating a common library makes them readily available.

To Create A CUSTOM LIBRARY

1 Create a new Flash document.

2 Create or import the items that you want to include in the custom library.

3 Choose Save from the File menu. The Save As dialog box appears.

4 Locate the Libraries folder, which is located in the Flash application folder on your hard drive.

5 Enter a name for the custom library, and then click Save. The custom library appears in the Common Libraries submenu the next time that you launch Flash.

Using Context Menus

Flash provides several context menus that contain commands and options that pertain to the current selection. For example, the context menu for a symbol on the Stage, as shown in Figure 1-14, contains commands to modify the symbol, plus ready access to pertinent panels.

To Access A CONTEXT MENU

▶ Right-click (Windows) or Control-click (Macintosh) a selected item in the Timeline,
Library, or on the Stage.

FIGURE 1-14

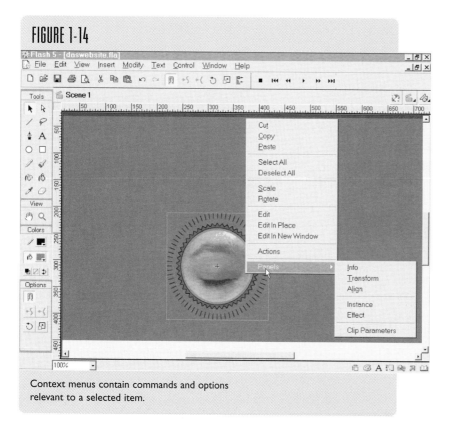

Context menus contain commands and options relevant to a selected item.

Customizing the Workspace

When you first launch Flash, the default workspace is set up with a row of floating panels and a floating toolbox. This arrangement may seem cluttered, especially if you are working with a smaller desktop. Fortunately, you can customize the workspace to suit your needs.

Docking the Toolbox

If you prefer to have the tools in a fixed location, you can dock the Toolbox. However, you cannot resize the Toolbox.

To Dock THE TOOLBOX

▶ **Drag it to the top left or top right side of the application window. The Toolbox will snap into place.**

TIP To re-dock the Toolbox to its last position, double-click its title bar.

To Undock THE TOOLBOX

▶ **Click the title bar and drag.**

Docking the Controller

By default, the Controller is a floating toolbar. If you frequently use it to preview your work, docking it may help speed up your workflow.

To Dock THE CONTROLLER

1 Choose Toolbars from the Window menu, and then choose Controller.

2 Drag the Controller below the menu bar.

Docking the Timeline

The default position for the Timeline is at the top of the application window. You can dock the Timeline on either side of the interface, or you can display it in a floating window. You can make the following modifications to the Timeline:

To move the Timeline, click the area above the layer window, and then drag.

To dock the Timeline, move it from its default position, and then drag it to either corner of the workspace.

To resize the Timeline while it is docked, drag the bar separating the Timeline from the workspace.

To resize the Timeline while it is floating, drag the lower-right corner (Windows), or drag the Size box in the lower-right corner (Macintosh).

Creating Keyboard Shortcuts

Keyboard shortcuts are a great way to speed up your production. Flash provides you with a number of built-in shortcuts. However, you can create a custom set of Keyboard Shortcuts to match a program that you are already familiar with. You can also choose one of the other built-in sets that match Keyboard Shortcuts used in Fireworks, Freehand 9, Illustrator, or Photoshop.

To Create A CUSTOM SET OF KEYBOARD SHORTCUTS

1 Choose Keyboard Shortcuts from the Edit menu. The Keyboard Shortcuts dialog boxappears, as shown in Figure 1-15.

2 Click the Duplicate Set button. The Duplicate dialog box appears.

3 Enter a name for the new set, and then click OK.

4 Select a set of commands from the Commands drop-down menu.

5 From the selected command set, choose a command to which you want to assign a shortcut. If a shortcut is currently assigned to the command, it will be displayed in the Press Key window. To change an existing shortcut, proceed to step 6.

6 Click inside the Press Key window. Perform the new shortcut on your computer's keyboard. The shortcut sequence appears in the Press Key window. If the shortcut is being used by another command, a warning dialog box appears below the Press Key window.

FIGURE 1-15

Keyboard Shortcuts

Current Set: Fireworks

Commands: Drawing Menu Commands

- Insert
  - Convert to Symbol...   F8
  - New Symbol...   Ctrl+F8
  - Layer
  - Motion Guide
  - Frame   F5
  - Remove Frames   Shift+F5
  - Keyframe   F6
  - Blank Keyframe   F7
  - Clear Keyframe   Shift+F6

Description: Create a new symbol that can be used in multiple places.

Shortcuts: + −

Ctrl+F8

Press Key: Ctrl+F8   Change

Help   OK   Cancel

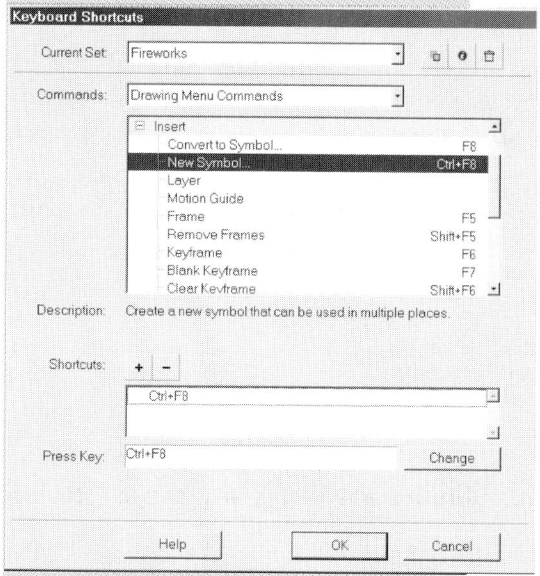

You can create a custom set of Keyboard Shortcuts to suit your working preference.

7 To accept the new shortcut, click Change.

8 Repeat steps 4 through 7 to finish assigning keyboard shortcuts for the new set and then click OK.

To Open AN EXISTING SET OF KEYBOARD SHORTCUTS

1 Choose Keyboard Shortcuts from the Edit menu.

2 Select the desired set from the Current Set menu.

To Add or delete a set Keyboard Shortcuts

1 Choose Keyboard Shortcuts from the Edit menu.

2 From the Current Set menu, select a set to modify.

3 To add a shortcut, click the Add Shortcut (+) button.

4 Click the Press Key window, and then enter the desired shortcut from your computer's keyboard.

5 To finish adding the new shortcut, click Change.

6 To delete a shortcut, select the desired shortcut, and then click the Delete Shortcut (-) button.

7 To add or delete additional shortcuts, repeat steps 3 through 6.

8 Click OK.

To Rename an existing set of Keyboard Shortcuts

1 Choose Keyboard Shortcuts from the Edit menu.

2 Select the set that you want to rename.

3 Click the Rename Set button.

4 In the Rename dialog box, enter a new name for the set.

5 Click OK to assign the name.

6 Click OK to exit the Keyboard Shortcuts dialog box.

> **note** The Flash 5 set of Keyboard Shortcuts cannot be modified.

To Delete an existing set of Keyboard Shortcuts

1 Choose Keyboard Shortcuts from the Edit menu to open the Keyboard Shortcuts dialog box.

continues

continued

2 Select the set that you want to delete.

3 Click the Delete Set button.

4 Click OK.

Editing Flash Preferences

In addition to customizing the workspace, you can also set other Flash parameters to suit your working habits and processor speed.

To Edit FLASH PREFERENCES

1 Choose Preferences from the Edit menu to open the Preferences dialog box.

2 Click the General tab.

3 In the Undo Levels field, enter a value from 0 to 200 to set the number of undo and redo levels. Using more undo levels uses more of your computer's memory.

4 In the Printing Options section (Windows only), select Disable PostScript to disable PostScript when printing to a PostScript printer. This option is deselected by default. Enable this option to correct problems when printing to a PostScript printer. Note that selecting this option will slow down printing to a PostScript printer.

5 In the Select Options section, Shift Select controls how you select multiple objects. With Shift Select enabled, pressing the Shift key while clicking additional objects adds them to a selection. With Shift Select disabled, clicking additional objects adds them to the selection.

6 Enable Show Tooltips to display tooltips when the cursor pauses over a button or icon.

7 In the Timeline Options section, select Disable Timeline Docking to display the Timeline as a free-floating window.

8 In the Timeline Options section, enable Use Flash 4 Selection Style to select frames as you did in Flash 4. This option allows you to create additional frames by dragging the last frame on the Timeline.

continues

continued

9 Enable Flash 4 Frame Drawing to display blank keyframes with unfilled circles.

10 In the Highlight Color section, select Use This Color, and then click the Color swatch to select a highlight color from the palette. Choose Use Layer Color to use the current layer's outline color for highlights.

11 In the Actions Panel section, choose Normal Mode or Expert Mode. In Normal Mode, you automatically generate ActionScript when you select an action. In Expert Mode, you can enter lines of ActionScript code directly into the Action Panel's text box.

12 Click the Edit tab to adjust settings for the Pen tool and drawing. These settings will be addressed in Chapter 2.

13 Click the Clipboard tab to determine how Flash handles Clipboard items copied from other programs.

14 In the Bitmaps section (Windows only), select an option from the Color Depth menu. The setting that you choose determines the Color Depth and Resolution that Flash assigns to objects that you copy to the Clipboard from other programs and then paste into a movie.

15 In the Bitmaps (Windows only) section, select Smooth to anti-alias clipboard bitmaps. Enter a value in the Size Limit field to determine how much RAM is used when copying a bitmap image to the Clipboard. Increase this value if you are working with large or high-resolution bitmap images. Choose None from the Color Depth menu if your computer has limited memory.

16 In the Gradients section (Windows only), choose an option from the menu to determine the quality of gradient fills. Choosing a higher quality increases the time needed to copy graphics. This setting affects only gradient quality when you paste copied objects to applications other than Flash. Gradient quality of clipboard items is preserved when pasting within Flash.

17 In the PICT Settings section (Macintosh only), for Type, choose Objects to represent Clipboard data as vector artwork. Alternately, select one of the bitmap formats to convert Clipboard data to a bitmap. Enter a value for Resolutions. To include PostScript data, select Include Postscript. Specify a Gradient setting to determine the quality of a gradient used in a PICT when pasted to an application outside of Flash. This setting does not alter Gradient quality when a PICT is pasted within Flash.

18 In the Freehand Text section, enable Maintain Text as Blocks so that you will be able to edit text pasted from Freehand to the Clipboard in Flash.

Creating Graphic Objects

2

With the drawing tools in Flash 5's Toolbox, you can create a moving visual feast for Web site visitors that will download quickly into their browsers. Using the drawing tools, you can create anything from simple geometric forms to complex cartoon characters. In this chapter, you will learn how to use the drawing tools to create basic shapes. In Chapter 3, you will learn how to modify and combine these shapes to create complex artwork for your movies.

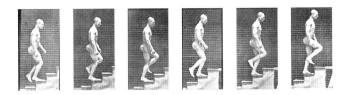

Exploring the Drawing Tools

The drawing tools are conveniently housed in the Toolbox, as shown in Figure 2-1. You can use these tools to create lines, shapes, and filled objects. To select a drawing tool, you click it. The tool's modifiers appear in the Options section of the Toolbox. When you use a drawing tool, Flash applies the current stroke and fill attributes to the object that you create. Flash applies stroke color to a line or an object's outline and fill color to a shape's fill.

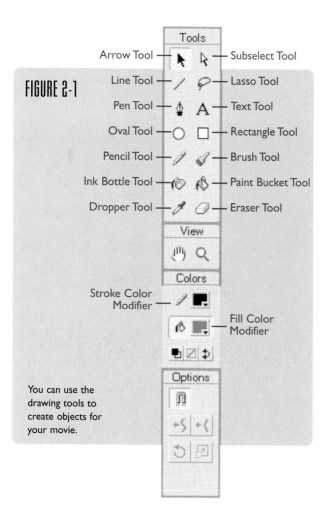

FIGURE 2-1

You can use the drawing tools to create objects for your movie.

Selecting Stroke and Fill Attributes

When you select a drawing tool, Stroke Color and Fill Color modifiers appear in the Colors section of the Toolbox. You use the Stroke Color modifier to select the color for a line or a shape's outline. The Fill Color modifier lets you select a color or gradient fill for a shape. The Colors section of the Toolbox and its controls are shown in Figure 2-2.

To Specify A STROKE AND FILL COLOR FOR A DRAWING TOOL

1 Select a drawing tool.

2 Click the **Stroke Color** swatch or **Fill Color** swatch to reveal the color palette shown in Figure 2-3.

3 Select a stroke or fill color by doing one of the following:

> Click a color or fill from the palette, as shown in Figure 2-3. You can apply gradients only to filled shapes. The gradients do not appear on the palette when you click the **Stroke Color** swatch.

> Enter a value in the Hexadecimal color value field.

> Click the **None** button to create a transparent stroke or fill.

> Click the **Color Picker** button to select a color from the **Color Mixer**.

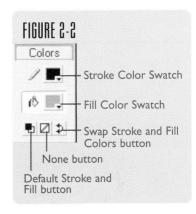

FIGURE 2-2

Stroke Color Swatch
Fill Color Swatch
Swap Stroke and Fill Colors button
None button
Default Stroke and Fill button

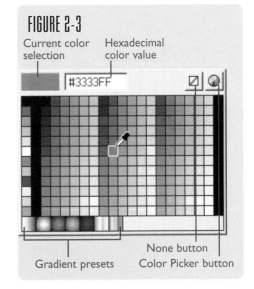

FIGURE 2-3

Current color selection
Hexadecimal color value
Gradient presets
None button
Color Picker button

To Modify CURRENTLY SELECTED STROKE OR FILL COLORS

 Select one of the following buttons at the bottom of the Color section of the toolbar:

Default Colors: Click this button to restore the default stroke and fill colors, black and white.

None: Click this button to create a transparent stroke or fill.

Swap Colors: Click this button to swap existing stroke and fill colors.

see also For more information on modifying stroke and fill colors, refer to the following sections in Chapter 3: Using the Ink Bottle Tool, Using the Paint Bucket Tool, Using the Dropper Tool, and Creating Custom Colors and Gradients.

Using the Eyedropper

To sample a color from an existing object, click the Stroke Color or Fill Color swatch, and then drag the eyedropper onto the Stage. When the eyedropper icon is over the object whose color you want to sample, release the mouse button, and the sampled color will appear in the swatch's window.

Selecting a Line Style

When you create a line or an object with an outline, the default line (or stroke as it is referred to in Flash) style is solid, one pixel thick. Using the Stroke panel shown in Figure 2-4, you can change stroke style, height, and color, or you can create a custom line style.

To Select A LINE STYLE

1 If the Stroke panel isn't displayed, choose Panels from the Window menu, and then choose Stroke. The Stroke panel appears.

2 Click the triangle to the right of the Stroke Style window, and then choose a style from the menu.

3 Click the triangle to the right of the Stroke Height window, and then drag the slider to specify stroke height. Alternately, you may enter a value between .1 and 10 in the text field.

4 Click the Stroke Color swatch, and then select a color from the palette.

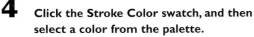

FIGURE 2-4 Stroke Style menu

Stroke preview window — Stroke height — Stroke color

n°te You can also use the Stroke panel to modify the stroke characteristics of a selected object.

Creating a Custom Line Style

If none of the preset stroke styles work for you, you can create a custom line style. Creating a custom line style and applying it to lines and outlines adds a creative touch to a movie; however, applying a custom line style to an object may increase file size.

To Create A CUSTOM LINE STYLE

1 Click the Stroke panel's option triangle. A button labeled Custom appears.

2 Click the Custom button to reveal the Line Style dialog box, as shown in Figure 2-5.

continues

3 Click the triangle to the right of the Type field, and then select a style from the drop-down menu. Each style has a different set of parameters that you can adjust to modify the preset.

4 Select an option from each of the style's parameter menus. As you modify each parameter's different options, Flash updates the custom line style in the preview window.

5 Click the triangle to the right of the Thickness field, and then select a line weight from the menu.

6 Enable the Sharp Corners options to have abrupt transitions in the line rendered as sharp corners.

7 Click OK to apply the new line style. Flash displays the new line style in the Stroke panel's Stroke Style window.

FIGURE 2-5

Line Style		

☐ Zoom 4x

Thickness: [4] pts
☐ Sharp Corners

Type: Hatched
Thickness: Hairline
Space: Distant
Jiggle: None
Rotate: None
Curve: Straight
Length: Equal

OK
Cancel
Help

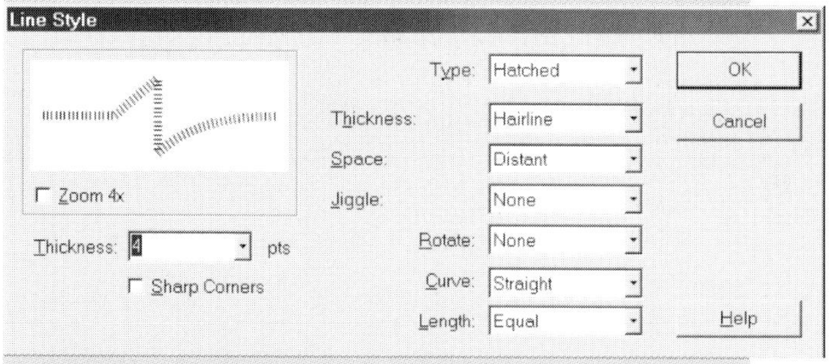

Create a custom line style to put a stamp of originality on your work.

Creating Lines, Ovals, and Rectangles

You can use lines, ovals, and rectangles as stand-alone objects or as the basis for more complex artwork.

To Create A STRAIGHT LINE, OVAL, OR RECTANGLE

1 Select the Line, Oval, or Rectangle tool.

2 Accept the default stroke style and stroke height, or use the Stroke panel to modify these attributes as outlined in the preceding steps. Select stroke color and fill color. You cannot apply fill colors to the Line tool.

TIP To modify the corner radius of a rounded rectangle, press the Up or Down Arrow keys while creating the object. To constrain the objects to circles or squares, press the Shift key while dragging the Oval or Rectangle tool. To constrain a line to 45-degree angles, press the Shift key while dragging the Line tool.

continues

chapter 2: creating graphic objects

continued

3 To create a rectangle with rounded corners, click the **Round Rectangle** modifier, and then enter a value in the **Rectangle Settings** dialog box, as shown in **Figure 2-6**. **Click OK** to apply the setting.

4 Drag the tool onto the Stage.

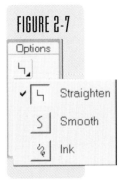

FIGURE 2-6

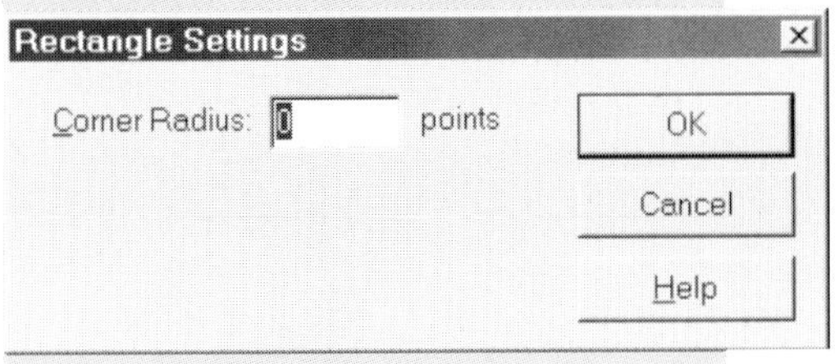

Rectangle Settings

Corner Radius: [0] points   OK
                              Cancel
                              Help

Using the Pencil Tool

The Pencil tool is the equivalent of a trusty No. 2 pencil that never needs sharpening. You can use it to create freeform lines or outlines that you can color using the Ink Bottle tool. Depending upon the Pencil Mode modifier that you choose, Flash will transform a squiggle drawn with a mouse into straight line segments or smooth, flowing curves. If you prefer, Flash can leave the line unmodified.

To Create A LINE WITH THE PENCIL TOOL

1 Select the Pencil tool.

2 Specify line style, line weight, and stroke color.

3 In the Options section, click the **Pencil Mode** modifier, as shown in **Figure 2-7**, and then select one of the following modes:

> **Straighten: Select this modifier to create a line comprised of straight line segments and interconnecting curves.**

> **Smooth: Select this modifier to draw smooth, flowing curved lines.**

> **Ink: Select this mode to create a free-form line with no assistance from Flash. Use this mode if you are an accomplished artist working with a digital tablet or if your design calls for an irregular line.**

4 To draw the line, drag onto the Stage.

TiP When you use the Pencil tool's Straighten mode, Flash will transform mouse-drawn shapes resembling ovals, rectangles, and triangles into their proper geometric forms.

FIGURE 2-7

Options

✓ Straighten
  Smooth
  Ink

Using the Brush Tool

Use the Brush tool as if you were painting with a brush to add artistic splashes of color to your movie. The tool's modifiers let you specify the width and style of the brush tip. The tool even has a modifier that lets you vary the width of the stroke with most pressure-sensitive tablets.

To Paint A SHAPE

1 Select the Brush tool. Figure 2-8 shows the modifiers that appear after you select the tool.

2 Select a fill color for the Brush.

3 Click the Brush Mode modifier and choose one of the following options from the list shown in Figure 2-9:

> **Paint Normal** paints over existing lines and fills on the selected layer.
>
> **Paint Fills** paints all filled shapes and blank areas on the Stage, leaving lines unaffected.
>
> **Paint Behind** paints behind existing lines and fills, applying color to blank areas of the Stage.
>
> **Paint Selection** applies paint within a selected filled shape, leaving lines and blank areas of the Stage unaffected.
>
> **Paint Inside** applies paint within the filled shape where you begin the stroke without affecting surrounding lines, surrounding fills, and blank areas of the Stage. If you like to paint within the lines, this mode is for you. Figure 2-10 shows how you can modify brush stokes with the different brush modes.

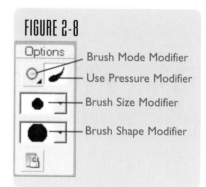

FIGURE 2-8

Brush Mode Modifier
Use Pressure Modifier
Brush Size Modifier
Brush Shape Modifier

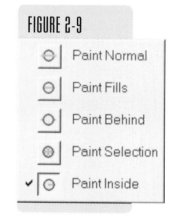

FIGURE 2-9

Paint Normal
Paint Fills
Paint Behind
Paint Selection
Paint Inside

note When using the Paint Inside Brush mode, you need to start your brush stroke inside the correct object. If you have several items stacked on top of one another, it's easy to apply paint to the wrong one. Furthermore, if you begin to paint outside an object, Flash applies the paint as if you were using the Paint Behind mode.

continues

chapter 2: creating graphic objects

FIGURE 2-10

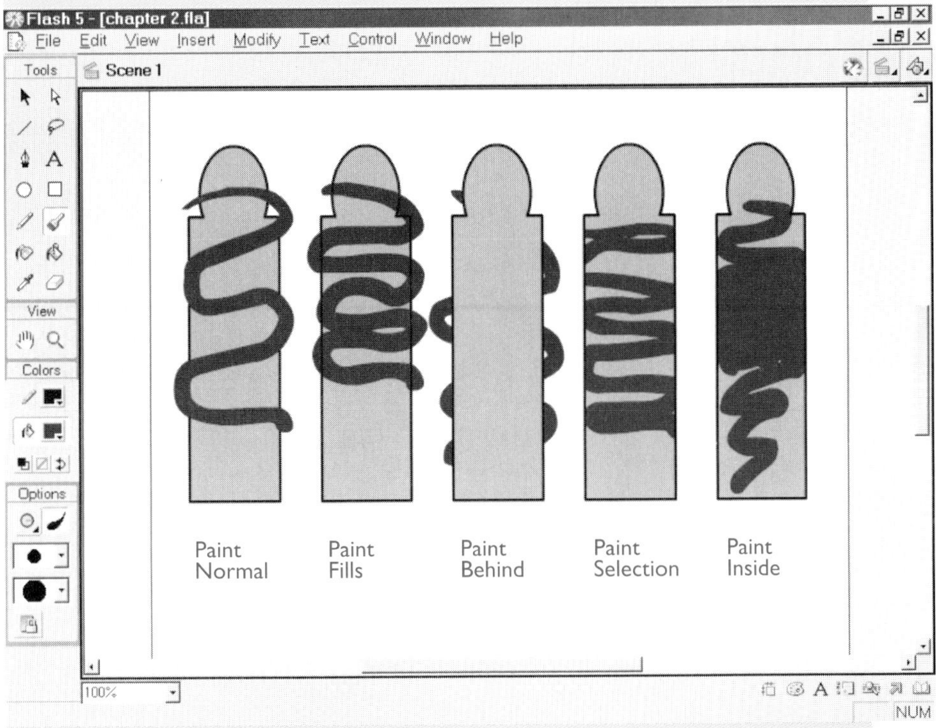

Flash 5 - [chapter 2.fla]

File Edit View Insert Modify Text Control Window Help

Scene 1

Paint   Paint   Paint   Paint   Paint
Normal   Fills   Behind   Selection   Inside

100%   NUM

You can control the effect of a brush stroke
with the Brush Mode modifier.

continued

4 To paint a stroke of varying width with your
computer's pressure-sensitive tablet, click the
Pressure Sensitive button.

5 Select a Brush Size from the menu shown
in **Figure 2-11**.

6 Select a Brush Shape from the menu shown
in **Figure 2-12**.

7 Drag on the Stage to apply a brush stroke.
Press the Shift key while dragging to constrain
strokes to horizontal or vertical directions.
Depending upon the speed of your processor,
you may find it necessary either to
momentarily pause before changing from
vertical to horizontal or to release the mouse
button before changing direction.

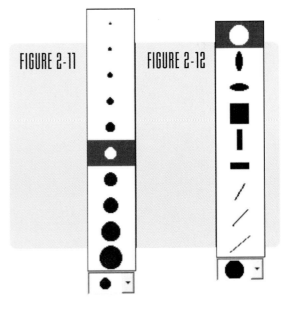

FIGURE 2-11   FIGURE 2-12

33

Using the Pen Tool

The Pen tool gives you pinpoint control when you are creating lines, shapes, and paths. Flash's other drawing tools create a path as you drag them across the Stage. With the Pen tool, you create a path by clicking to add corner or curve points. Flash connects the points to create segments.

To Create A STRAIGHT LINE WITH THE PEN TOOL

1 Select the Pen tool.

2 Accept the default stroke style and stroke height, or use the **Stroke** panel to modify these attributes as outlined previously. Select a stroke color and a fill color.

3 Click on the Stage where you want the first point of the path to appear. As you click, an arrow appears to the right of the cursor.

4 Click where you want the second point of the path to appear. A line segment connects the two points, as shown in Figure 2-13. Hold down the **Shift** key while adding points to constrain a line segment to 45-degree increments.

5 Click to add segments to the path.

6 To complete an open path, double-click the last point. Alternately, **Control-click** (Windows) or **Command-click** (Macintosh). A small *x* appears to the right of the Pen tool, signifying that it is ready to create a new line segment.

continues

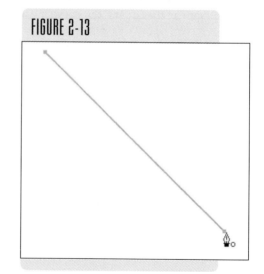

n°te While the Pen tool is selected, Flash displays points and segments along a path with the currently selected layer's display color. When you deselect the tool, Flash displays the path with the stroke and fill colors that you selected.

FIGURE 2-13

continued

7 To complete a closed path, move the Pen tool over the first point in the path, and then click. The path closes, and the outline that you created fills with the selected fill color, as shown in Figure 2-14.

To Create A CURVED PATH WITH THE PEN TOOL

1 Select the Pen tool.

2 Accept the default stroke style and stroke height, or use the Stroke panel to modify these attributes as outlined previously. Select a stroke color and a fill color.

3 Click on the Stage where you want the first point of the path to appear.

4 Click and drag to create the second point of the curved path. As you drag, two handles appear that define the curve, as shown in Fgure 2-15. The length and slope of the handles are defined as you drag. To constrain the handles to 45-degree increments, hold down the Shift key while dragging.

5 Release the mouse button to complete the curved segment.

6 Click and drag to add additional curved segments to the path. Click without dragging to add a straight segment to the path.

7 To complete an open path, double-click the last point. Alternately, Control-click (Windows) or Command-click (Macintosh) anywhere on the Stage. A small x appears to the right of the Pen Tool icon, signifying that the tool is ready to create a new path.

8 To complete a closed path, position the Pen tool over the first point in the path, and then click. The path closes, and Flash fills the shape with the fill color that you selected.

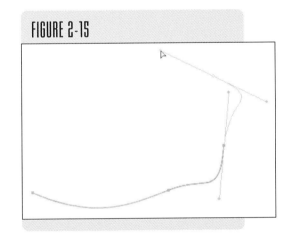

FIGURE 2-14

FIGURE 2-15

Adjusting Pen Tool Preferences

The Pen tool is a powerful weapon in your drawing tool arsenal. You can adjust the tool to change the appearance of the Pen tool cursor, display line segments as you draw, or change the appearance of selected points.

To Modify PEN TOOL PREFERENCES

1 Choose Preferences from the Edit menu, and then click the Edit tab.

2 In the Pen tool section, adjust the following options:

Show Pen Preview: Select this option and Flash creates a preview of line segments as you move the cursor across the Stage before you create the end point of the segment.

Show Solid Points: Select this option to display selected points as hollow points and unselected points as solid points.

Show Precise Cursors: Select this option to display the Pen tool as a crosshair. This option comes in handy when you need to align path points to precise locations along the grid.

Modifying a Path Created with the Pen Tool

Once you have created a path with the Pen tool, you can modify its shape by adding, deleting, or converting points. You can also reposition points and adjust the length and slope of handles for curve points by using the Subselect tool.

Adding Points to a Path

To fine-tune the shape of a path, you can add additional points to it with the Pen tool.

To Add A POINT TO A PATH

1 Select the Pen tool. Notice that the color of all paths on the current layer changes to the layer's display color.

Warning You cannot add a point to a straight line segment with the Pen tool.

continues

continued

2 Move the Pen tool towards the point on the line segment where you want to add a point. As the tool approaches the line segment, a plus sign appears in front of the cursor, as shown in Figure 2-16.

3 Click to add the point.

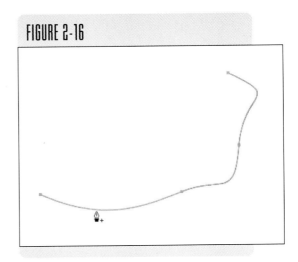

FIGURE 2-16

Deleting Points from a Path

You can also modify a path by deleting points. Deleting excess points optimizes the path and reduces file size. You cannot delete the start or end point of a path. If you delete the last point of a closed path, the path will still be closed but will conform to a new shape.

To Delete A CORNER POINT FROM A PATH

1 Select the Pen tool.

2 As you approach a corner point, a minus sign appears next to the cursor, as shown in Figure 2-17. Click to delete the point. Alternately, select the point with the Subselect tool, and then press Delete.

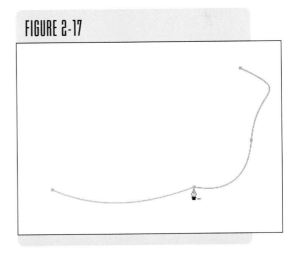

FIGURE 2-17

To Delete A CURVE POINT FROM A PATH

1 Select the Pen tool.

2 As you approach a curve point, an angled less than sign appears next to the cursor, as shown in Figure 2-18. To delete the curve point, double-click the point. (The first click converts the point to a corner point; the second click deletes it.) Alternately, select the point with the Subselect tool, and then press Delete.

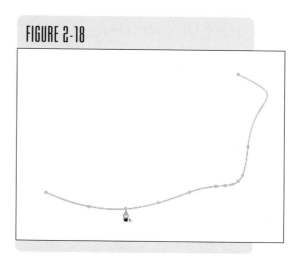

FIGURE 2-18

Modifying Points Along a Path

By default, Flash displays selected corner points as hollow squares and selected curve points as hollow circles. Once you have created a shape with the Pen tool, you can modify it by moving points or by adjusting the slope and length of a curve point's handles. You can convert corner points to curve points and vice versa. You can also move individual points or a group of points.

To Move A POINT

1 Select the Subselect tool.

2 Click a point to select it, and then drag it to the desired location.

To Nudge A POINT

1 Select the Subselect tool.

2 Click a point to select it.

3 To select more than one point, drag the Subselect tool around the points that you want to select. Alternately, select the first point, and then hold down the Shift key and click to add points to the selection.

4 Use the Arrow keys to nudge the point(s) to a new position.

38

Converting Points

You can also modify a path by converting one or more points. For example, to smooth an abrupt transition from one segment to the next, you can convert a corner point to a curve point.

To Convert A CORNER POINT TO A CURVE POINT

1   Select the point that you want to convert with the Subselect tool.

2   Hold down the **Alt** key and drag the point (**Windows**); or hold down the **Option** key and drag the point (**Macintosh**).

To Convert A CURVE POINT TO A CORNER POINT

1   Select the **Pen** tool.

2   Click a corner point.

Modifying a Curve

You can modify a curved path segment by selecting a curve point and dragging either of its handles with the Subselect tool.

To Modify A CURVE

1   Select the Subselect tool.

2   Click a curve point. The point's handles appear. If the point that you selected is in the middle of a curved segment, the handles for the adjoining points also appear.

3   Click and drag one of the handle's end points to modify the curved segment, as shown in Figure 2-19.

FIGURE 2-19

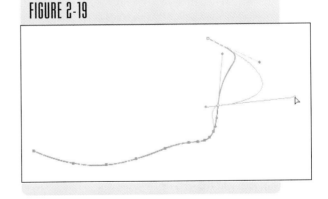

Using the Zoom and Pan Tools

As you gain experience with the Flash drawing tools, you will find yourself creating objects of increasing complexity. When this occurs, the Zoom and Pan tools will enable you to change your viewpoint of the Stage and zoom in to get a better look at individual objects in your movie.

To Zoom In (INCREASE MAGNIFICATION) ON AN OBJECT

 Select the Zoom tool, as shown in Figure 2-20, and then do one of the following:

> Click the tool's Enlarge modifier, and then click anywhere on the Stage to increase to the next highest level of magnification.

> Drag the tool around an object or an area of the Stage that you want to zoom in on.

To Zoom Out (DECREASE MAGNIFICATION)

 Select the Zoom tool, and then click the tool's Reduce Modifier button to zoom out to the next lowest level of magnification.

To Use ZOOM CONTROL

 At the lower-left corner of the workspace is the Zoom Control window. Click the triangle to the right of the window to choose a preset magnification from the menu, or enter a value from 8 to 2000 in the Zoom Control window.

To Change YOUR VIEW OF THE STAGE

> Select the Hand tool, and then drag up, down, right, or left.

TIP To momentarily switch from one zoom mode to the other, press the Alt key (Windows) or Option key (Macintosh). The tool's icon changes to reflect the new mode. Click to change magnification. Release the Alt/Option key to return to the tool's previously selected mode.

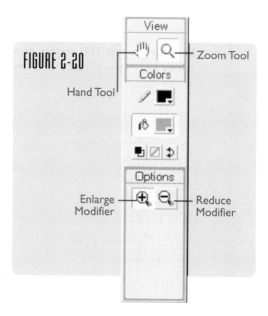

FIGURE 2-20

Hand Tool — Zoom Tool

Enlarge Modifier — Reduce Modifier

TIP To momentarily activate the Hand tool, press the Spacebar, and then drag to pan to a new position. Release the Spacebar to switch back to the previously selected tool.

chapter 2: creating graphic objects

Modifying Drawing Settings

You can adjust drawing settings to suit your working preference. These settings determine the snapping, smoothing, and straightening behaviors of the drawing tools. The actual behavior of each setting varies, depending upon your desktop size and which level of magnification you applied to the Stage.

To Modify DRAWING SETTINGS

1 Select Preferences from the Edit menu to reveal the Preferences dialog box.

2 Click the Editing tab.

3 In the Drawing Settings section, adjust the following settings:

Connect Lines: This setting determines how close the end of one line must be to another before snapping to it. Choose from Must Be Close, Normal, or Can Be Distant. The setting also determines how close a line must be to true vertical or horizontal before Flash draws it that way.

Smooth Curves: This setting determines how much Flash smoothes a curve created with the Pencil tool in the Smooth or Straighten mode. Normal works well for most users. If your drawing skills with a mouse are a bit shaky, choose the Smooth option.

Recognize Lines: This setting determines how close to straight a line must be before Flash straightens it. If you are an accomplished computer artist, Normal or Strict will probably work well for you. Select Tolerant for maximum assistance from Flash.

Recognize Shapes: This setting determines how accurately you must draw shapes such as rectangles, ovals, or triangles before Flash redraws them that way. The Normal or Tolerant settings work well for most users. Turn this option Off for no assistance.

Click Accuracy: This setting determines how close your mouse must be to an item before it can be recognized by Flash. Choose Strict, Normal, or Tolerant.

Creating Text Objects

Text objects are often a dynamic part of a Flash movie. As you will learn in future chapters, you can animate text and transform it into other shapes. When you create a text object, you can adjust its alignment, color, font face, kerning, size, and style.

To Create A TEXT OBJECT IN FLASH

1 Select the Text tool.

2 Click anywhere on the Stage to create a text block. The default text block widens as you enter text and is signified by a round handle at the top-right corner of the box. If you enter enough text, the default text box expands beyond the boundaries of the Stage.

To Create A TEXT BOX OF A SPECIFIED WIDTH

▶ Drag the handle to the right. The round handle becomes a square, indicating that the text block is a fixed width. When text reaches the end of a fixed width text box, it wraps to a new line. Both types of text boxes are shown in Figure 2-21.

FIGURE 2-21

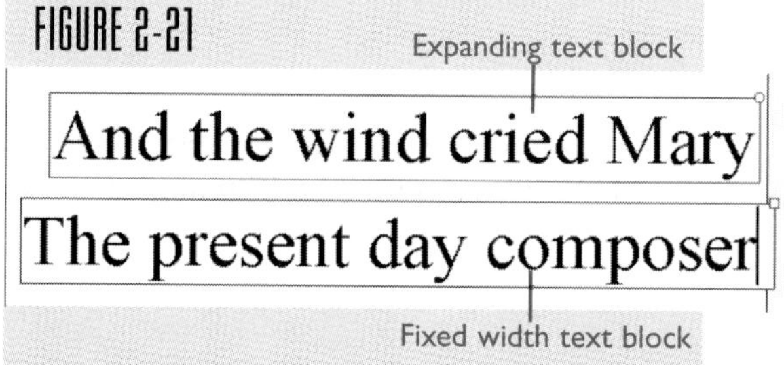

Expanding text block

And the wind cried Mary

The present day composer

Fixed width text block

Adjusting Character Options

When you create a new text object, the current character options are applied. You use the Character panel to modify character options, such as font size, font style, and color.

To Adjust TEXT CHARACTER OPTIONS

1 Choose Panels from the Window menu, and then choose Character to display the Character panel, as shown in Figure 2-22.

2 Click the triangle to the right of the Font Style window, and then select a style from the drop-down menu.

continues

chapter 2: creating graphic objects

continued

3 Click the triangle to the right of the Font size window, and then drag the slider to set font size. Alternately, type a value in the Text window.

4 Click the Bold and/or Italic buttons to boldface or italicize the text.

5 Click the Text (Fill) Color swatch, and then select a color from the palette.

6 To adjust the tracking (spacing) between text characters, click the triangle to the right of the tracking window, and then drag the slider. Alternately, type a value in the tracking text window.

7 To use the selected font's built-in kerning information, click the Kern box.

8 To modify the baseline shift, click the arrow to the right of the Baseline Shift window, and then choose one of the following options:

> **Normal** places the text on the baseline.
>
> **Superscript** places the text above the baseline.
>
> **Subscript** places the text below the baseline.

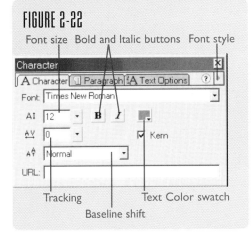

FIGURE 2-22

Font size Bold and Italic buttons Font style

Tracking

Baseline shift

Text Color swatch

n°te When you specify a font, Flash embeds the font's information with the published movie so that the text is displayed properly in the user's browser. However, Flash does not recognize all fonts and will not export unsupported fonts with a movie. To verify that Flash can export a chosen font, choose Antialias Text from the View menu. If the edges of the text appear jagged, select another font style; Flash does not recognize the currently selected font and will not export the text.

Adjusting Paragraph Options

If your Flash movie has blocks of paragraph text, you can specify the alignment of the text in the paragraph, as well as the margins, indentation, and line spacing. The Paragraph panel is used to set these options.

To Adjust PARAGRAPH OPTIONS

1 Choose Panels from the Window menu, and then choose Paragraph. The Paragraph panel appears, as shown in Figure 2-23.

2 Click one of the Align buttons to fully justify the text or to align it to the left, center, or right.

3 To set margins, line spacing, and indentation, click the triangle to the right of the option's window, and then drag the slider. Alternately, enter a value in the Text window. The minimum and maximum allowable values vary for each field. A warning dialog box appears if you enter an inappropriate value for the field.

FIGURE 2-23

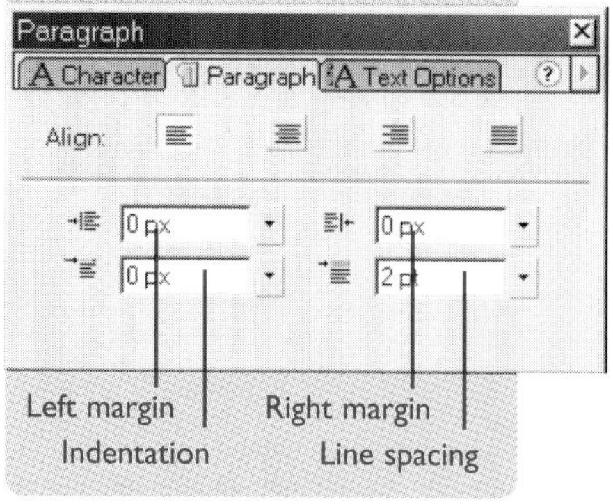

Editing Text Objects

To Edit A BLOCK OF TEXT

 Select the Text tool, and then click the text that you want to edit. A box appears around the selected text. Drag the Text tool over the text to select it, and then modify its parameters with either the Character or Paragraph panel.

To Modify THE WIDTH OF A TEXT BOX

 Select it with the Text tool, and then drag the box's handle.

see also The Text Options panel is primarily used with ActionScript and is discussed in Chapter 14.

To Spell CHECK A BLOCK OF TEXT

Select it with the Text tool, drag the tool over the text to highlight it, and then choose Copy from the Edit menu. Launch your word processor, paste the text into a new document, and then use the program's spell checker to catch any typographical errors.

Modifying Graphic Objects

After creating an object with one of the
drawing tools, you can modify it using Flash 5's
full array of tools and menu commands. In
this chapter, you will learn how to use these
features to move, smooth, straighten, rotate,
scale, and recolor objects in your movies.

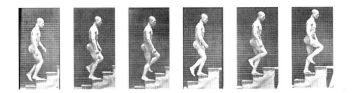

Modifying Objects with Tools

In Flash 5, you can directly modify objects with tools from the toolbar. You learned how to use tools to create objects in Chapter 2. The focus of this chapter is modifying objects. The tools you will use to modify objects were shown previously in Figure 2.1. Each tool has a specific set of modifiers that will be discussed in detail in the upcoming sections.

Using the Arrow Tool

The Arrow tool in the upper-left corner of the toolbox is a multi-faceted workhorse. You use it to select, move, smooth, straighten, rotate, and modify shapes created with the drawing tools. The Arrow tool's modifiers affect how the tool functions. Figure 3-1 shows the modifiers that you have at your disposal once you select the Arrow tool.

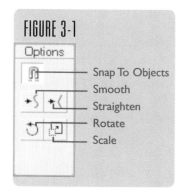

FIGURE 3-1

Selecting Objects

One of the primary functions of the Arrow tool is to select. Using the Arrow tool, you can select a single object or multiple objects on the Stage. An object created with a stroke and fill looks like one object, but it is actually two: the stroke outline and the filled shape. Furthermore, lines created in Flash appear to be continuous but are actually comprised of segments. You can use the Arrow tool to select an entire object, its fill, its outline, or one of its line segments. When the Arrow tool is in selection mode, a rectangular icon appears below the cursor.

To Select AN OBJECT, CHOOSE THE ARROW TOOL AND THEN DO THE FOLLOWING:

To select a filled object, click its center. The selected fill is highlighted, as shown in Figure 3-2.

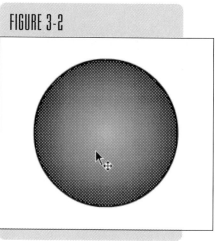

FIGURE 3-2

continues

chapter 3: modifying graphic objects

continued

2 To select a filled object and its outline, double-click the fill. Figure 3-3 shows a selected fill and outline.

3 To select a line segment, click it. The selected line segment is highlighted, as shown in Figure 3-4.

4 To select a series of connected line segments, double-click any segment. The selected segments are highlighted, as shown in Figure 3-5.

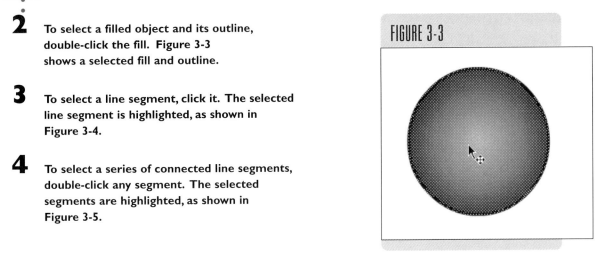

FIGURE 3-3

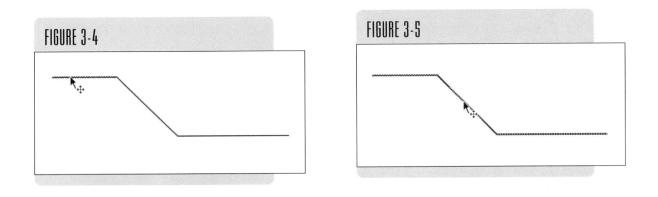

FIGURE 3-4

FIGURE 3-5

Creating Selections

In addition to selecting single objects, you can use the Arrow tool to select multiple objects. You can edit the selected objects as a whole or combined into a group, a technique you will learn in Chapter 4. After you select a single object, the default method is to hold down the Shift key and click objects to add them to the selection. If you prefer to add objects to a selection by just clicking them, you can change to this selection mode by changing selection methods as outlined in the Editing Flash Preferences section in Chapter 1. You can also use the Arrow tool to create a rectangular selection, also known as a marquee selection.

To Create A MARQUEE SELECTION

1 Select the Arrow tool.

2 Click to define the upper-left corner of the selection.

3 Drag down and to the right to encompass the items that you want to select, as shown in Figure 3-6.

4 Release the mouse button to complete the selection.

To Slice AN OBJECT

▶ Create a rectangular selection around part of an object, and then drag the selection to create a new object, as shown in Figure 3-7.

FIGURE 3-6

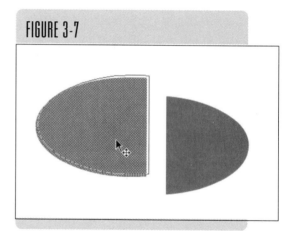

You can use the Arrow tool to create a marquee selection.

FIGURE 3-7

Moving Objects

After you create a selection with the Arrow tool, an icon with arrows pointing left, right, up, and down appears below the tool. This signifies that you can move the selection manually with the tool. To move the selection, you drag it and then release the mouse button when the selection is in the desired location.

Smoothing and Straightening Objects

Objects that you draw with a mouse are generally too irregular to be acceptable for a finished production. The Arrow tool has two modifiers that will remove the bumps from mouse-drawn objects. Figure 3-8 shows the results of applying these modifiers to mouse-drawn objects. The Arrow tool's Smooth modifier optimizes a curved shape or line by smoothing it and thereby reducing the number of points used to define it. The Smooth modifier does not affect straight line segments.

To Smooth A CURVED SHAPE OR LINE WITH THE ARROW TOOL

1 Select the Arrow tool, and then select the object that you want to smooth. If the object you are smoothing is a curved line, make sure to double-click to include all segments that make up the line.

2 Click the Smooth modifier in the Options panel. Click as many times as needed to optimize the curve.

To Straighten A LINE WITH THE ARROW TOOL

1 Select the Arrow tool, and then select the line that you want to straighten.

2 Click the Straighten modifier button in the Options section. To apply further straightening, click again.

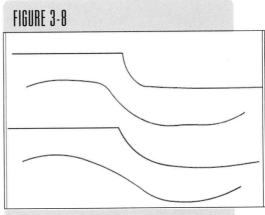
TIP Use the Arrow tool's Straighten modifier to remove minor kinks from a selected line. An alternate method for smoothing or straightening a shape is to choose the Smooth or Straighten command from the Modify menu.

Modifying Shapes

In addition to smoothing and straightening selected objects, the Arrow tool can also be used to alter an object's basic shape. As you move the tool close to an editable shape, its cursor changes to reflect the type of change it can apply. When the Arrow tool approaches a curved segment, a small curve appears below the cursor. An angled line appears when the tool approaches a corner point.

To Modify A SHAPE WITH THE ARROW TOOL

1 Select the Arrow tool, and then move it towards the shape that you want to modify. The tool's cursor changes, as shown in Figure 3-9.

2 Click and drag to modify the shape. You can move only a corner point to a new position whereas you can reshape a curved segment.

To Add A NEW CORNER POINT TO A SHAPE OR LINE WITH THE ARROW TOOL

1 Select the Arrow tool.

2 Hold down the Ctrl key and drag (Windows), or hold down the Option key and drag (Macintosh) where you want to add a corner point on a segment.

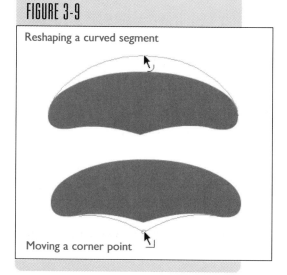

FIGURE 3-9

Reshaping a curved segment

Moving a corner point

Rotating Objects

You use the Arrow tool's Rotate modifier to rotate and skew objects. You also use this modifier to position objects on the Stage as well as animate them.

To Rotate AN OBJECT WITH THE ARROW TOOL

1 Select the Arrow tool, and then select the object that you want to rotate.

continues

continued

2 Click the Rotate modifier in the Toolbar's Options section. Eight unfilled circles appear around the perimeter of the object.

3 Move the tool towards one of the corner circles. Four curved arrows appear.

4 Click and drag to rotate the object, as shown in Figure 3-10.

To Skew AN OBJECT WITH THE ARROW TOOL

1 Select the Arrow tool, and then click the object that you want to skew.

2 Click the Rotate modifier in the Toolbar's Options section.

3 To skew the object along the vertical axis, move the tool towards the center point on either the left or right side. To skew along the horizontal axis, move the tool towards the center point on the top or bottom of the object.

4 Click and drag in the direction that you want to skew the object, as shown in Figure 3-11.

 note Alternately, you can rotate an object by choosing Transform from the Modify menu, and then choosing Rotate.

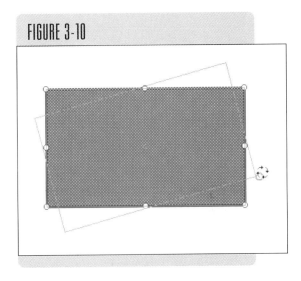

FIGURE 3-10

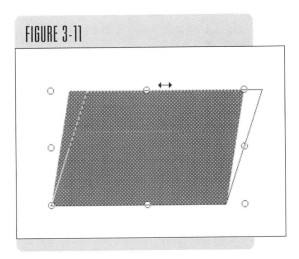

FIGURE 3-11

Scaling Objects

Use the Arrow tool with its Scale modifier enabled to resize objects interactively. In the Scale mode, you can use the Arrow tool to scale objects proportionately or to resize their width or height.

To Resize AN OBJECT WITH THE ARROW TOOL

1 Select the Arrow tool, and then select the object that you want to resize.

2 Click the Scale modifier in the Toolbar's Options section. Eight unfilled squares appear on the object's perimeter.

3 To rescale an object proportionately, click a square at the object's corner. Drag diagonally to scale the object.

4 To resize an object's height, click the middle square on the object's top or bottom, and then drag up or down.

5 To resize an object's width, click the middle square on the object's right or left side, and then drag right or left.

Using the Snap to Objects Modifier

The Snap to Objects modifier makes it possible for you to precisely align objects to one another. When the modifier is enabled, a black circle appears under the cursor when you drag a selected object. The black circle becomes larger when it is close enough to snap to another object. The point where one object snaps to another depends upon the reference point of the black circle. For instance, if you drag the object by its center, the center of the object will snap to other objects.

To Enable THE SNAP TO OBJECTS MODIFIER, DO ONE OF THE FOLLOWING:

■ ....Select the Arrow tool, and then click the Snap to Objects button in the Options section.

■ ....Choose Snap to Objects from the View menu.

■ ....If the Main toolbar (Windows only) is enabled, click the Snap to Objects button.

see also You can also snap objects to the grid or guides. See Modifying the Grid section in Chapter 1 for more information.

Using the Lasso Tool

You can also create selections with the Lasso tool. Use the tool to create a freeform selection and round up objects on the Stage or to create a point-to-point selection area using the tool's Polygon modifier.

To Create A FREEFORM SELECTION WITH THE LASSO TOOL

1 Select the Lasso tool.

2 Drag onto the Stage to define the boundaries of the selection, as shown in Figure 3-12.

3 Release the mouse button to close the selection.

To Create A POINT-TO-POINT SELECTION WITH THE LASSO TOOL

1 Select the Lasso tool.

2 Click the tool's Polygon modifier.

3 Click to set the location of the first point.

4 Click to add the second point. A straight line connects the two points, shown in Figure 3-13.

5 Continue adding points to define the selection area.

6 Double-click to close the selection.

FIGURE 3-12

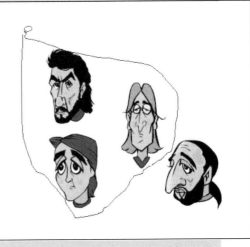

You can create a freeform selection with the Lasso tool.

FIGURE 3-13

You can create a point-to-point selection using the Lasso tool with the Polygon modifier selected.

Modifying Objects with the Menu Commands

The Arrow tool and its modifiers allow you to manually modify objects. There are also menu commands that allow you more options when modifying objects. However, many menu commands achieve the same results as tools. The only commands that will be covered in this book are those that offer different options than their respective tools.

Modifying Objects with the Transform Menu

The Transform menu contains commands that allow you to reposition objects with unerring accuracy. These commands come in handy when you animate objects.

To Access THE TRANSFORM MENU

▶ **Choose Transform from the Modify menu, and then choose the desired command, as shown in Figure 3-14. The Flip Vertical and Flip Horizontal commands are especially useful for animating text objects.**

FIGURE 3-14

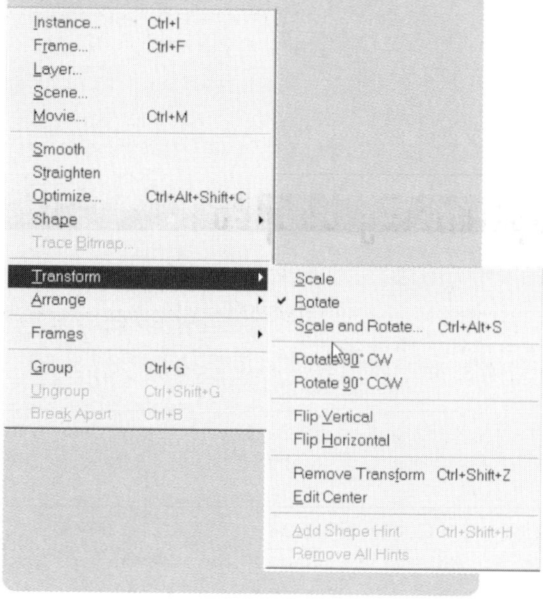

Instance...	Ctrl+I
Frame...	Ctrl+F
Layer...	
Scene...	
Movie...	Ctrl+M
Smooth	
Straighten	
Optimize...	Ctrl+Alt+Shift+C
Shape	▶
Trace Bitmap...	
Transform	▶
Arrange	▶
Frames	▶
Group	Ctrl+G
Ungroup	Ctrl+Shift+G
Break Apart	Ctrl+B

Transform submenu:

Scale	
✓ Rotate	
Scale and Rotate...	Ctrl+Alt+S
Rotate 90° CW	
Rotate 90° CCW	
Flip Vertical	
Flip Horizontal	
Remove Transform	Ctrl+Shift+Z
Edit Center	
Add Shape Hint	Ctrl+Shift+H
Remove All Hints	

Using the Scale and Rotate Command

The Scale and Rotate command is useful when you need to scale and rotate an object with mathematical precision.

To Scale AND ROTATE AN OBJECT

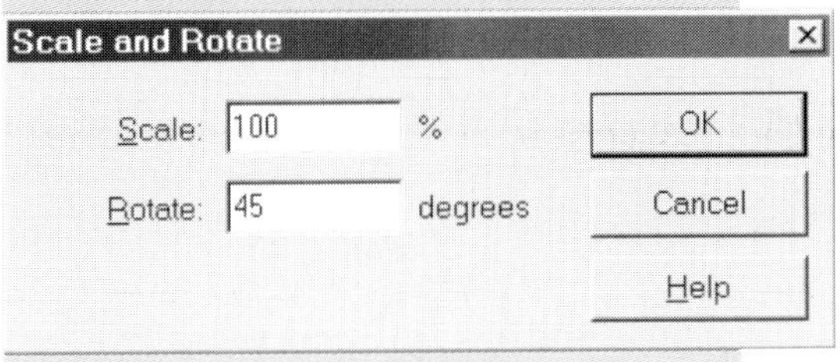

1 Choose Transform from the Modify menu, and then choose Scale and Rotate. The Scale and Rotate dialog box appears, as shown in Figure 3-15.

2 Enter a value in the Percentage field. Higher values increase size; lower values reduce size.

3 Enter a value in the Rotate field. Enter a negative value to rotate the object counter-clockwise.

4 Click OK.

FIGURE 3-15

Scale and Rotate

Scale: 100 %

Rotate: 45 degrees

OK Cancel Help

Optimizing Shapes

The Optimize command is another method of smoothing curved segments. Optimizing an object reduces the number of curves used to define it and reduces the file size of the completed Flash movie.

To Optimize AN OBJECT

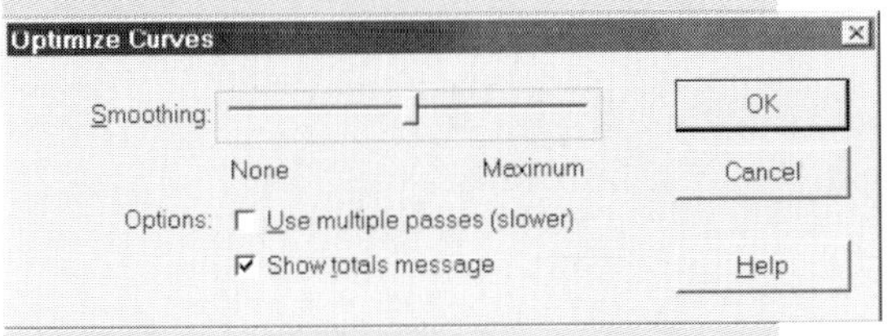

1 Select the shape that you want to optimize, and then choose Optimize from the Modify menu. The Optimize dialog box appears, as shown in Figure 3-16.

2 Drag the slider in the Smoothing section to determine the amount of optimization.

3 Enable the Use Multiple Passes option to have Flash repeat the process until further smoothing is not possible.

FIGURE 3-16

Optimize Curves

Smoothing:

None Maximum

Options: ☐ Use multiple passes (slower)
         ☑ Show totals message

OK Cancel Help

continues

55

continued

4 Enable the **Show Totals Message** option to display the results of the process.

5 Click **OK**.

Converting Lines to Fills

Converting lines to fills allows you to apply a gradient fill to a line. You can modify a converted line with the Arrow tool like any other filled shape, a technique that comes in handy when you are animating. Figure 3-17 shows a line before and after being converted to a fill. The converted line has been modified with the Arrow tool.

To Convert A LINE TO A FILL

1 Select the line that you want to convert.

2 Choose **Shape** from the **Modify** menu, and then choose **Convert Lines To Fills**.

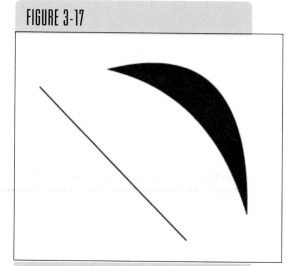

FIGURE 3-17

When you convert a line to a fill, you can edit it as if it is a filled shape.

Expanding Fills

Use the Expand Fill command to precisely expand the size of a filled shape. This command works best if the filled shape has no stroke.

To Expand A FILLED SHAPE

1 Select the shape, choose **Shape** from the **Modify** menu, and then choose **Expand Fill**. The Expand Fill dialog box appears, as shown in Figure 3-18.

continues

continued

2 In the Distance field, enter the value in pixels by which you want to enlarge or reduce the fill's size.

3 Select Expand to enlarge the size of the fill; select Inset to reduce the size of the fill.

4 Click OK.

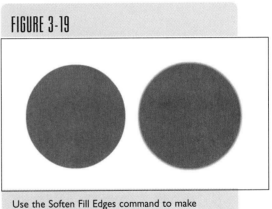

FIGURE 3-18

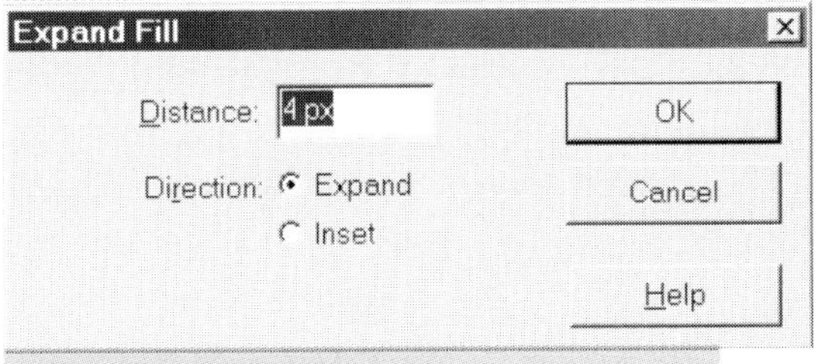

Softening Fill Edges

Use the Soften Fill Edges command to create a blurring effect at the edge of a filled object. This command works best on objects with no stroke. Figure 3-19 shows a filled object before and after the Soften Fill Edges command was applied.

To Soften A FILLED SHAPE'S EDGES

1 Select the filled object, choose Shape from the Modify menu, and then choose Soften Edges. The Soften Edges dialog box appears.

2 In the Distance field, enter a value in pixels. This value determines the width of the softened edge.

3 Enter a value in the Number of Steps field. This value determines how many bands Flash creates to blend the softened edge. More steps create a smoother blend but increase file size.

4 Select Expand to enlarge the shape when the edge is softened; select Inset to reduce the shape's size.

5 Click OK. Notice that the softened edge is actually a new object. To have the shape and softened edge behave as one object, select both, and then group them.

FIGURE 3-19

Use the Soften Fill Edges command to make an object appear as if it is out of focus.

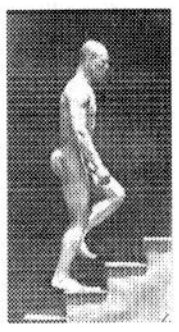

Modifying Text Shape

When you initially create a text object, you cannot edit it with the Arrow tool or use any of the menu commands to modify its shape. You can, however, change text into an editable shape by using the Break Apart command. Once you have converted a text object into an editable shape, you can no longer edit it as text.

To Modify A TEXT SHAPE

► Select the text object, and then choose **Break Apart** from the **Modify** menu. Flash converts the text object into editable shapes that you can modify using the **Arrow** tool or menu commands. **Figure 3-20** is a text object that was converted into editable shapes using the **Break Apart** command.

FIGURE 3-20

Modifying Objects with the Info and Transform Panels

The Arrow tool and its modifiers enable you to interactively move and modify a shape. When you need to transform or move an object with mathematical precision, use the Info and Transform panels.

Using the Info Panel

The Info panel gives you the exact dimensions of an object and its position on the Stage. You can modify an object's size or location by entering new values in the Info panel.

To Modify AN OBJECT USING THE INFO PANEL

▌ Select the object that you want to modify.

continues

2 Choose Panels from the Window menu, and then choose Info. Alternately, click the Info button on the Launcher bar. The Info panel appears, as shown in Figure 3-21.

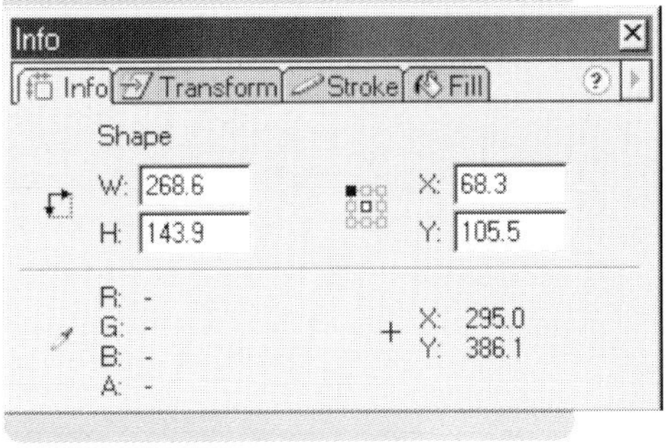

3 To resize an object, enter a new value in the W (width) or H (height) field.

4 To reposition an object, enter new values in the X (horizontal axis) and Y (vertical axis).

FIGURE 3-21

Info

| Info | Transform | Stroke | Fill |

Shape

W: 268.6   X: 68.3
H: 143.9   Y: 105.5

R: -
G: -   + X: 295.0
B: -   Y: 386.1
A: -

To the left of the object's coordinates on the Info panel is an icon with nine small squares. By default, the square in the top-left corner is black, and the center square is white. The black square denotes which point of the object is being used as the point of reference, in other words, the point on the object that Flash uses to compute its position. To switch to a center point of reference, click the square in the center.

To understand the difference between the two reference points, consider a square object, 100 pixels by 100 pixels, in the upper-left corner of the Stage. Using the default reference point, the Info panel shows its position as X:0,Y:0. Using the center reference point, the Info panel shows its position as X:50,Y:50.

The bottom section of the Info panel shows the current position of the cursor on the Stage, plus the RGB and Alpha values of objects that the cursor moves over.

Using the Transform Panel

You use the Transform panel to resize an object by a specified percentage and to rotate or skew an object by a specified number of degrees. You can also use it to duplicate and transform an object in one operation.

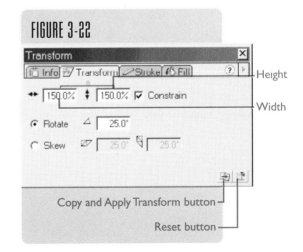

FIGURE 3-22

Transform

| Info | Transform | Stroke | Fill |

150.0% ↕ 150.0% ☑ Constrain — Height / Width

⦿ Rotate △ 25.0°

○ Skew ⊿ 25.0° ⧄ 25.0°

Copy and Apply Transform button
Reset button

To Access THE TRANSFORM PANEL

► Choose Panels from the Window menu, and then choose Transform. Alternately, click the Info button on the Launcher bar, and then click the Transform tab.

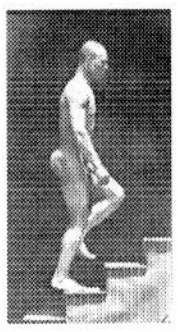

To Modify A SELECTED OBJECT USING THE TRANSFORM PANEL, DO ONE OF THE FOLLOWING:

■ ....To resize the object proportionately, click the Constrain box, enter a value in either the Width or Height text box, and then press Enter or Return.

■ ....To resize an object's width, enter a percentage value in the Width text box, and then press Enter or Return.

■ ....To resize an object's height, enter a value in the Height text box, and then press Enter or Return.

■ ....To rotate a selected object using the Transform panel, click the Rotate option, enter a value, and then press Enter or Return. To rotate the object counterclockwise, enter a negative value.

■ ....To skew a selected object using the Transform panel, click the Skew option, and then enter a value in either or both text fields. The left field skews an object along its horizontal axis; the right field skews an object along its vertical axis.

■ ....To transform an object while creating a duplicate, enter the transformations that you want to apply to the duplicated object, and then click the Copy and Apply Transform button at the bottom of the panel.

TiP Flash remembers the last transformation that you apply with the Transform panel. This comes in handy when you need to create multiple objects and apply the same transformation to each duplicate. For example, to create the spokes of a wheel, draw a vertical line with the Line tool. Open up the Transform panel, select the Rotate option, and then enter a value of 30 degrees. Click the Copy and Apply Transform button to create the first duplicate, and then click the button to create additional duplicates that rotate 30 degrees. Continue clicking the button to spin the spokes of the wheel.

To Undo THE LAST TRANSFORMATION THAT YOU APPLIED WITH THE TRANSFORM PANEL

▶ Click the Reset button at the bottom of the panel.

Using the Ink Bottle Tool

You use the Ink Bottle tool to change an object's stroke color. You click the tool on a line or an outline to apply the currently selected stroke color, line style, and line weight. The Ink Bottle tool comes in handy when you need to change the stroke characteristics of several items in your scene. You simply fill the Ink Bottle with the desired stroke color, line style, and line weight, and then you apply the tool to every object whose stroke you need to change.

To Use THE INK BOTTLE TOOL

1 Select the Ink Bottle tool.

2 Select a stroke color.

3 Choose Panels from the Window menu, and then choose Stroke. The Stroke dialog box appears. Select the desired line style and weight.

4 Click an object on the Stage to apply the stroke. If you click the middle of a filled object, the Ink Bottle tool applies the stroke to its outline.

see also For more information on stroke style, stroke height, and stroke color, see the Selecting Stroke and Fill Attributes section in Chapter 2.

Using the Paint Bucket Tool

You use the Paint Bucket tool to fill enclosed areas with solid, gradient, or bitmap fills. You can use it to fill an enclosed outline created with one of the drawing tools, or you can use it to change an existing fill. The Paint Bucket tool has modifiers that allow you to fill an outline with a gap.

To Apply A FILL WITH THE PAINT BUCKET TOOL

1 Select the Paint Bucket tool.

2 Select a solid color or gradient for the fill.

3 If you are filling an outline with gaps, click the Gap Size Modifier button, and then select one of the options, as shown in Figure 3-23.

4 Click an object on the Stage to apply the fill.

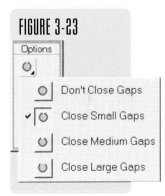

FIGURE 3-23

see also For more information on selecting a fill color, refer to the Selecting Stroke and Fill Attributes section in Chapter 2.

Editing a Fill with the Paint Bucket Tool

You can modify a bitmap or gradient fill with the Paint Bucket tool's Transform Fill modifier. In this mode, the Paint Bucket tool can adjust the position, size, and rotation of the fill relative to the object that you apply it to.

To Edit A FILL

1 Select the Paint Bucket tool, and then click the Transform Fill modifier, as shown in Figure 3-24.

2 Click the filled object. The fill's center point and a bounding box with handles appear, as shown in Figure 3-25.

3 Click and drag the circle in the center of the object to move the fill's center, as shown in Figure 3-26.

continues

FIGURE 3-24

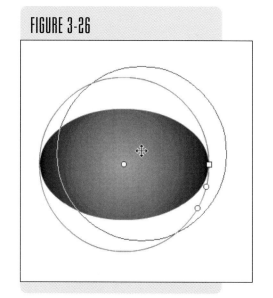

FIGURE 3-25

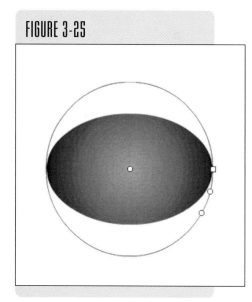

FIGURE 3-26

continued

4 To change the width of the fill, click and drag the square handle on the side of the bounding box, as shown in Figure 3-27.

5 To proportionately resize the fill, click and drag the round handle below the square handle, as shown in Figure 3-28.

6 To rotate the fill, click and drag the last round handle, as shown in Figure 3-29. As you drag one of the fill's handles to move it to a new position, a black bounding box appears, giving you a preview of the fill's new location. Release the mouse button to finish transforming the fill.

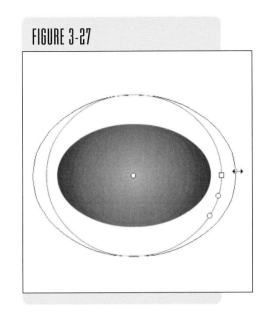

FIGURE 3-27

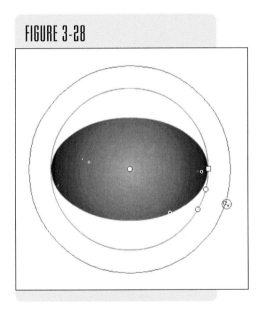

FIGURE 3-28

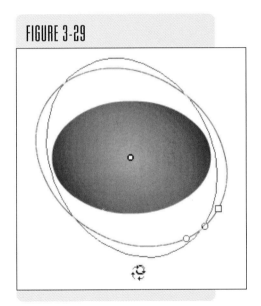

FIGURE 3-29

Locking a Fill with the Paint Bucket Tool

A locked fill appears to emanate from a central point on the Stage. When you apply a locked gradient or bitmapped fill to objects, they act as windows to an underlying gradient or image that covers the entire Stage.

To Create A LOCKED FILL

1 Select the Paint Bucket tool, and then choose a gradient or bitmap as a fill.

2 Click the Lock Fill Modifier button (the padlock in the tool's Options section).

3 To apply the locked fill, click an object on the Stage, as shown in Figure 3-30.

FIGURE 3-30

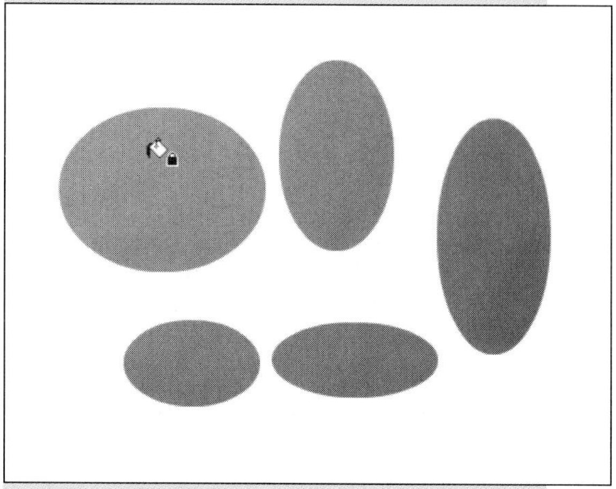

When you apply a locked fill to objects, they act as masks to an underlying gradient that covers the Stage.

Using the Dropper Tool

You use the Dropper tool to sample a fill and apply it to another object. You can use the tool to sample a bitmap as a fill, a technique you will learn in Chapter 5.

To Sample AN OBJECT'S STROKE OR FILL USING THE DROPPER TOOL

1 Select the Dropper tool, and then click the object whose stroke or fill you want to sample. Clicking a stroke turns the Dropper tool into the Ink Bottle tool. Sampling a fill turns the Dropper tool into the Paint Bucket tool with the Lock Gradient modifier enabled.

2 Click a line or outline to apply a sampled stroke. Click an enclosed outline or filled object to apply a sampled fill.

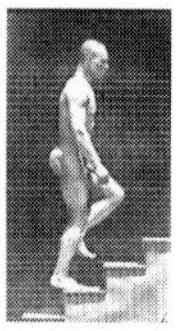

Using the Eraser Tool

Even the best graphic artist makes a mistake every now and then. Use the Eraser tool like a normal eraser, or use it to erase only lines or fills.

To Completely ERASE A STROKE OR FILL

1 Select the Eraser tool.

2 Click the Faucet modifier.

3 Drag the tool onto the Stage. Notice that the cursor changes into an icon that looks like a dripping faucet, as shown in Figure 3-31. Click a stroke or filled shape to completely remove it.

FIGURE 3-31

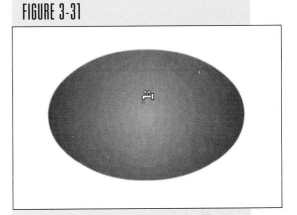

To Erase EVERYTHING ON STAGE

▶ Double-click the Eraser tool.

Erasing Shapes

In addition to using the Eraser tool to totally delete a stroke or fill, you can use the tool like a conventional eraser and drag to erase part of an object. The tool's modifiers let you specify the size of the eraser and exactly which part of an object to erase.

To Erase A SHAPE USING THE ERASER TOOL

1 Select the Eraser tool.

2 Click the Eraser Mode button, and then select from the following modes:

Erase Normal erases strokes and fills on a layer as you drag the tool across them.

Erase Fills erases only filled shapes; strokes and outlines are not affected.

continues

continued

Erase Lines erases strokes only; filled objects are not affected.

Erase Selected Fills erases a fill from a selected shape without affecting its stroke.

Erase Inside erases the fill from an object where you begin the eraser stroke without affecting surrounding fills or strokes.

note When using the Eraser tool's Erase Inside mode, make sure that you begin the stroke inside the object that you want to erase. Otherwise, you may end up erasing the wrong item, especially if you have several items stacked on top of one another.

3 Click the Eraser Shape modifier, and then select a size and shape from the pop-up menu.

4 Drag the tool onto the Stage to erase the stroke or fill.

Creating Custom Colors and Gradients

The standard Web 216 color palette is the default color palette used in Flash. You can, however, change the default palette to one of your own creation. You can also save frequently used color combinations as custom palettes and load them as needed. You use the Mixer and Swatches panels to select and create colors and load palettes. You use the Fill panel to create solid, linear, and radial gradients. You can add a color or gradient that you create to the palette used in the movie that you are creating. You can even save the modified color palette for future use.

Using the Mixer Panel

The Mixer panel, as shown in Figure 3-32, is another method of specifying or editing a stroke or fill color. The Mixer panel gives you considerably more latitude than the Color section of the Toolbox. You can apply a stroke or fill to an object by dipping your cursor into the Color Bar to select a color, or you can enter known color numeric values in the R, G, and B fields.

FIGURE 3-32

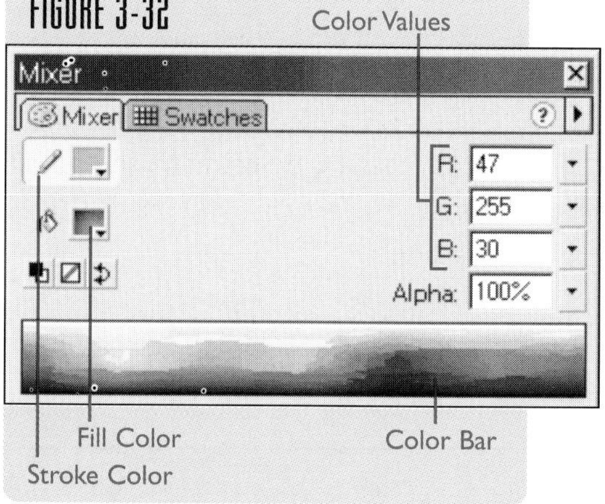

Color Values

Mixer		
Mixer	Swatches	

R: 47
G: 255
B: 30
Alpha: 100%

Fill Color
Stroke Color
Color Bar

To Create A CUSTOM COLOR WITH THE MIXER PANEL

1 Choose Panels from the Window menu, and then choose Mixer. The Mixer panel appears.

2 Click the Fill or Stroke Color swatch to select an existing color from the palette.

3 Click either the Stroke Color or Fill Color window, and then drag the cursor in the Color Bar to mix a custom color. As you drag, the Color swatch changes to reflect the new color in both the Mixer panel and the Color section of the Toolbox. Release the mouse button to select a color.

4 To match a known color, enter its values into the R, G, and B color value fields. Click the triangle in the upper-right corner of the Mixer panel, and then from the menu choose to enter values in either RGB, HSB, or Hex (hexadecimal) format. Alternately, click the small triangle to the right of each field, and then drag the slider to the desired value.

5 To add transparency to the color, enter a value from 0 (transparent) to 100 (opaque) in the Alpha field.

6 To add a custom color to the currently loaded palette, click the triangle in the upper-right corner of the Mixer panel, and then choose Add Swatch.

note It is possible to apply a transparent stroke or fill to a new object but not an existing one. To apply transparency to an existing stroke or fill, you must first delete it and then create a new one.

Using the Swatches Panel

The Swatches panel, as shown in Figure 3-33, is conveniently grouped with the Mixer panel. Use the Swatches panel to select a color or gradient from the currently loaded palette, duplicate a swatch, delete a swatch, load a custom color palette, add colors to the current palette, replace the existing palette, or sort the palette by colors.

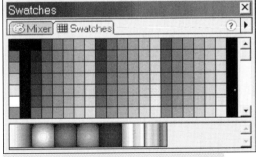

FIGURE 3-33

To Load AN EXISTING COLOR SET

1 Choose Panels from the Window menu, and then choose Swatches. The Swatches panel appears.

continues

continued

2 Click the triangle in the panel's upper-right corner, and then choose one of the following menu options:

Add Colors to add a saved palette's colors to the currently loaded palette.

Replace Colors to replace the currently loaded palette with another one.

Load Default to replace the currently loaded palette with the default palette.

Web 216 to load the Web safe 216 color palette.

3 The Import Color Swatch dialog box appears. Locate the desired color set file, and then click Open.

To Save A CURRENTLY LOADED COLOR PALETTE

1 Click the triangle in the upper-right corner of the panel, and then choose one of the following:

Save Colors to save the currently loaded color palette.

Save as Default to replace the current default palette with the existing one.

2 If you select the Save Colors command, the Export Color Swatch dialog box appears. Locate the folder in which you want to save the palette, enter a name for the color set, and then click Save.

To Clear ALL COLORS FROM THE PALETTE EXCEPT BLACK AND WHITE

 Choose Clear Colors from the Swatches panel's Option menu.

To Sort THE PALETTE BY HUES OF THE SAME COLOR

Choose Sort by Color from the panel's Option menu.

Creating a Custom Fill

The default color set gives you seven gradient fills to choose from. You can modify these fills to suit an object in your movie. When creating a custom gradient, it is beneficial to have both the Fill and Mixer panels open at the same time so that you can switch back and forth between panels when modifying a gradient's colors.

To Create A CUSTOM FILL

1 Choose Panels from the Window menu, and then choose Fill. The Fill panel appears.

2 Select one of the preset gradients from the Mixer panel as a starting point. The selected gradient appears in the Fill panel. The selected fill in **Figure 3-34** is a Linear Gradient. A Linear gradient blends two or more colors in a Linear pattern, and you apply them to Rectanglar objects in most instances. A Radial gradient blends two or more colors concentrically.

3 To change a fill's color, click one of its color pointers. The Pointer Color window appears to the right of the Gradient Definition bar and displays the pointer's current color. Click the Color swatch to choose a color from the palette. To apply transparency to the color, in the Mixer panel adjust the Alpha setting to the desired degree of transparency. Alternately, you can choose a color from the Mixer.

4 To change a pointer's position, click and drag it to a new position on the Gradient Definition bar. To add a color pointer to the gradient, click below the Gradient Definition bar at the point where you want to add the color. Select a color for the pointer as outlined in step 3.

continues

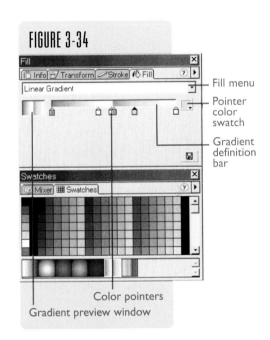

FIGURE 3-34

Fill menu

Pointer color swatch

Gradient definition bar

Color pointers

Gradient preview window

TIP To convert a horizontal Linear gradient to vertical, select the Paint Bucket tool, enable the Transform Fill modifier, and then rotate the gradient to a vertical position.

see also For more information on creating Bitmap gradients, refer to Chapter 5.

continued

5 Add more pointers and colors as needed. To save the gradient to the movie's palette, click the triangle in the **Fill** panel's upper-right corner, and then choose **Add Gradient**.

TIP To create a Linear or Bitmap gradient, click the arrow to the right of the Fill menu, and then select the desired gradient type.

chapter 3: modifying graphic objects

Creating Complex Graphic Objects

4

To add complex graphic objects to your Flash 5 movies, you can create simple shapes with the drawing tools and unite them into a whole greater than the sum of its parts. Flash has a decidedly different way of treating intersecting lines and overlapping shapes. At first, you may find this departure from time-honored vector-drawing functionality strange, but you will soon learn to use it to your advantage. In this chapter, you will learn how to master the way that Flash handles vector-drawn objects to create complex graphics for your movies.

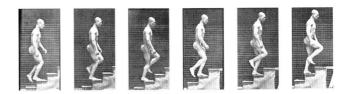

Working with Intersecting Lines

A line that you create with the Line tool is a single line segment. However, when one line intersects another, the top line neatly cleaves the lower line into two segments, each of which you can select and move to another location. However, if you select the top line first, it breaks into two segments. Figure 4-1 shows an identical pair of intersecting lines. The set on the right has been separated with the Arrow tool.

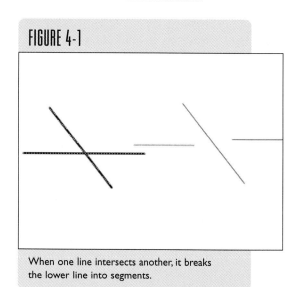

FIGURE 4-1

When one line intersects another, it breaks the lower line into segments.

Working with Overlapping Shapes

Flash also differs from conventional vector-based drawing programs in how it handles overlapping shapes. In Flash, when you place one shape on top of another in the same layer and deselect the shape, the two shapes lose their identity. The overlapping shapes either combine to create a new shape, or one shape cuts away from another, much like Boolean modeling in 3-D programs. Figure 4-2 shows some objects created by overlapping shapes.

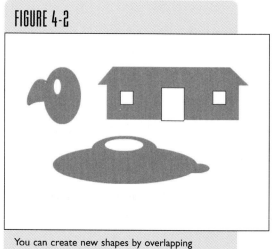

FIGURE 4-2

You can create new shapes by overlapping one shape with another.

Expanding a Filled Shape

When you overlap two shapes of the same color on a layer, they merge to become a new shape. You can further modify the resulting shape with either the Arrow tool or, if you prefer point-by-point editing, the Subselect tool.

To Expand A FILLED SHAPE

1 Create a filled object using the **Oval, Rectangle,** or **Brush** tool.

2 Create another object of the same color.

3 Using the **Arrow** tool, overlap the two shapes as desired.

4 Deselect the shape that you just positioned. The two shapes are now one, as shown in Figure 4-3.

FIGURE 4-3

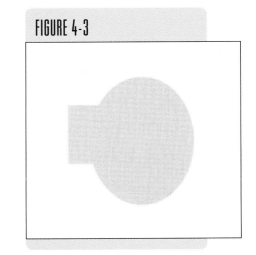

> **note** When you combine shapes to create a new shape, the result is easier to control if the shapes have a transparent stroke.

Subtracting from a Filled Shape

When you overlap shapes of different colors on the same layer, deselect the shapes, and then select and remove one shape. The shape that you remove cuts a piece out of the remaining shape. You use this characteristic to create a character's eye sockets, windows for a building, or tire rims.

To Subtract ONE SHAPE FROM ANOTHER

1 Create a filled shape using the **Oval, Rectangle,** or **Brush** tool.

2 Create a second shape of a different fill color.

continues

3 Using the Arrow tool, overlap it with the first, as shown in Figure 4-4.

4 Deselect the second shape by clicking anywhere on the Stage.

5 Select and drag the second shape away from the first shape to create a new object, as shown in Figure 4-5.

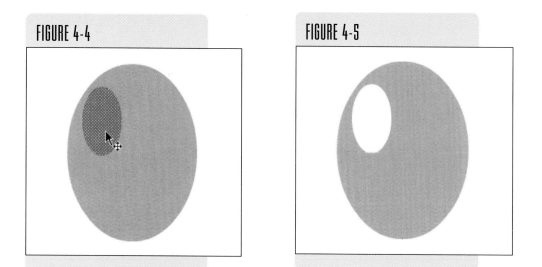

FIGURE 4-4

FIGURE 4-5

Overlapping Lines and Filled Shapes

You can place a line on top of a fill to create new shapes. The resulting shapes depend upon whether you select the line or the filled shape after creating the objects. The following steps illustrate the different results possible when you place lines on fills and vice-versa.

To Create NEW SHAPES BY PLACING A FILL OVER A LINE

1 Using the Line, Pen, or Pencil tool, draw a line on the Stage.

2 Using the Oval, Rectangle, or Brush tool, create a filled shape with no stroke.

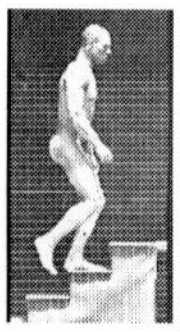

continued

3 Position the filled shape on top of the line, as shown in Figure 4-6.

4 Deselect the filled shape. The line will be segmented, as shown in Figure 4-7. For the purpose of this figure, the new segments were repositioned with the Arrow tool.

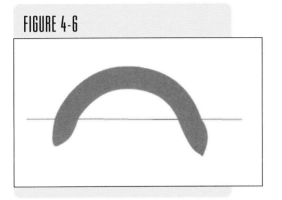

FIGURE 4-6

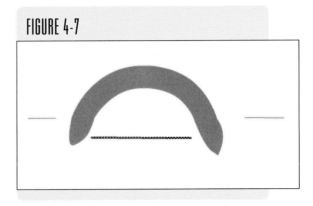

FIGURE 4-7

To Create NEW SHAPES BY PLACING A LINE OVER A FILL

1 Create a filled shape using the Oval, Rectangle, or Brush tool. It is easier to control the final outcome if the filled shape has no stroke.

2 Create a line using the Line, Pen, or Pencil tool.

3 Using the Arrow tool, position the line over the filled shape, as shown in Figure 4-8.

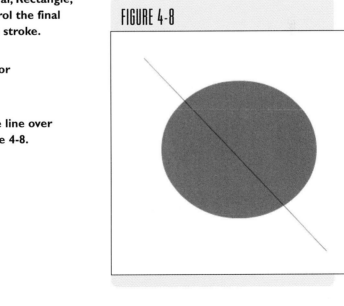

FIGURE 4-8

continues

continued

4 The shapes that are left depend upon which item you select first. If you first select the filled shape with the Arrow tool, two new filled shapes and the original line remain, as shown in Figure 4-9.

5 If you first select the line with the Arrow tool, the filled shape will remain unchanged, but three new line segments appear, as shown in Figure 4-10.

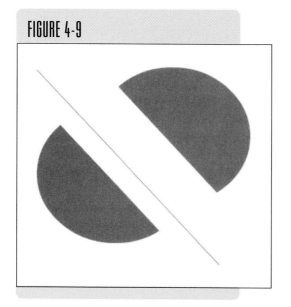

FIGURE 4-9

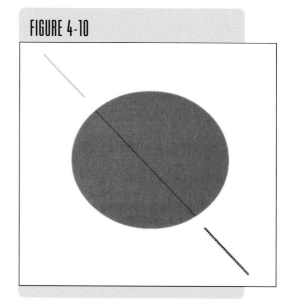

FIGURE 4-10

Aligning Objects

You can align objects to each other and to the Stage by using the Grid and the Arrow tool. However, the most precise way to align and position objects to each other and to the Stage is to use the Align panel.

The Align panel has options to align, distribute, and space objects along the vertical axis, horizontal axis, or along both axes. You can also use the panel to match the width, height, or both dimensions of selected objects and evenly space them along the vertical axis, horizontal axis, or both. You can perform these alignment options relative to the position of the selected objects or to the Stage. You can combine the options in the Align panel to perform more than one modification on an object. For example, you can align a selection of objects, space them, and match their dimensions simultaneously by clicking the proper buttons.

chapter 4: creating complex graphic objects

Aligning Objects to Each Other

You use the buttons in the top section of the Align panel to perform alignment operations. Use a combination of these buttons to perform necessary alignment tasks.

To Align OBJECTS RELATIVE TO EACH OTHER

1 Select the objects that you want to align.

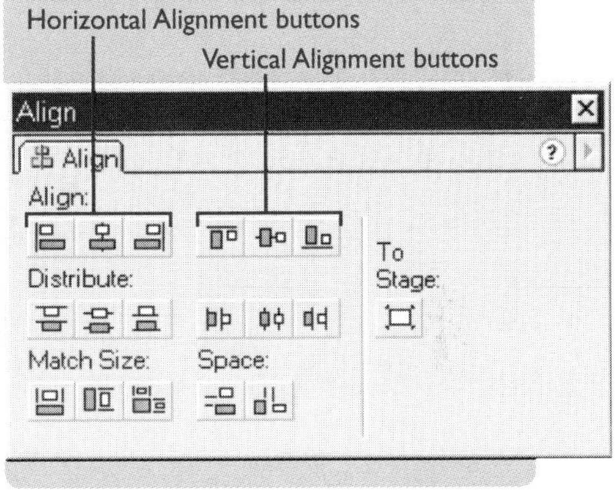

2 Choose Panels from the Window menu, and then choose Align. The Align panel appears, as shown in Figure 4-11.

3 In the Vertical Alignment section, click a button to apply one of the following alignment options:

Vertically align selected objects along the top edge of the highest selected object.

Vertically align selected objects to the center point between the top and bottom objects.

Vertically align selected objects along the bottom edge of the lowest selected object.

FIGURE 4-11

Horizontal Alignment buttons

Vertical Alignment buttons

4 In the Horizontal Alignment section, click a button to apply one of the following alignment options:

Horizontally align selected objects relative to the left edge of the object on the farthest left side of the Stage.

Horizontally align selected objects relative to the center point between the farthest left and farthest right objects.

Horizontally align selected objects relative to the right edge of the object on the farthest right side of the Stage.

5 To align objects both vertically and horizontally, click the desired alignment button from each section.

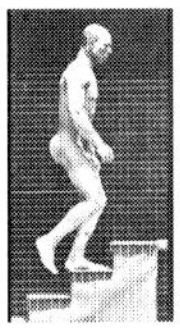

To Align OBJECTS RELATIVE TO THE STAGE

1 Select the objects that you want to align.

2 Open the Align panel.

3 Click the To Stage button.

4 In the Horizontal Alignment section, click a button to apply one of the following options:

Align selected objects to the left edge of the Stage.

Align selected objects to the horizontal center point of the Stage.

Align selected objects to the right edge of the Stage.

5 In the Vertical Alignment section, click a button to apply one of the following options:

Align selected objects to the top edge of the Stage.

Align selected objects to the vertical center point of the Stage.

Align selected objects to the bottom edge of the Stage.

6 To simultaneously align objects to the Stage vertically and horizontally, click the desired alignment button in each section.

Distributing and Spacing Objects

The Distribute section of the Align panel allows you to distribute objects evenly by their edges or centers.

To Distribute OBJECTS

1 Select the objects that you want to distribute. If you are distributing objects relative to their areas, select more than two objects.

2 Open the Align panel. The Align panel appears, as shown in Figure 4-12.

continues

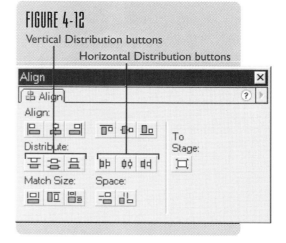

FIGURE 4-12
Vertical Distribution buttons
Horizontal Distribution buttons

chapter 4: creating complex graphic objects

continued

3 In the Vertical Distribution section, select Distribute Top, Distribute Vertical Center, or Distribute Bottom.

4 In the Horizontal Distribution section, select Distribute Left, Distribute Horizontal Center, or Distribute Right.

To Evenly SPACE OBJECTS

1 Select three or more objects that you want to space evenly.

2 To space the selected objects relative to the Stage, click the To Stage button.

3 Click the Space Vertically button to space the objects along the vertical axis.

4 Click the Space Horizontally button to space the objects along the horizontal axis.

Matching the Dimensions of Objects

You can also use the Align panel to modify the width, height, or both dimensions of selected objects. The selected objects' dimensions are changed relative to the largest selected object.

To Match THE DIMENSIONS OF OBJECTS

1 Select the objects whose dimensions you want to modify.

2 Open the Align panel.

3 In the Match Size section, select Match Width, Match Height, or Match Width and Height.

note If you click the To Stage button when matching dimensions of objects, Flash resizes the objects relative to the Stage's dimensions.

Creating Object Groups

As you learned previously, editable objects in Flash lose their identity when placed over other objects. One way to avoid this is by creating object groups. When grouped, objects are no longer editable and don't interact with other elements on the Stage. A group of objects behaves as a single unit. When you move, resize, or rotate a group, all of the elements that comprise the group do likewise. If you create several groups on a layer, they stack one on top of the other.

To Create A GROUP

1 Select the items that you want to group.

2 Choose Group from the Modify menu. Alternately, simultaneously press the Ctrl and G keys (Windows) or the Command and G keys (Macintosh). A bounding box appears around the group, as shown in Figure 4-13.

To Return THE OBJECT IN A GROUP TO EDITABLE STATUS

1 Select the group that you want to ungroup.

2 Choose Ungroup from the Modify menu. Alternately, simultaneously press the Ctrl and Shift and G keys (Windows), or simultaneously press the Command and Shift and G keys (Macintosh).

FIGURE 4-13

You group objects to organize the graphic objects used in your movies.

Arranging the Hierarchy of Grouped Objects

When you create several object groups on a layer, they stack on top of each other. As you add groups to the movie, they form a hierarchy; the last group created is at the top of the heap. Editable objects are always at the lowest level of the hierarchy. You can change the hierarchy of grouped objects and symbols. However, editable objects are always positioned at the bottom of the hierarchy.

To Change A GROUP'S OR SYMBOL'S POSITION IN THE HIERARCHY

1 Select the group or symbol whose position in the stacking order you want to rearrange.

continues

chapter 4: creating complex graphic objects

continued

2 Choose Arrange from the Modify menu to open the menu shown in Figure 4-14, and then choose one of the following options:

> **Bring to Front** brings a group or symbol to the top level.
>
> **Bring Forward** moves a group or symbol to the next highest level in the hierarchy.
>
> **Send Backward** moves a group or symbol to the next lowest level.
>
> **Send to Back** moves a group or symbol to the lowest level but above any editable objects on the Stage.

Figure 4-15 shows a group on the Stage with several editable objects. All the items have been selected. The object group is readily identifiable by the rectangular bounding box that surrounds it.

see aLso For more information on symbols, refer to Chapter 6.

TIP After creating a group and moving it to the desired position on Stage, you can lock it to prevent accidental editing. You can also lock symbols.

FIGURE 4-14

Modify	Text	Control	Window	H
Instance...	Ctrl+I			
Frame...	Ctrl+F			
Layer...				
Scene...				
Movie...	Ctrl+M			
Smooth				
Straighten				
Optimize...	Ctrl+Alt+Shift+C			
Shape	▶			
Trace Bitmap				
Transform	▶			
Arrange	▶			
Frames	▶			
Group	Ctrl+G			
Ungroup	Ctrl+Shift+G			
Break Apart	Ctrl+B			

Bring to Front	Ctrl+Shift+Up
Bring Forward	Ctrl+Up
Send Backward	Ctrl+Down
Send to Back	Ctrl+Shift+Down
Lock	Ctrl+Alt+L
Unlock All	Ctrl+Alt+Shift+L

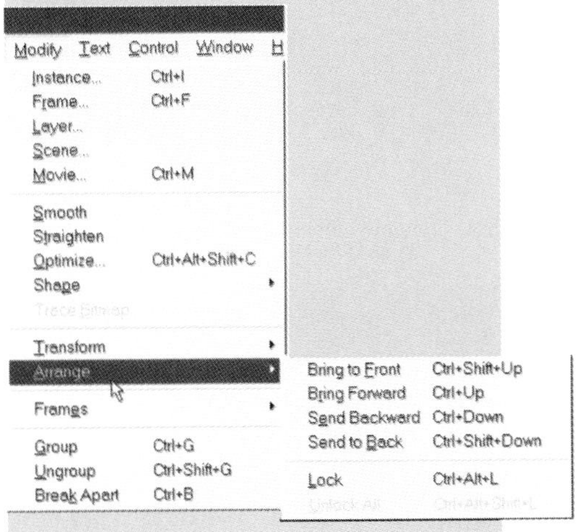

FIGURE 4-15

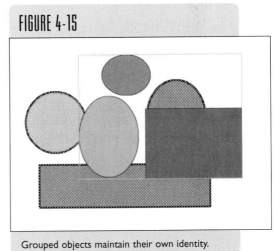

Grouped objects maintain their own identity.

To Lock A GROUP OR SYMBOL

1 Select the group or symbol that you want to lock.

2 Choose Arrange from the Modify menu, and then choose Lock. The symbol or group is locked and cannot be selected.

To Unlock ALL LOCKED GROUPS OR SYMBOLS

▶ Choose Arrange from the Modify menu, and then choose Unlock All.

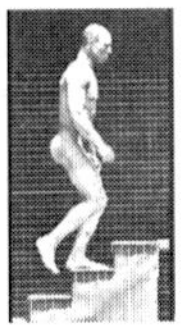

Editing Groups

Creating object groups is a convenient way to organize graphics in your movie. However, there will be times when you change your mind, or the client for whom you are creating the movie decides that a change is in order. Fortunately, you can edit individual items in a group by ungrouping it.

To Edit A GROUP

1 Select the group that you want to edit.

2 Choose Edit Selected from the Edit menu. Alternately, double-click the group, or choose Edit Selected from the pop-up context menu. Flash enters group-edit mode. The word "Group" is displayed in the upper-left corner, just above the Timeline, as shown in Figure 4-16. When you work in group-edit mode, objects not In the group are dimmed, indicating that they are not editable.

3 Perform the desired modifications on the items in the group.

4 To return to movie-editing mode, double-click anywhere on the Stage, or click the name of the current scene.

FIGURE 4-16

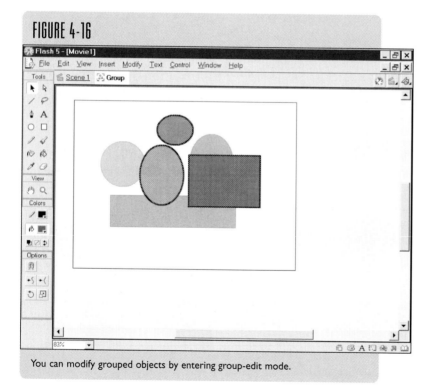

You can modify grouped objects by entering group-edit mode.

chapter 4: creating complex graphic objects

Creating Glowing Text

The Internet is bristling with examples of creative text usage in Flash. Glowing text is a relatively easy effect to create and can add visual interest to your Flash presentation.

To Create GLOWING TEXT

1 The glowing text effect works best against a dark background. Choose Movie from the Modify menu, and then choose a dark color for the background.

2 Create a block of text, as shown in Figure 4-17.

3 With the text still selected, choose Copy from the Edit menu.

4 Choose Paste from the Edit menu. A copy of the original text block appears on the Stage.

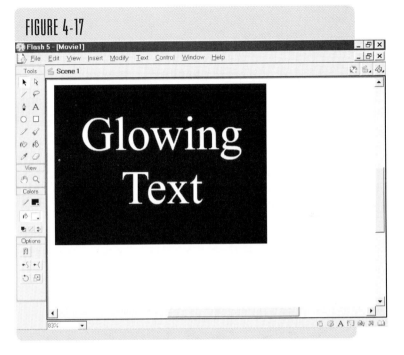

FIGURE 4-17

5 With the copied text still selected, click the Fill Color window, and then select a glow color. Bright greens and reds work well for this.

6 Choose Break Apart from the Modify menu, to turn the text block into editable shapes.

7 Choose Shape from the Modify menu, and then choose Soften Edges. The Soften Fill Edges dialog box appears.

8 In the Soften Edges dialog box, enter a value of 10 in both the Distance field and the Steps field. For the Direction option, select Expand, and then click OK.

> **note** The Distance and Steps values that you choose depend upon the size of the text to which you apply the glow. Use large values for big text.

9 To unify the block of broken apart text, choose Group from the Modify menu.

continues

continued

10   Choose Arrange from the Modify menu, and then choose Send to Back.

11   Select both blocks of text with the Arrow tool, choose Panels from the Window menu, and then choose Align.

12   Align the two blocks of text vertically and horizontally, and then group them. The completed glowing text effect appears, as shown in Figure 4-18.

You can use a variation of this technique to create the ubiquitous but effective drop shadow. Choose a light gray color for the copied text. To create a soft-edged drop shadow, use the Soften Fill Edges command. To create a hard-edged drop shadow, use the Expand Fill command. After sending the text to the back, use the Arrow tool to move it to the desired position. Shown in Figure 4-19 are hard-edged and soft-edged drop shadows.

FIGURE 4-18

FIGURE 4-19

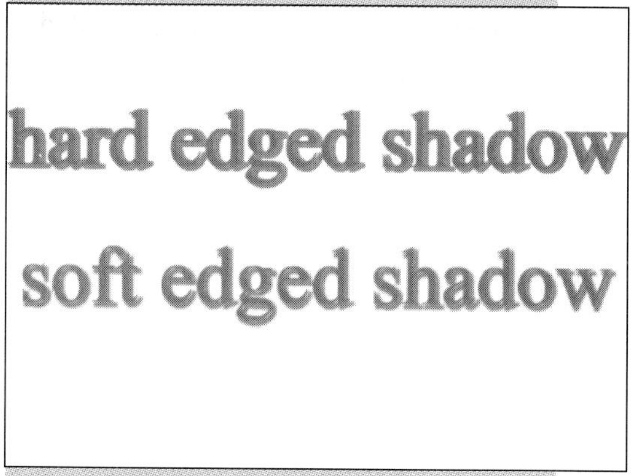

Painting Complex Graphics

When you have many graphic objects on the Stage, painting them can be an arduous task. Fortunately, the designers of Flash have provided you with modifiers for the Brush tool that allow you to control exactly where to apply paint. The Brush Mode modifiers determine exactly where Flash applies paint. Listed on the following page are some common uses for the different brush modes.

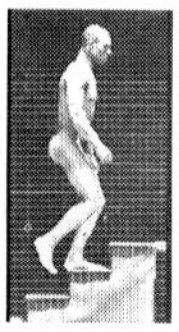

To apply paint anywhere on the Stage without disturbing lines, choose the Brush tool's Paint Fills mode.

To apply paint without disturbing existing fills and lines, choose the Brush tool's Paint Behind mode.

To apply paint to selected fills only, choose the Brush tool's Paint Selection mode. Flash applies paint within the areas of selected fills, leaving surrounding lines, unselected fills, and blank areas of the Stage unaffected. This mode comes in handy when you need to apply paint to several different objects on the Stage. Figure 4-20 shows the Brush tool in the Paint Selection mode. Paint is being applied in a haphazard fashion all over the Stage. When you release the mouse button, Flash applies the paint to only the selected fills, as shown in Figure 4-21.

To apply paint to the inside of a filled area, choose the Brush tool's Paint Inside mode. Begin your brush stroke inside a filled shape, and the surrounding Stage area, fills, and lines are unaffected.

FIGURE 4-20

Selected fills

You can use the Brush tool's Paint Selection mode to apply paint to several selected objects.

FIGURE 4-21

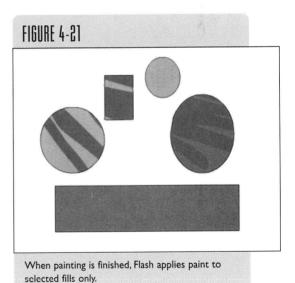

When painting is finished, Flash applies paint to selected fills only.

see aˡˢᵒ For more information on the Brush tool and its modifiers, refer to Chapter 2.

Filling Complex Graphics

Editing a complex graphic with many objects can be a time-consuming task. Creating selections is one way to speed up the editing process, especially when changing fill characteristics. By creating a selection of objects, you have the flexibility of applying the same fill to several objects in one operation.

To Apply A SOLID FILL TO SEVERAL OBJECTS

1 Using the **Arrow** tool, select the objects that you want to fill, as shown in **Figure 4-22.** If you are using Flash's default selection mode, click the first object to select it, and then hold down the **Shift** key and click additional objects to add them to the selection.

2 After you select the objects, the **Fill** button in the **Colors** section of the **Toolbox** becomes active. Click the **Fill Color** window, and then choose a color from the palette. Alternately, select a color from the **Mixer Panel.** Flash applies the color to the selected objects, as shown in **Figure 4-23.**

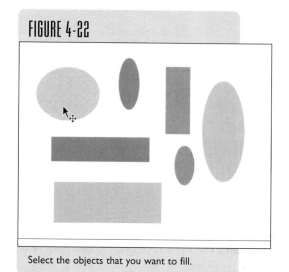

FIGURE 4-22

Select the objects that you want to fill.

FIGURE 4-23

Applying a gradient fill to several objects is a different process. If you use the method described previously and select a gradient from the palette, Flash applies the gradient as if each object were filled separately, as shown in Figure 4-24. Filling a selection in this manner makes the objects appear as if they are separate entities. To have the objects in a selection appear as parts of a single entity, you must apply a single gradient to the selection.

To Apply A SINGLE GRADIENT FILL TO SELECTED OBJECTS

1 Select the objects to which you want to apply the gradient.

2 Select the **Paint Bucket** tool.

3 Click the **Fill Color** swatch, and then select a gradient from the palette.

4 Click one of the selected objects to apply the fill. Flash fills the objects with a single gradient, as shown in **Figure 4-25**.

FIGURE 4-24

FIGURE 4-25

Organizing Complex Graphics with Layers

Layers are a valuable tool for organizing the graphic elements in your movies. When you add a layer to a movie, it's like placing a transparent sheet of acetate over the Stage. Objects on the layers above or below are visible, yet they are not affected by edits applied to the current layer. You can move between layers, lock layers, hide objects on a layer, and cut and paste objects between layers. Figure 4-26 shows graphic objects segregated by layers. Notice that where objects on upper layers overlap objects on lower layers, the underlying object is partially eclipsed.

FIGURE 4-26

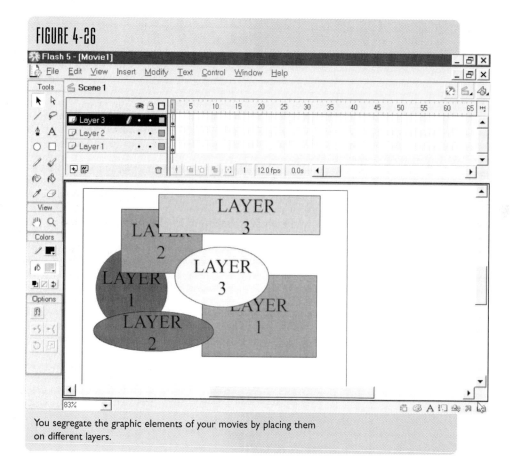

You segregate the graphic elements of your movies by placing them on different layers.

see aLso In Flash, you can use layers for more than just graphics. The mechanics of creating layers and navigating between them is covered in detail in Chapter 7.

Importing
Non-Flash
Graphics

At times, you will find it necessary to augment Flash 5's drawing tools by using imported graphics, such as clip art or perhaps a graphics file supplied by a client. With Flash, you have the capability of importing both vector and bitmap graphics. If the graphics were created in either Macromedia's Freehand or Fireworks, they can be imported as editable objects, preserving layers, text, and other document elements.

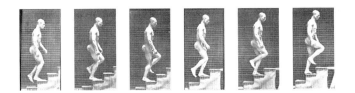

Importing Vector Graphics

All graphic objects that you create in Flash are vector-based. You can import vector images created in other programs directly into Flash. Flash supports the following vector-based images:

Adobe Illustrator AI and EPS (*.ai,*.eps) formats version 6.0 and earlier can be imported into Flash. Once you import files in these formats, you must ungroup the objects on each layer before you can edit them.

Enhanced Metafile (*.emf) is a Windows format that supports vector and bitmap images.

Freehand (*FH7, *FT7, *FH8,*FT8,*FH9,*FT9) is the best choice for importing vector graphics into Flash. If you are creating a vector image for a Flash project in Freehand, do not exceed eight colors when creating gradients. Flash creates a blending path when you import Freehand files with gradients exceeding eight colors. Also note that if you save the Freehand file with the CMYK color format, colors are converted to RGB when imported into Flash.

Windows Metafile (*.wmf) is another proprietary Windows vector format that imports directly into Flash.

To Import A VECTOR GRAPHIC INTO FLASH

1 Choose Import from the File menu. The Import dialog box opens, as shown in Figure 5-1.

2 Locate the file that you want to import.

3 Click Open to import the file.

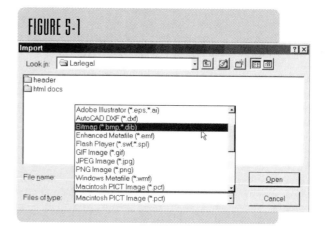

FIGURE 5-1

To Import A FreeHand file into Flash

1 Follow the preceding steps and select the desired FreeHand file. When you click **Open**, the FreeHand Import dialog box appears, as shown in Figure 5-2.

FIGURE 5-2

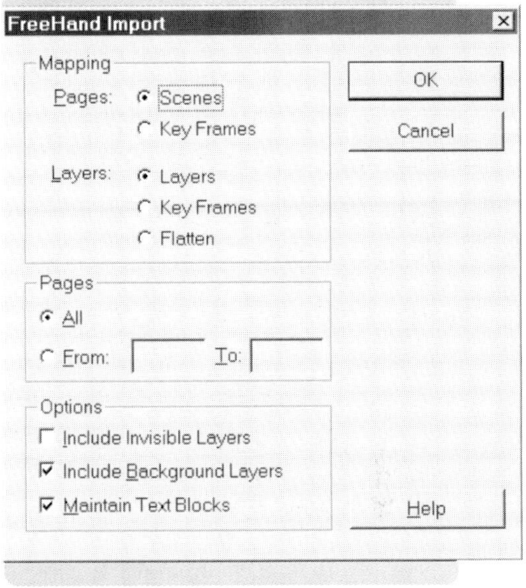

2 In the Mapping Pages section, select one of the following options:

Scenes converts each page of a FreeHand document into a scene.

Key Frames converts each page of a FreeHand document into a keyframe.

3 In the Mapping Layers section, select one of the following options:

Layers converts each layer in a FreeHand document into a layer in Flash.

Key Frames converts each layer in a FreeHand document into a keyframe in Flash.

4 In the Pages section, select one of the following options:

All imports all pages from the FreeHand document.

From imports selected pages from the FreeHand document. After selecting this option, enter the beginning and ending pages that you want to import into Flash by entering their numbers in the text fields.

5 In the Options section, select any of the following options:

Include Visible Layers imports all layers from the FreeHand document except those that are hidden.

Include Background Layers imports background layers from the FreeHand document.

Maintain Text Blocks imports text blocks from the FreeHand document as editable text.

6 Click **OK** to import the file.

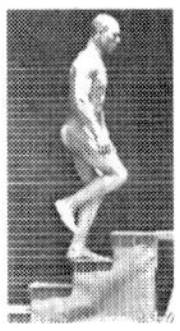

Importing Bitmap Images

Bitmap is the generic name for images comprised of pixels, little dots of color that combine to create the image. As a rule, bitmap files are larger than vector files and increase the download time of the published movie. However, there are times when only a bitmap image will give you the definition and color you are after, for example if your client is in the fashion business and you are displaying his or her wares in a Flash movie. Flash supports the following bitmap file formats:

Bitmap (*.bmp) is a Windows-based format. BMP files are not compressed and are therefore quite large. Don't confuse this format's name with the generic use of the name "bitmap" as it applies to all pixel-based images.

GIF (*.gif) is an acronym for Graphics Interchange Format. Images in this format have 256 colors or less. GIF files may also be multi-frame animations. GIF files are best suited to images with large areas of solid color. GIF files are available for both Windows and Macintosh. Animated GIF files import into Flash with frames intact. However, you have to remove some of the frames to get the timing right.

JPEG (*.jpg) is an acronym for Joint Photographic Experts Group. JPEG files support millions of colors, are compressed, and are well suited for displaying photographs on the Internet. The format is available for both Windows and Macintosh.

PICT (*pct,*.pic) format is available only for Macintosh Flash users. PICT images may be comprised of both vector and bitmap images. If the original file has an Alpha channel, it remains intact when imported, as long as the image was saved with 32 bit color and no compression.

PNG (*.png) is an acronym for Portable Network Group. Files saved in this format are not compressed. PNG files can be saved with an Alpha channel for compositing in Flash. The format is available for both Macintosh and Windows users and supports 8 bit and 24 bit color.

To Import a bitmap into Flash

1   **Choose Import from the File menu. The Import dialog box appears.**

continues

note If you create a movie that you intend to import into Flash, save it as sequenced images. When you import the first image into Flash, a dialog box appears, telling you that the file appears to be part of a sequence of images. Click Yes, and Flash imports the entire sequence and places each image on its own keyframe.

chapter 5: importing non-Flash graphics

continued

2 Locate the file that you want to import.

3 Click Open to import the file.

To Import A FIREWORKS PNG FILE INTO FLASH

1 After you follow the previous steps to open a Fireworks file, the Fireworks **PNG** Settings dialog box appears, as shown in Figure 5-3.

2 The Import Editable Items option is selected by default, and the following options are chosen by default:

> Include Images imports all bitmap images used in the original file. The bitmap images are included in the Flash Library but cannot be edited in an external editor.

> Include Text imports text as editable blocks.

> Include Guides imports all guides used in the Fireworks document. You can drag the imported guides to new positions as needed.

note PNG is the native format for files created in Macromedia's Fireworks. You can import these files into Flash as editable objects or flattened images. If you import the image flattened, you can launch Fireworks from within Flash to edit the original PNG file, complete with vector data, guides, and layers.

FIGURE 5-3

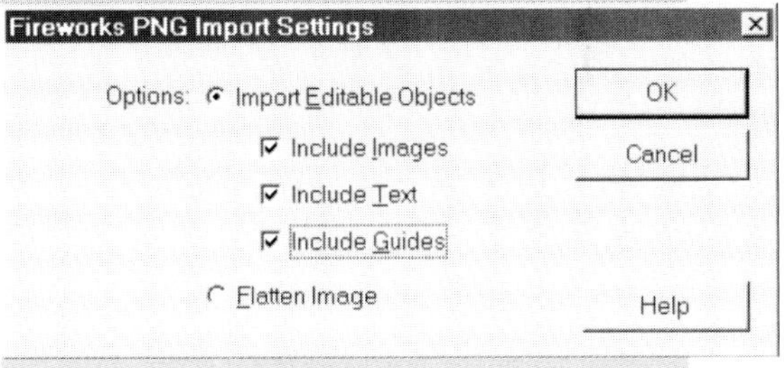

Fireworks PNG Import Settings	✕
Options: ⊙ Import Editable Objects	OK
☑ Include Images	Cancel
☑ Include Text	
☑ Include Guides	
○ Flatten Image	Help

3 Select Flatten Image to import the Fireworks **PNG** file as a bitmap on the currently selected layer.

4 Click **OK** to complete the import. Flash adds the image to the document Library.

To Edit A FLATTENED FIREWORKS FILE IN FIREWORKS

1 Select the image in the Library, and then choose Edit in Fireworks 3 from the Library Options menu. Fireworks 3 launches, and you are prompted to locate the original Fireworks file.

2 Locate the original file, perform the needed edits, save the file in Fireworks, and then close the program.

continues

3 From the Flash document Library, select the flattened image that you just edited.

4 Select Update from the Library Options menu.

5 Click Update to apply the edits that you performed in Fireworks.

see also For more information on updating imported Library items, refer to the Updating Imported Files in the Library section in Chapter 1.

Editing Bitmap Export Settings

All bitmaps in Flash movies are compressed before they are exported. You can modify the default compression of an individual image to suit your needs.

To Edit BITMAP EXPORT SETTINGS

1 Select the imported bitmap in the document Library.

2 Open the Library Options menu, and then choose Properties from the menu. The Bitmap Properties dialog box appears with the default export settings, as shown in Figure 5-4.

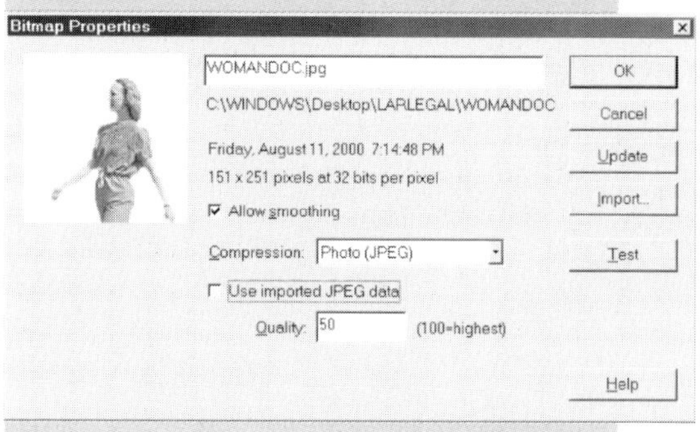

3 The Allow Smoothing option is checked by default and applies antialiasing to the exported image.

FIGURE 5-4

4 Click the arrow to the right of the Compression Settings field, and then choose Photo (JPEG), or Lossless (PNG/GIF).

5 If you select Photo, the Quality window opens. Enter a value to determine the amount of compression that Flash will apply to the exported image. For example, entering a value of 50 compresses the image by 50 percent. Higher values produce better looking images but increase file size. To apply a different compression value, disable the Use Document Default Quality option.

6 Click the Test button. The thumbnail image in the preview window updates to reflect the changes that you applied. A message appears at the bottom of the dialog box, showing you the image's file size at the new settings. Change the settings in steps 3 through 6 until you have the image quality and file size that you desire.

Converting Bitmaps to Flash Vector Objects

You can convert imported bitmaps to vector objects by using the Trace Bitmap command. The Trace Bitmap command breaks an image down into editable objects of similar colors. After converting the bitmap, you can modify the resulting vector objects with any of the editing tools or commands.

To Convert A BITMAP IMAGE INTO VECTOR OBJECTS

1 Select the bitmap image that you want to convert.

2 Choose Trace Bitmap from the Modify menu to open the Trace Bitmap dialog box, shown in Figure 5-5.

FIGURE 5-5

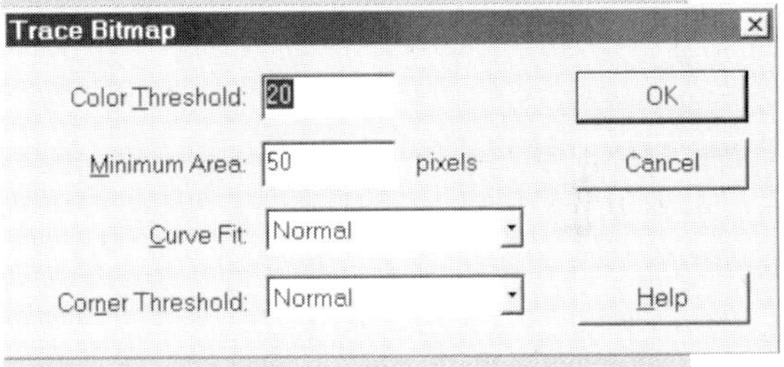

Trace Bitmap

Color Threshold: 20 OK

Minimum Area: 50 pixels Cancel

Curve Fit: Normal

Corner Threshold: Normal Help

3 In the Color Threshold field, enter a value between 1 and 500. This setting determines how close in color neighboring pixels must be before Flash considers them the same color. Lower values produce a more faithful rendition of the original bitmap but bloat the movie's file size.

4 In the Minimum Area field, enter a value between 1 and 1000. This setting determines how many neighboring pixels are included when Flash assigns color to an individual pixel.

5 Select an option from the Curve Fit menu. This setting determines how the outlines around the newly created vector objects are drawn. The Smooth or Normal options work well in most cases.

6 Select an option from the Corner Threshold menu. This setting determines how Flash draws corners when it creates the vector objects. The Many Corners option creates smooth, rounded objects; Few Corners creates blocky-looking vector objects with sharp corners. Normal is generally the best choice for creating good-looking shapes without breaking the bandwidth barrier.

7 Click OK to convert the bitmap to vector objects.

After the bitmap is traced, you can edit the individual vector objects with any of the Toolbox tools or menu commands. After editing the traced bitmap, you need to group it so that it behaves as a single entity. Figure 5-6 shows the original bitmap at the left and two traced versions to the right. The middle object resulted from a bitmap trace with a Color Threshold of 300 and a Minimum Area setting of 200 pixels. The object on the right was traced with a Color Threshold of 20 and a Minimum Area of 50 pixels. The object on the far right looks more like the original image, but if used in a Flash movie would result in a larger file size than if the object in the middle were used.

FIGURE 5-6

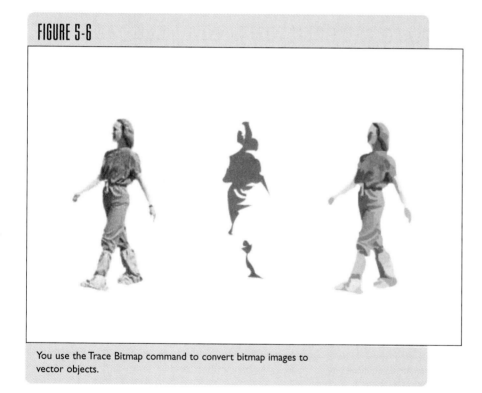

You use the Trace Bitmap command to convert bitmap images to vector objects.

Using the Break Apart Command

The Break Apart command is another way of converting a bitmap into editable objects. The objects that this command creates are areas of similar color that you can select and modify. You can convert a broken apart bitmap into a fill.

To Break APART A BITMAP

1 Select the bitmap that you want to break apart.

2 Choose Break Apart from the Modify menu. After the command is executed, the bitmap's bounding box disappears. Use the Lasso tool's Magic Wand modifier to select individual areas of color, or use the Dropper tool to convert the bitmap to a fill. After modifying a broken apart bitmap, group it, and it behaves as a single object.

Using the Magic Wand

You use the Lasso tool's Magic Wand modifier to select like areas of color from a broken apart bitmap. You can then modify the selection's shape with the Arrow or Subselect tool, or you can modify the selection's fill with the Paint Bucket tool.

To Select LIKE AREAS OF COLOR WITH THE MAGIC WAND

1 Break apart a bitmap.

2 Select the Lasso tool, and then click the Magic Wand modifier, as shown in Figure 5-7.

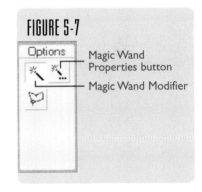

FIGURE 5-7

Magic Wand Properties button

Magic Wand Modifier

continues

3 Click the Magic Wand Properties button to open the Magic Wand Settings dialog box, as shown in Figure 5-8.

4 In the Threshold field, enter a value between 0 and 200. This setting determines how closely adjacent pixel colors must match before they are included in the selection. High settings create a selection with a wide band of colors. Enter a value of 0 to select pixels identical in color to the pixel that you click.

5 Select an option from the Smoothing menu. This setting determines how the edges of the selection are smoothed. The default Normal mode works well in most instances. The Pixel mode uses the pixels in the selection to determine how the edge is smoothed. This is similar to your photo-paint program's antialiasing feature.

6 Move the tool onto the Stage. Notice that the cursor changes from a lasso to a magic wand as it nears the broken apart bitmap. Click an area of color that you want to select on the bitmap. Hold down Shift, and then click to add other areas to the selection. Figure 5-9 shows a bitmap before and after the Magic Wand was used to make a selection. The bitmap on the right was broken apart. The Magic Wand was used to create a selection whose fill color was modified with the Paint Bucket tool.

FIGURE 5-8

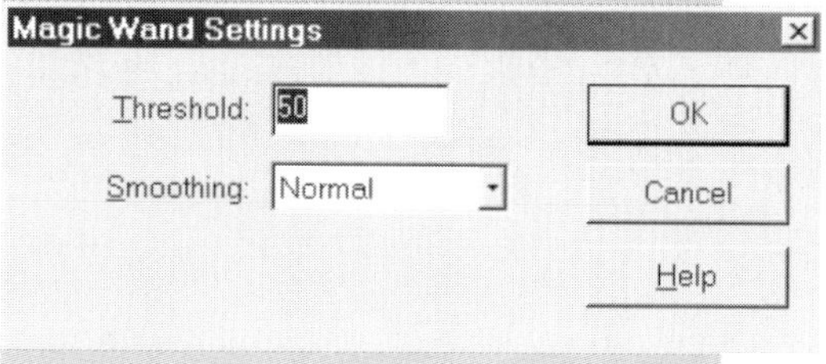

Magic Wand Settings

Threshold: 50

Smoothing: Normal

OK

Cancel

Help

n°te The Magic Wand modifier is a convenient way to remove unwanted background colors from a bitmap image that has been broken apart. Select the colors with the tool, and then press Delete to remove them.

FIGURE 5-9

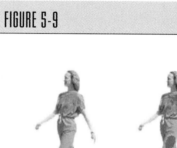

You use the Break Apart command to convert a bitmap into areas of like color.

Using Bitmaps as Fills

Once you break apart a bitmap, you can use it as a fill. A bitmap fill creates a tiling pattern within the object that you apply it to, or you can use it with the Brush tool to paint areas of a bitmap on the Stage or within a filled area.

To Convert A BITMAP TO A FILL

1 Select a bitmap that you want to sample as a fill.

2 Choose Break Apart from the Modify menu.

3 Select the Dropper tool, and then click the broken apart bitmap. The Dropper tool becomes the Paint Bucket tool. Notice that a minute image of the sampled bitmap appears in the Current Fill window, as shown in Figure 5-10.

4 After sampling the broken apart bitmap, delete it. Flash stored the original bitmap in the document Library when you first imported the file. If you need to use it again, select the bitmap in the document Library, and then drag it onto the Stage.

FIGURE 5-10

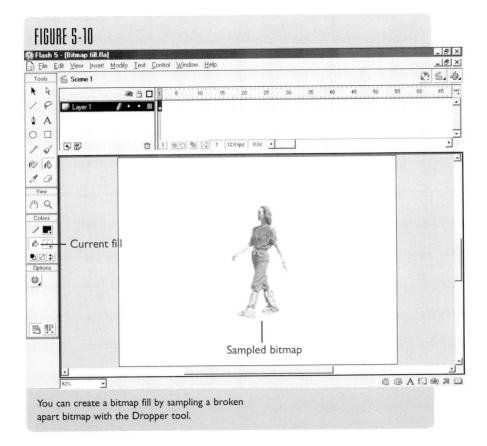

Current fill

Sampled bitmap

You can create a bitmap fill by sampling a broken apart bitmap with the Dropper tool.

To Apply A BITMAP FILL, DO ONE OF THE FOLLOWING:

■ ....After creating the bitmap fill, create an object on the Stage using either the **Oval** or **Rectangle** tool. Flash fills the object with a tiling pattern of the sampled bitmap.

■ ....After creating a bitmap fill, select the **Brush** tool, and then drag the tool on the Stage to apply brush strokes with the tiling bitmap pattern.

■ ....To fill an existing object with the bitmap fill, select the **Paint Bucket** tool, and then click the object.

Figure 5-11 shows an example of bitmap fills at work.

FIGURE 5-11

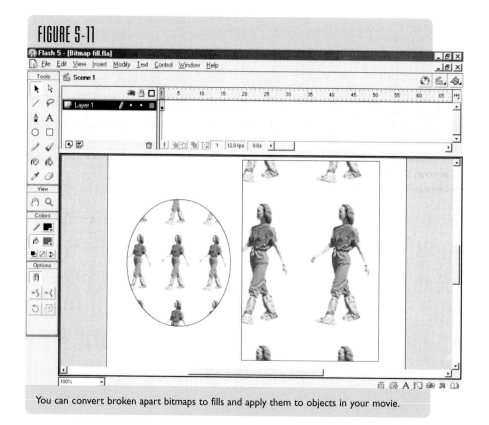

You can convert broken apart bitmaps to fills and apply them to objects in your movie.

Editing a Bitmap Fill

When you initially create the bitmap fill, the tiling images may need to be modified. You can scale, rotate, reposition, or skew the tiling images in the bitmap fill by using the Paint Bucket tool's Transform Fill modifier.

To Edit A BITMAP FILL

1 Select the Paint Bucket tool, and then click the Transform Fill modifier.

2 Click one of the tiling images within the bitmap. A bounding box with handles appears around the selected image. Figure 5-12 shows a selected image from within the bitmap fill.

3 To resize the image tile proportionately, drag the square handle to the lower left of the tile's bounding box. As the cursor approaches the handle, it changes into a diagonal double-headed arrow. Drag towards the tile's center to make the image smaller; drag away from the center to increase its size.

4 To change the image tile's height, drag the square handle at the bottom edge of the bounding box. As the cursor approaches the handle, it changes into a vertical double-headed arrow. Drag toward the tile's center to shorten it; drag away from the center to lengthen it.

5 To change the image tile's width, drag the square handle on the left side of the bounding box. As the cursor approaches the handle, it changes into a horizontal double-headed arrow. Drag away from the image's center to increase width; drag towards the center to decrease width.

6 To skew the tile horizontally, drag the round handle at the image tile's top center. The cursor becomes a horizontal double-headed arrow as it approaches the handle. Drag left or right to skew.

FIGURE 5-12

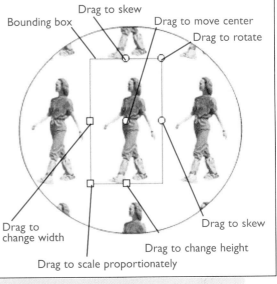

Drag to skew

Bounding box

Drag to move center

Drag to rotate

Drag to change width

Drag to skew

Drag to change height

Drag to scale proportionately

continues

continued

7 To skew the tile vertically, drag the round handle on the right side of the image tile's bounding box. The cursor becomes a vertical double-headed arrow as it approaches the handle. Drag up or down to skew.

8 To rotate the tile, drag the round handle on the top-right corner of the bounding box. The cursor changes to four curved arrows as it nears the handle. Rotate the tile clockwise or counterclockwise as desired.

9 To reposition the tile's center point, drag the center handle. As the cursor approaches the handle, it changes into a four-headed arrow. Drag up, down, left, or right.

A black bounding box appears as you drag a handle of the selected tile, giving you a preview of the tile's new position or size. When you release the mouse button, all tiles within the bitmap fill change to reflect the edit that you performed. Flash updates all objects using the bitmap fill. Click the edited bitmap fill with the Dropper tool to apply the changes to the current fill.

Creating Reusable Graphic Symbols

The ability to pack a lot of content into a small file is one of Flash 5's greatest assets. The compact file size of Flash movies is due in large part to the element known as the symbol. Symbols are reusable graphic artwork and other elements, such as buttons. By creating symbols and placing them in your movies, you have the capability of packing a lot of action in a very small file that downloads quickly into the user's Web browser.

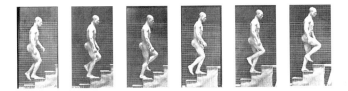

Understanding Symbols and Instances

When a graphic object is converted into a symbol, Flash stores all the pertinent instructions needed to recreate the object. A symbol is stored once in the document's Library and can be used repeatedly in a Flash production without adding additional elements to the file, which greatly reduces the file size of the finished production. Every time that you use a symbol in a movie, Flash creates an instance of the original. Flash recreates the instance by referring to the symbol's master instructions. When you create a symbol, you assign a behavior to it. You have three symbol behaviors at your disposal. They are as follows:

Symbols created with the Graphic behavior assigned to them are static images placed along the Timeline. You can animate instances of graphic symbols by changing their size, position, or rotation along the Timeline. When you create a symbol with the Graphic behavior, it is identified by the icon as shownin Figure 6-1.

FIGURE 6-1

Symbols created with the Button behavior assigned to them are interactive elements that react to mouse clicks and rollovers. You can assign a different graphic element to each rollover state. You can add sounds to buttons as well as actions. You will learn how to create interactive buttons in Chapter 11. When you assign the Button behavior to a symbol, it is identifiable by the icon as shown in Figure 6-2.

FIGURE 6-2

Symbols created with the Movie Clip behavior assigned to them are reusable pieces of animation with their own Timelines. Movie clips play independently of the main movie's Timeline. Use them wherever you need an animation on-call. For example, many Flash designers create a movie clip that plays when a user's mouse rolls over a button. You can identify Movie Clip symbols by the icon shown in Figure 6-3.

FIGURE 6-3

Creating Symbols

Creating instances of symbols offers a decided design advantage for you. You can create a symbol for any object that you use more than once in a movie. This not only reduces the file size of the finished production but also reduces the amount of time you spend creating graphic elements. For example, you can create a rectangular object and convert it into a symbol; then you can create an instance of this symbol whenever you need a rectangular object in your production. You can change the scale or rotation of the rectangle as needed. Even though you can modify other properties, such as brightness, tint, transparency, and color effect, you cannot modify the basic shape of an instance. However, you can edit the shape of the original symbol. Modifying the shape of a symbol will change all instances of it in your production.

Creating New Symbols

Create a new symbol when you know that you will use a basic element repeatedly in your movie.

To Create A NEW SYMBOL FROM SCRATCH

1 Choose **New Symbol** from the **Insert menu.** Alternately, simultaneously press the **Ctrl** and **F8** keys (**Windows**) or the **Command** and **F8** keys (**Macintosh**). The **Symbol Properties** dialog box appears, as shown in **Figure 6-4.**

FIGURE 6-4

Symbol Properties		✕
Name: Symbol 8		OK
Behavior: ● Movie Clip		Cancel
○ Button		
○ Graphic		Help

2 Select a behavior for the symbol.

3 Enter a name for the symbol, or use the default name that Flash assigns the symbol. It's good practice to assign a name for every symbol that you create. Giving symbols unique names makes them easier to identify when the document Library starts filling up.

4 Click **OK** to enter symbol-editing mode, as shown in **Figure 6-5.**

5 Use the drawing tools to create and position the graphic elements used for the symbol, or import elements created in other programs.

continues

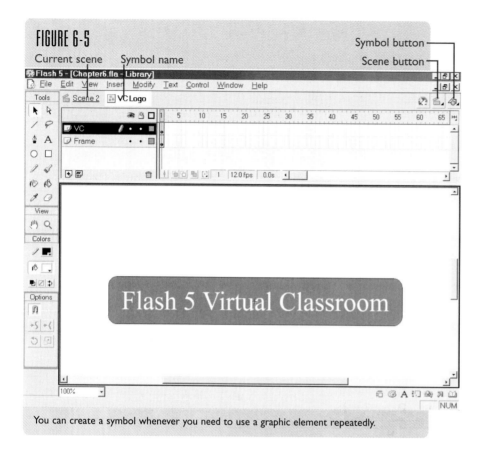

FIGURE 6-5

You can create a symbol whenever you need to use a graphic element repeatedly.

continued

6 After creating the symbol, exit symbol-editing mode by doing one of the following:

Click the Scene button, and then choose a scene from the pop-up menu.

Click the current scene's name to the left of the symbol's name.

Flash adds the completed symbol to the document Library for future use.

Creating New Symbols from Within the Library

You can also create symbols from within the document Library. This technique comes in handy when you are perusing the Library for a symbol and decide that you need to create a new one.

To Create A SYMBOL FROM WITHIN THE LIBRARY

1 Click the triangle in the upper-right corner of the **Library** window to open the **Options** menu, as shown in Figure 6-6.

2 Choose **New Symbol** from the menu. Alternately, click the **New Symbol** icon in the lower-left corner of the window.

3 The **Symbol Properties** dialog box opens. Assign a behavior to the symbol, and then use any of the drawing tools to finish creating the symbol, as outlined in the preceding steps.

FIGURE 6-6

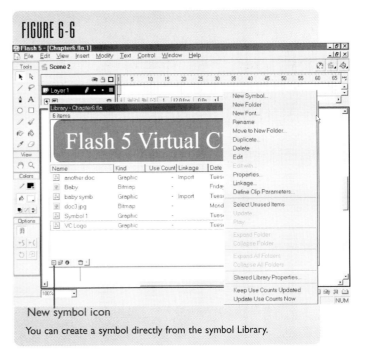

New symbol icon

You can create a symbol directly from the symbol Library.

Converting Objects to Symbols

You can also add a symbol to the Library by converting an object on the Stage. This technique comes in handy when you create a graphic object and decide to use it more than once in a movie.

To Convert AN OBJECT TO A SYMBOL

1 Select the object that you want to convert to a symbol.

2 Choose **Convert to Symbol** from the **Modify** menu. Alternately, press **F8**.

3 The **Symbol Properties** dialog box appears.

4 Enter a name for the symbol, and then assign a behavior to it.

5 Click **OK**. Flash adds the symbol to the document Library for future use.

Creating Symbol Instances

Once you create a symbol, you can use it repeatedly throughout a movie. You can modify and animate symbol instances by changing their properties.

To Create A SYMBOL INSTANCE

1 In the Timeline, select the layer and frame where you want to insert a symbol instance.

2 Choose Library from the Window menu to open the document Library. Alternately, click the Library button on the Launcher bar.

3 Find the symbol's name in the Library window, and then click it to select it. The chosen symbol's name is highlighted and displayed in the preview window.

4 Click the symbol in the preview window, and then drag it onto the Stage. As you drag the symbol, a bounding box appears, previewing the current location on the Stage.

5 Release the mouse button when the instance is in the desired position, as shown in Figure 6-7.

see aLso For more information on layers, refer to Chapter 7. For more information on the Timeline, refer to Chapter 8.

TiP You can quickly create an instance by dragging the symbol's name directly to the Stage.

FIGURE 6-7

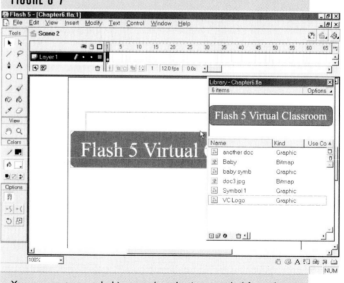

You can create a symbol instance by selecting a symbol from the document Library and then dragging it onto the Stage.

Modifying Symbol Instances

Variety is the spice of life. The beauty of symbol instances is that you can reuse the same symbol within your movie yet modify it so that it appears to be a different object. After adding an instance to a movie, you can modify it with Toolbox tools or menu commands. You can scale, rotate, or skew an instance by using the Arrow tool, Info Panel, Transform panel, or the appropriate menu command. You animate instances by modifying them in keyframes, a technique you will learn in Chapter 9.

Applying Effects to Symbol Instances

Another way to modify an instance's appearance is by applying an effect to it. There are four effects that you can apply to an instance: Brightness, Tint, Alpha, and Advanced. You can apply only one effect to an instance. You animate an effect by applying it in one keyframe and changing its settings in another.

To Apply AN EFFECT TO AN INSTANCE

1 Select an instance.

2 Choose Panels from the Window menu, and then choose Effect. Alternately, click the Instance button on the Launcher bar, and then click the Effect tab on the Instance panel. The Effect panel opens, as shown in Figure 6-8.

3 Click the triangle to the right of the window, and then select an effect from the drop-down menu.

4 Adjust the effect's parameters. Refer to the next four sections for specific instructions on how to apply each effect.

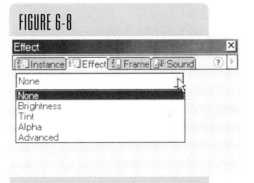

FIGURE 6-8

Figure 6-9 shows the original symbol instance on the left and four additional instances, each with a different effect applied.

FIGURE 6-9

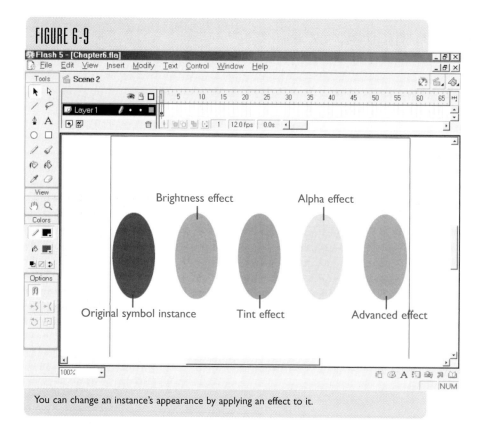

You can change an instance's appearance by applying an effect to it.

Modifying an Instance's Brightness

The Brightness effect allows you to vary the relative brightness of an object. Use the Brightness effect to make an object brighter or dimmer on a scale from -100% (black) to 100% (white).

To Modify AN INSTANCE'S BRIGHTNESS

1 Open the Effect panel.

2 Select Brightness, and then drag the slider to the desired setting.

Figure 6-10 shows the range of the effect. A setting of -100% has been applied to the instance on the left, the original is in the middle, and the instance to the right has been modified with a setting of 100%.

FIGURE 6-10

Modifying an Instance's Tint

Applying the Tint effect to an instance is another way to differentiate it from other instances of the same symbol. With the tint effect, you can vary the strength of an instance's color or tint it with another color.

To Vary THE STRENGTH OF AN INSTANCE'S COLOR

1 Select the instance that you want to tint, and then open the Effect panel.

2 Select Tint. The Tint controls appear, as shown in Figure 6-11.

3 Click the triangle to the right of the Tint Value slider at the top of the panel, and then drag to set the degree of saturation. Alternately, enter a value from 0% (transparent) to 100% (saturated) in the Tint Text Field box.

To Change AN OBJECT'S TINT COLOR

1 Select the instance to which you want to apply the effect, and then open the Effect panel.

2 Select Tint.

3 To select a tint color, drag your cursor in the color bar. The selected color appears in the Tint Color window.

4 To tint the instance with a known color, enter the color's value in the R, G, and B fields.

5 Drag the Tint slider at the top of the panel to adjust the degree of saturation for the selected color.

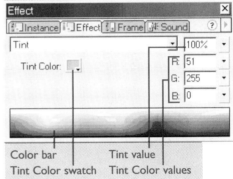

FIGURE 6-11

Color bar | Tint value
Tint Color swatch | Tint Color values

note The default color for the Tint effect is black. When you vary the strength of an instance's color, it will be based on black, enabling you to make the color of the instance darker. To lighten the instance's color, click the Tint Color swatch, and then select white from the palette.

TIP You can also select a tint color by clicking the Tint Color swatch. When you click the swatch, the cursor changes into an eyedropper, and the current color palette appears. Click a color to select it from the palette, or drag your cursor anywhere within the workspace to sample a color from another object. Click to finish selecting the color.

Modifying an Instance's Alpha Property

Applying the Alpha effect to an instance allows you to control its opacity. Apply this effect when you want objects underneath an instance to be partially visible. You can also make an instance appear out of nowhere by applying 0% Alpha in one keyframe and 100% in the next.

To Apply THE ALPHA EFFECT TO A SELECTED INSTANCE

1 Open the Effect panel, and then select Alpha.

2 Drag the slider at the top-right corner of the panel to adjust opacity. Alternately, enter a value from 0% (completely transparent) to 100% (completely opaque).

Applying Advanced Effects to an Instance

The Advanced effect modifies an instance by adjusting each color's value and the transparency of the object. The effect's controls, as shown in Figure 6-12, let you vary the instance's red, green, blue, and transparency values. The controls in the left column let you vary the original color red, green, blue, and transparency values by a specified percentage. The controls in the right column allow you to increase or decrease the color or transparency values by a constant value. This constant is added to the color produced by the left column controls to create the end result. The values for the right column controls correspond to the 8 bit (256 color) scale. For example, entering values of 255 in the R, G, and B fields is the equivalent of whitewashing the original color. Entering values of -255 in the R, G, and B fields is the equivalent of dropping a bucket of black paint over the object.

To Apply THE ADVANCED EFFECT TO A SELECTED INSTANCE

1 Open the Effect panel, and then choose Advanced from the Effect menu.

2 In the left column, drag the Red, Green, Blue, and Alpha sliders to modify the original color. Alternately, enter a value from -100% to 100% in each field.

3 In the right column, drag the Red, Green, Blue, and Alpha sliders to modify the color produced by the left column controls. Alternately, in each field, enter a value from -255 to 255.

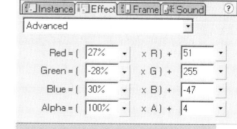

FIGURE 6-12

Swapping Symbols

To err is human, which is why most graphic design programs are equipped with an eraser tool. To change one's mind is the divine right of graphic designers everywhere, and much to their chagrin, their clients also enjoy this divine right. Fortunately, when mind changing runs rampant, you can swap an instance of one symbol with another symbol. The new symbol instance inherits any effects applied to the old instance. For example, you have created a movie that displays pictures of your client's corporate officers. The CEO wants you to replace his photograph in the movie with a more recent one. Instead of repositioning the new image and reapplying an effect to it, you can import the image, convert it to a symbol, and then swap the new symbol with the old.

To Swap A SYMBOL

1 Select the instance that you want to change.

2 Open the Instance panel by choosing Panels from the Window menu, and then choose Instance.

3 Click the Swap Symbol button, as shown in Figure 6-13.

4 The Swap Symbol dialog box appears, as shown in Figure 6-14. All symbols used in the movie are displayed in the window.

5 Click a symbol to select it. A thumbnail preview appears in the small window to the left of the dialog box.

6 Double-click the symbol to swap it, or click OK.

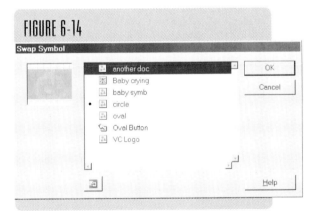

FIGURE 6-13

Swap Symbol button

FIGURE 6-14

Duplicating Symbols

Many symbols used in a Flash movie are similar in design, with one or two elements differing slightly. Buttons are a perfect example of this. The basic shape is the same, but the text that appears when a mouse rolls over the button is different. When you need a symbol that's similar to other symbols in your movie, you don't need to create a new symbol from scratch. You can simply duplicate a symbol and use it as the starting point for the new symbol.

To Duplicate A SYMBOL

1 Select a symbol in the Library.

2 Right-click (Windows) or Control-click (Macintosh), and then choose Duplicate from the context menu. Alternately, choose Duplicate from the Library's Option menu.

3 The Symbol Properties dialog box appears, as shown in Figure 6-15.

4 Enter a name for the duplicated symbol.

5 Select a behavior for the duplicated symbol.

6 Click OK.

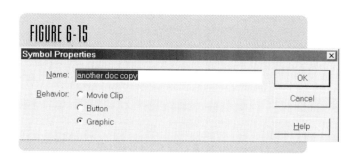

FIGURE 6-15

A symbol can also be duplicated from its instance.

To Duplicate A SYMBOL FROM AN INSTANCE

1 Select the instance whose symbol you want to duplicate.

2 Open the Instance panel.

3 Click the Duplicate Symbol button, as shown in Figure 6-16.

continues

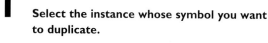

FIGURE 6-16   Symbol Name dialog box

Duplicate Symbol button

continued

4 The Symbol Name dialog box appears, as shown previously.

5 Enter a name for the duplicated symbol, and then click **OK**.
The duplicated symbol appears in the Library, ready for editing.

Modifying Symbols

After creating a symbol, Flash recreates the basic shape and elements that you used to create the symbol whenever you place an instance of it on the Stage. This is a tremendous benefit to you, the Flash Web designer. Creating a symbol and then peppering the movie with instances of it as needed save you time when you are designing the movie and editing it. When you edit a symbol, all instances of it are instantly changed.

Modifying Symbols in Symbol-Editing Mode

When you edit a symbol in symbol-editing mode, Flash opens up a new window, complete with all the tools and commands that you need to edit the symbol and add elements to it.

To Edit A SYMBOL IN A NEW WINDOW

FIGURE 6-17

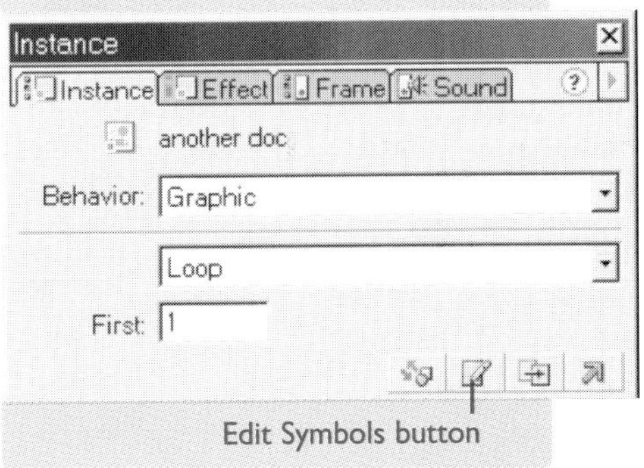

1 To enter symbol-editing mode, do one of the following:

Select an instance of the symbol that you want to edit on the Stage, right-click (Windows) or Control-click (Macintosh), and then choose **Edit** from the context menu.

Select an instance of the symbol that you want to edit on the Stage, open the Instance panel, and then click the Edit Symbol button, as shown in Figure 6-17.

Edit Symbols button

In the Library, select the symbol that you want to edit, and then double-click the icon to the left of its name.

In the Library, select the symbol that you want to edit, and then double-click it in the preview window.

In the Library, select the symbol that you want to edit, and then choose **Edit** from the Options menu.

Click the Edit Symbol button, in the upper-right corner of the interface, and then select the symbol to edit from the drop-down menu.

continues

continued

2 The symbol opens up in a new window with the symbol's name displayed to the right of the current scene's name. Edit the symbol with any of the drawing tools or menu commands, or import other elements if necessary.

3 To exit symbol-editing mode, click the current scene name. Alternately, double-click anywhere on the Stage. All instances of the symbol automatically update to reflect the changes that you made.

Modifying Symbols in Place

Flash has another symbol-editing mode that is beneficial in certain situations. When you choose to edit a symbol in place, everything on the Stage—except the symbol that you are editing—is dimmed. When you edit in this mode, the effects of your edits are immediately visible.

To Edit A SYMBOL IN PLACE

1 Select an instance of the symbol that you want to edit.

2 Double-click the symbol. Alternately, right-click (Windows) or Control-click (Macintosh) the symbol, and then choose Edit in Place from the context menu.

3 Flash enters edit-in-place mode. The name of the symbol being edited is displayed next to the current scene's name. All other elements on the Stage are dimmed.

4 Edit the symbol as needed. As you edit the symbol, you immediately see the effect that your editing has on the scene. If you have other instances of the symbol on the Stage, they update to reflect the results of your editing as well.

5 To return to movie-editing mode, double-click anywhere on the Stage. Alternately, click the current scene's name.

Nesting Symbols

When you create a new symbol, it may seem logical to create everything from scratch. However, you can greatly reduce the file size of your movie if you use symbols already at your disposal. For example, you need to create a new symbol, a square with several circles inside it. You have already created a circular symbol for a button. Instead of creating circles for the new symbol, you can create instances of the circular symbol. This process of placing a symbol within a symbol is known as nesting. Once you nest the symbol within a symbol, it becomes an instance that you can modify like any other instance.

To Nest A SYMBOL IN A SYMBOL

1 Create a new symbol by choosing New Symbol from the Insert menu.

2 In the Symbol Properties dialog box, enter a name for the symbol, and then specify a behavior. Click OK to enter symbol-editing mode.

3 Use the drawing tools to create new elements for the symbol.

4 To nest existing symbols in the new symbol, open the Library by choosing Library from the Window menu. Alternately, click the Library button on the Launcher bar.

5 Select the desired symbol from the Library, and then drag it onto the Stage.

6 Position and modify the symbol's instance as needed.

7 Add and position additional symbols from the Library as needed.

8 To exit symbol-editing mode, click the current scene's name. Flash adds the nested symbol to the document Library.

Using Symbols from Another Flash File

You can also use symbols created for another Flash movie. This may be beneficial when you are under a tight deadline or otherwise pressed for time. Once you have the symbol in your movie, you can edit it as needed.

To Use SYMBOLS FROM ANOTHER FLASH FILE

1 Choose Open As Library from the File menu. The Open As Library dialog box appears.

2 Navigate to the location of the desired file on your hard drive, and then click Open. The other document's Library opens.

3 Click a symbol's name to select it, and then drag it onto the Stage. Alternately, drag the symbol directly into the current document's Library.

4 Add additional symbols as needed, and then close the other document's Library. The added symbols now appear in the current document's Library.

Creating a Shared Library

You can create a shared library when you need to use a document's assets in multiple Flash movies. When you create a shared library, you define the symbols to be shared with other movies, and then you create links. The shared library must be published as a .swf file and posted to the Web. When you use a symbol from a shared library in another movie, you create a link that Flash uses to import the symbol from the shared library's file. When a movie using assets from a shared library is played, the Flash Player downloads the .swf file containing the shared library from the Web. The Flash Player loads the entire shared library file when it encounters the first frame containing a symbol from the shared library. If a movie contains symbols from more than one shared library, the Flash Player downloads each file separately when the first occurrence of a symbol from that file occurs.

To Create A SHARED LIBRARY

1 Create a new Flash document.

2 Create and/or import the items that you want to use as shared assets. Remember to convert editable objects into symbols.

3 Choose Library from the Window menu, or click the Library button on the Launcher bar.

4 Click a Library item to be shared with other movies.

5 Right-click (Windows) or Control-click (Macintosh) the symbol, and then choose Linkage from the pop-up menu. Alternately, choose Linkage from the Options menu. The Symbol Linkage Properties dialog box appears, as shown in Figure 6-18.

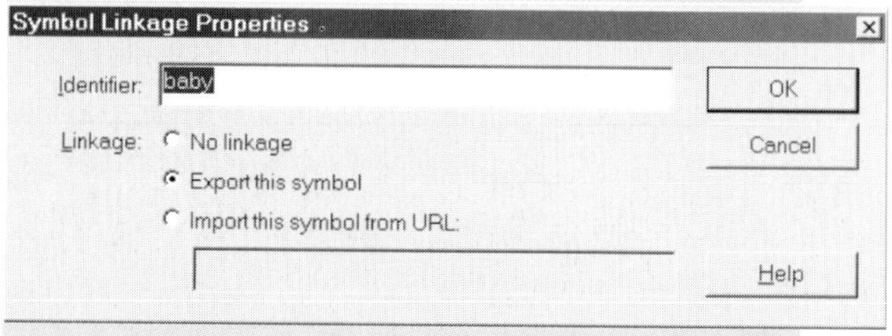

6 Select Export This Symbol.

7 Enter a name for the symbol in the Identifier field. Do not use spaces in the name.

Warning Make sure to properly link all symbols to and from a shared library. If an error occurs when the Flash Player is downloading a shared library, the movie will not play.

FIGURE 6-18

Symbol Linkage Properties

Identifier: baby

Linkage: ○ No linkage
● Export this symbol
○ Import this symbol from URL:

OK

Cancel

Help

continues

continued

8 Click OK.

9 Continue linking assets to be shared.

10 Save and publish the movie.

To Use A SYMBOL FROM A SHARED LIBRARY

1 Choose Open As Shared Library from the File menu to access the Open As Shared Library dialog box.

2 Navigate to the location of the shared library's .fla file on your hard drive. Click Open.

3 The shared library file's document Library opens. Notice that all commands on the Options menu are grayed out and unusable.

4 Drag the needed symbol from the shared library file's document Library into the current document's Library. The shared asset appears in the current document's Library. The word "Import" appears in the symbol's Linkage column, as shown in Figure 6-19. This designates that the symbol is linked to the current movie as an external file and is not added to the current movie.

FIGURE 6-19

You can create shared libraries to share common symbols with other movies.

Changing the Linkage of an Imported File

When you use a symbol from a shared library, Flash automatically creates the import link for you. If you ever move the shared library file to another Web site, you need to manually change the link.

To Change THE LINKAGE OF A FILE IMPORTED FROM A SHARED LIBRARY

1 Click the imported symbol's name in the current document's Library.

2 Right-click (Windows) or Control-click (Macintosh) to open the Symbol Linkage Properties dialog box, as shown in Figure 6-20.

3 Enter the URL of the Web site where the shared library's .swf file can be found.

4 Click OK.

note A shared library is a convenient way to manage a large Web site comprised of multiple linked movies. Create the common assets, such as buttons, logos, and any pictures to be used in the site, and then save them as a single .fla file. Create the proper links to export the assets that you want to share, and then publish the movie. Use the Open As Shared Library command whenever you need to use a symbol from the shared library in another movie. Publish and upload the movies to a Web site, and you are ready to entertain visitors.

FIGURE 6-20

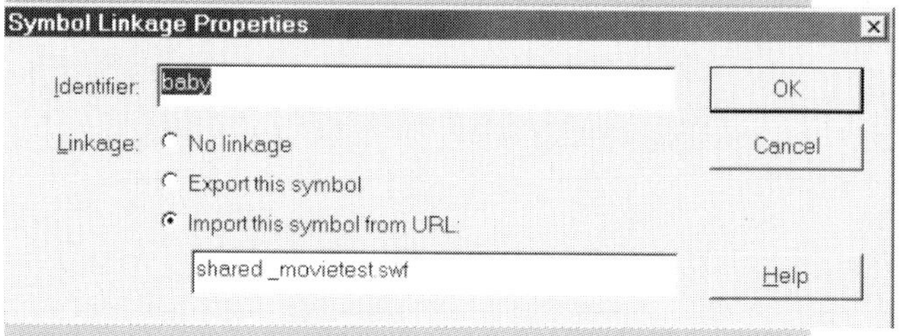

Symbol Linkage Properties		☒
Identifier: baby		OK
Linkage: ○ No linkage		Cancel
○ Export this symbol		
● Import this symbol from URL:		
shared_movietest.swf		Help

Working with Layers

7

Flash 5 uses layers to organize the various elements in a movie. Think of layers as thin sheets of clear acetate placed over the Stage. Objects created on the current layer obscure objects on the layers below and are obscured by objects created on layers above. You switch from layer to layer to edit the various components of your movie. When you create a complex movie, layers are invaluable. In fact, the only way to get predictable results when animating multiple objects is to create a separate layer for each animation. In this chapter, you will learn how to create and manipulate layers.

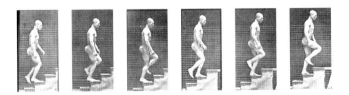

Organizing Movies with Layers

In Flash, you use layers to organize artwork, actions, and sound. When you edit objects on a layer, the actions that you perform do not affect objects on other layers. You can create guide layers to use as reference when aligning objects in your movies, motion guide layers to create a path which objects follow during an animation, and mask layers to act as windows to objects on linked layers beneath it.

Creating Layers

Creating separate layers for the elements of your movies speeds up your workflow considerably. Using layers allows you to find items more easily and to greatly reduce the chances of inadvertently selecting and moving the wrong object. It's a good idea to get in the habit of creating separate layers for artwork, sound, and actions. Each layer has its own Timeline. Figure 7-1 shows a movie that uses several layers to organize its content. Notice that each layer has a unique name.

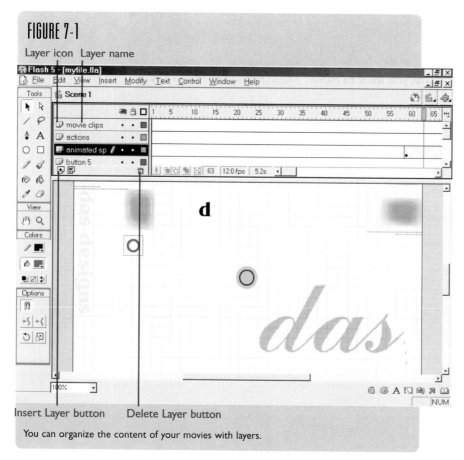

FIGURE 7-1

Layer icon   Layer name

Insert Layer button   Delete Layer button

You can organize the content of your movies with layers.

To Create A LAYER, DO ONE OF THE FOLLOWING:

■ ....Choose Layer from the Insert menu.

■ ....Click the Insert Layer button at the bottom of the Timeline.

■ ....Right-click (Windows) or Control-click (Macintosh) a layer's name, and then choose Insert Layer from the context menu.

The new layer appears above the layer that you selected when you invoked the Insert Layer command.

Naming Layers

The default name for a new layer is Layer, followed by the next available layer number. You can change the default name to reflect the content of the layer, a practice that you will find beneficial when editing your Flash movies. Naming layers makes it easier to find items and edit them when creating a complex movie.

To Name A LAYER

1 Double-click the layer that you want to name. The selected layer's name is highlighted.

2 Type a new name for the layer, and then press Enter or Return. Alternately, double-click the Layer Name icon (which looks like a pencil) to the right of a layer's name, type a new name for the layer, and then press Enter or Return.

Selecting Layers

Once you have created layers, you navigate from one layer to another to create frames and select items.

To Select A LAYER, USE ONE OF THE FOLLOWING TECHNIQUES:

■ ....Click a layer's name.

■ ....Click a frame in a layer's Timeline.

■ ....Select an item on the Stage that is on the layer that you want to select.

Selected layers are highlighted in black.

To Select MORE THAN ONE LAYER:

■ ....Hold down the **Shift** key and click to add neighboring layers to the selection.

■ ....Hold down the **Ctrl** key and click (**Windows**) or hold down the **Command** key and click (**Macintosh**) to add non-adjacent layers to the selection.

Deleting Layers

There will be times when you need a layer only temporarily, for example when creating a template for objects on another layer or for importing an object that you trace with the drawing tools and then delete.

To Delete A SELECTED LAYER, DO ONE OF THE FOLLOWING:

■ ....Click the **Delete Layer** button in the Timeline.

■ ....Drag the layer to the **Delete Layer** button.

■ ....Right-click (**Windows**) or Control-click (**Macintosh**), and then choose **Delete Layer** from the context menu.

Copying Layers

You can copy the contents of an entire layer's Timeline to a newly created layer. This technique comes in handy when you need to use elements from one layer in another layer. You can also copy a layer's Timeline and paste it into a new document.

To Copy A LAYER'S CONTENTS

1 Select the layer that you want to copy. The layer's Timeline is highlighted in black.

2 Choose **Copy Frames** from the **Edit** menu.

3 Create a new layer.

4 Choose **Paste Frames** from the **Edit** menu.

chapter 7: working with layers

Modifying a Layer's Properties

A layer has properties, just like any other item that you create in Flash. Figure 7-2 shows a typical Timeline with several layers. Above the layers list are three icons that you can use to modify the properties of a particular layer. Clicking one of these icons changes that property for all layers. To the right of each layer's name are three columns with corresponding icons that toggle a property on or off for an individual layer.

FIGURE 7-2

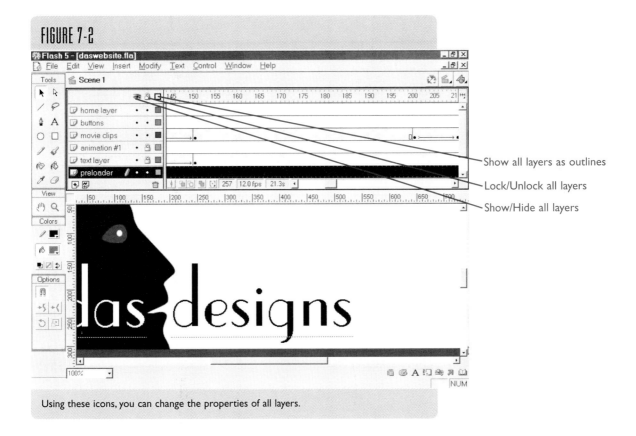

Using these icons, you can change the properties of all layers.

— Show all layers as outlines
— Lock/Unlock all layers
— Show/Hide all layers

Hiding Layers

When a layer is hidden, none of the objects on that layer are visible. Hiding layers is a convenient way to get a better look at things, especially when you need to edit items on a lower layer that are obscured by objects on an upper layer.

To Show or Hide ALL LAYERS

▶ **Click the Show/Hide All Layers icon (the eye) at the top of the Timeline. A red X icon appears below the eye icon in each layer, indicating that all layers are hidden. Click the eye icon to toggle all layers' visibility on and off.**

To Show or Hide AN INDIVIDUAL LAYER

 Click the dot in a layer's **Show/Hide** column, which is directly below the eye icon. A hidden layer is designated by a red *X*. Click the *X* to reveal a hidden layer.

Locking Layers

Even though you go to great pains to segregate different items on layers, you could still inadvertently select an object on another layer. With one slip of the mouse, you can destroy hours of work. Locking the layer will prevent accidental selection of the wrong item once you have the items on a layer just the way that you want them.

To Lock ALL LAYERS

 Click the **Lock/Unlock All Layers** icon (the padlock) at the top of the layers list. A padlock appears in every layer's **Lock** column.

To Unlock ALL LAYERS

 Click the **Lock/Unlock All Layers** icon.

To Lock AN INDIVIDUAL LAYER

 Click the dot in a layer's **Lock** column. A padlock appears, signifying that the layer is locked and its contents cannot be tampered with.

To Unlock AN INDIVIDUAL LAYER

 Click the padlock in that layer's **Lock** column.

Viewing Objects on Layers as Outlines

Another option available to you is to view the shapes on a layer as outlines. In this mode, each individual object on a layer is displayed as an outline, using that layer's specified outline color.

To View ALL LAYERS AS OUTLINES

 Click the Show All Layers as Outlines icon at the top of the layer list. Click the icon again to toggle off the outline display.

To View AN INDIVIDUAL LAYER AS AN OUTLINE

 Click the square icon in the layer's Outline column. The icon changes from a filled square to an outline. Click the icon again to toggle off the outline display.

TIP You can use layers as templates to trace objects. If you have a piece of complex vector artwork that you want to use in a movie but are afraid will result in a large file, you can import it into Flash on its own layer. Create a layer above it, and then use the Flash drawing tools to recreate a "bandwidth friendly" version of the original. After you trace all the elements that you want to use, delete the imported file, and then convert the traced version to a symbol.

Using the Layer Properties Dialog Box

You can also change a layer's properties through a dialog box. With the Layer Properties dialog box, shown in Figure 7-3, you can change any or all of a layer's properties.

FIGURE 7-3

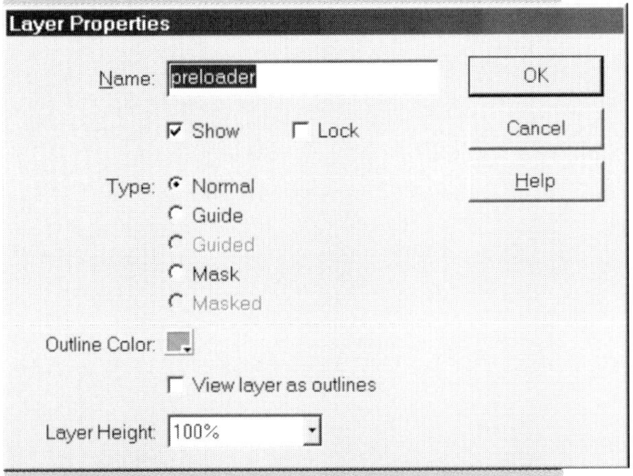

Layer Properties

Name: preloader	OK
☑ Show ☐ Lock	Cancel
Type: ⦿ Normal	Help
○ Guide	
○ Guided	
○ Mask	
○ Masked	
Outline Color: ▪	
☐ View layer as outlines	
Layer Height: 100%	

You can use the Layer Properties dialog box to change a layer's properties.

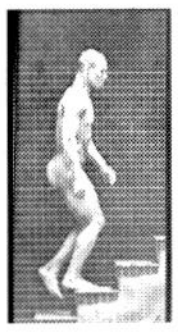

To Open THE LAYER PROPERTIES DIALOG BOX, DO ONE OF THE FOLLOWING:

■........**Right-click (Windows) or Control-click (Macintosh) a layer's name, and then choose Properties from the layer's context menu, as shown in Figure 7-4.**

■........**Double-click the icon to the left of a layer's name.**

■........**Choose Layer from the Modify menu.**

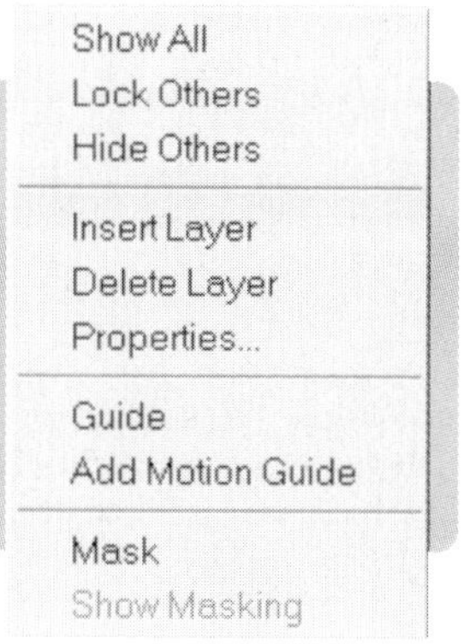

To Modify A LAYER'S PROPERTIES

1 Open the Layer Properties dialog box shown in Figure 7-3.

2 Name allows you to name the layer by entering a name in the Name field.

3 Show toggles a layer's visibility on and off.

4 Lock locks a layer to prevent any editing. Disable this option to edit items on a layer.

5 Type allows you to modify the layer's type by selecting one of the following:

> **Normal is the default layer for creating objects. You also use it when creating a layer for sounds or actions.**
>
> **Guide converts the layer into a guide layer. A guide layer is a visual aid that you use when creating and aligning objects.**
>
> **Guided specifies that the layer is linked to a motion guide layer. You use a motion guide layer to create a path that objects follow during an animation. You create motion guide layers by using a menu command or the layer's context menu.**
>
> **Mask converts the layer to a mask layer. You will learn how to create a mask layer before the end of this chapter.**
>
> **Masked is a normal layer that is linked to a mask layer.**

FIGURE 7-4

> Show All
> Lock Others
> Hide Others
>
> Insert Layer
> Delete Layer
> Properties...
>
> Guide
> Add Motion Guide
>
> Mask
> Show Masking

see al so For more information on motion guide layers, motion paths, and animation, refer to Chapter 9.

continues

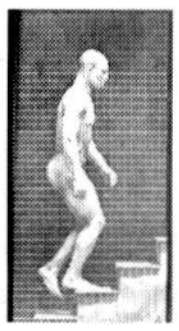

continued

6 The Outline Color section changes the layer's outline color. Click the Outline Color swatch, and then select the desired color from the palette. When creating a motion path, change the motion guide layer's outline color to one that contrasts with the movie's background color. This will make it easier to see and edit the motion path.

7 View Layer as Outlines displays all objects on the layer as outlines, using the color specified in the Outline Color section.

8 Layer Height lets you change how the layer's Timeline is displayed. Click the arrow to the right of the window, and then select 100%, 200%, or 300%. Increase a layer's height when you need to get a better look at items such as a sound's waveform.

Changing the Number of Layers Displayed

When you create complex movies, you generally end up with a lot of layers that cannot all be displayed in the standard window. One way to circumvent this problem is to use the scroll bar to scroll to another layer. If this is bothersome, you can increase the height of the Timeline window by dragging the bar that separates the Timeline window from the Stage, as shown in Figure 7-5.

FIGURE 7-5

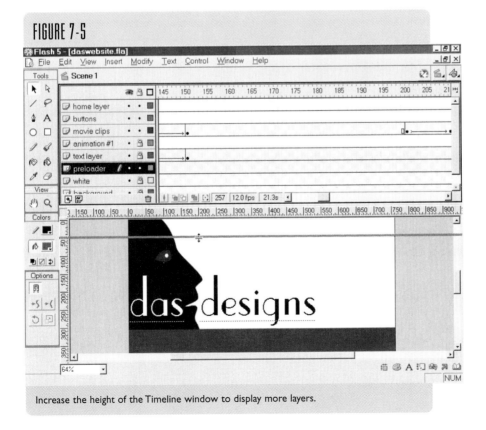

Increase the height of the Timeline window to display more layers.

To Float the Timeline

▶ Click the space to the left of the eye icon, and then drag the Timeline onto the Stage, as shown in Figure 7-6.

FIGURE 7-6

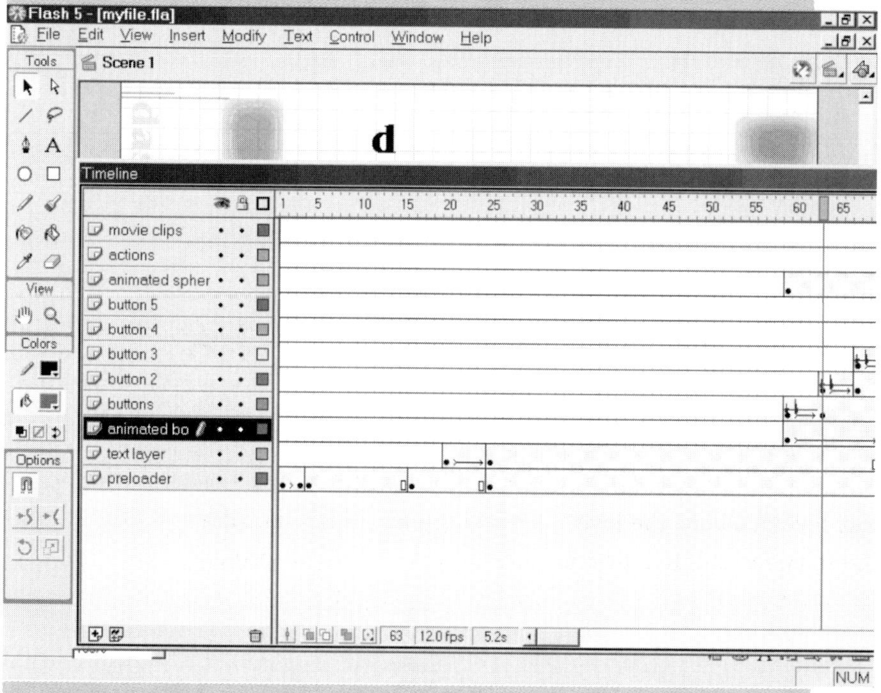

To display all layers at once, you can float the Timeline.

Changing the Length of the Layer Window

You can also change the length of the layer window. Increase the length of the window when you want to display a long layer name in its entirety; decrease it to display more of the Timeline.

To Change the length of a layer window

▶ Click the bar that separates the Layer window from the Timeline, and then drag left or right, as shown in Figure 7-7.

FIGURE 7-7

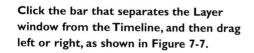

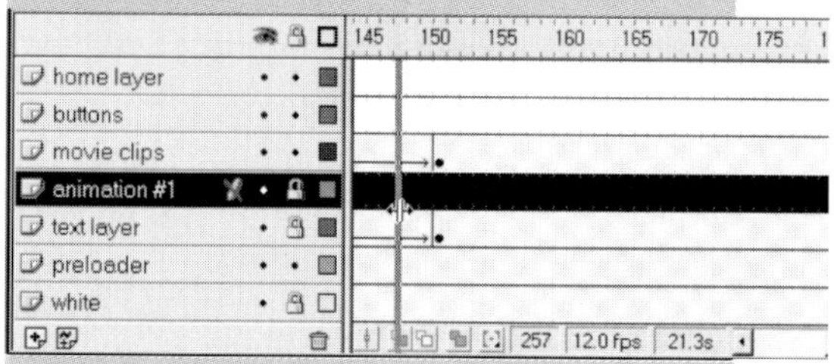

Organizing Layer Hierarchy

As you learned previously, the layers in your movie arrange themselves in a hierarchy, or pecking order. The first layer created is at the bottom of the heap. Flash positions new layers directly above the layer that you selected when you created the new layer. Objects on upper layers obscure objects on lower layers. Fortunately, you can rearrange the stacking order of layers to make artwork on a lower level more visible by moving the layer to a higher level.

To Change THE ORDER OF LAYERS

 Select a layer, and then drag it up or down. Release the mouse button when the layer is at the desired level in the list.

Working with Objects Across Layers

After organizing your movie with layers, you move from layer to layer to edit individual objects. If you select an object on the Stage, the object's Timeline is also selected. You can also edit items on several layers at once by creating a selection of objects. When you create a selection of objects across several layers, the layer of the last item selected becomes the current layer. However, the selection still remains intact. You can move the selected objects to another location, or you can use the Paint Bucket tool to change the fill of all selected objects at once.

Moving Objects Across Layers

You can arrange an object's relative position on the Stage by moving its layer to another position in the stacking order. This is the equivalent of moving a group on a single layer forward or backward with one of the Arrange commands. Moving an entire layer, however, changes the relative position of all objects on that layer. To affect a single object's position on the Stage, you must cut the object from its layer and then paste it to another layer. You can also copy an object and paste it to another layer.

Using the Paste in Place Command

When an object is pasted, it appears in the center of the Stage. This is handy when you are creating a new symbol. However, when you cut or copy an object from one layer and paste it to another, it is often desirable to paste it to the same exact location, for example, when you create eyes for a character and then decide to animate them on another layer. After you cut the eyes from the layer they are on, you use the Paste in Place command to put them in the same location on another layer.

To Paste AN OBJECT IN PLACE

1 Select an object on the Stage.

2 Choose Cut or Copy from the Edit menu.

3 Choose Paste in Place from the Edit menu.

Creating Guide Layers

There are two types of guide layers in Flash: guide layers and motion guide layers. You use guide layers to place elements that you use as visual aids when positioning and aligning objects. Motion guide layers are used in animation and are discussed in the Animating with Motion Paths section of Chapter 9.

To Create A NEW GUIDE LAYER

1 Create a new layer by clicking the Insert Layer button at the bottom of the Timeline.

2 Name the new layer.

3 Double-click the layer icon to the left of the layer's name to reveal the Layer Properties dialog box.

4 In the Type section, select Guide.

5 Click OK. The new layer is converted to a guide layer. The Guide Layer icon appears to the left of the layer's name, as shown in Figure 7-8.

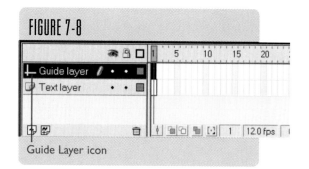

FIGURE 7-8

Guide Layer icon

Adding Guides to a Guide Layer

After you create a guide layer, you need to add the desired guides to it. Guides can take on many forms. You can use ovals and rectangles without fills as guides, or you can use straight and angled lines as guides, or you can quickly create a set of guides by dragging guides out of the rulers. You can drag a set of guides out of the rulers on any layer. Go to the trouble of setting up a guide layer when you need to use a specific set of guides for an entire project.

To Create GUIDELINES FROM RULERS

1 Create a guide layer as outlined previously.

2 To use the rulers, choose Rulers from the View menu.

3 To create a horizontal guideline, click the horizontal ruler, and then drag. As you drag, a gray line appears, giving you a preview of the guideline's position. Use the vertical ruler to measure the position of the guideline as you drag. Release the mouse button when the guideline is at the desired position.

4 To create a vertical guideline, click the vertical ruler, and then drag as shown in Figure 7-9. Use the horizontal ruler to measure the position of the guideline.

5 Release the mouse button when it is at the desired position.

6 To reposition a guide, click it with the Arrow tool, and then drag it to a new position.

> **note** You can add as many guidelines as you need. Any guidelines or objects used as guides on a guide layer do not show up when the movie is published.

FIGURE 7-9

Vertical ruler   Guidelines   Horizontal ruler

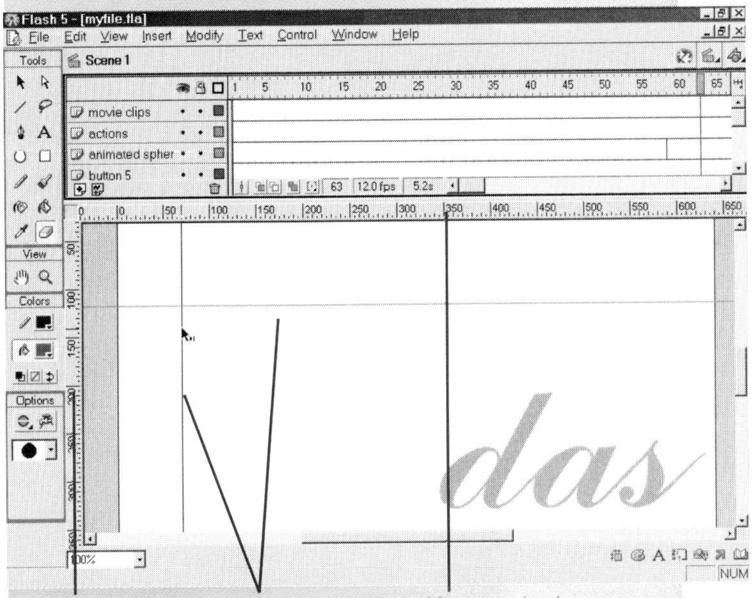

To create guidelines, you click a ruler and then drag.

Adjusting Guideline Properties

Once you have a guide layer and guidelines set up, you can modify guideline properties to suit your working preference. You can show or hide guidelines, lock the position of guidelines, have objects snap to guides, or change the color of guides.

To Show or Hide ALL GUIDELINES

 Choose Guides from the View menu, and then choose Show. This command toggles guideline visibility on and off.

To Lock THE POSITION OF GUIDELINES

 Choose Guides from the View menu, and then choose Lock. A checkmark appears next to the command, signifying that all guides are locked. To unlock locked guidelines, apply the command again.

To Snap TO GUIDES

Choose Guides from the View menu, and then choose Snap to Guides.

This option is turned on by default. The actual point of an object that snaps to a guide depends on where you select the object with the Arrow tool before dragging. If you click an item and drag it near its center, snapping takes place at the item's registration point, its center by default. If you click an item and drag it by a corner, snapping takes place at that corner. If you click an item and drag it by the center of an edge, snapping takes place at the edge. When Snap to Guides is turned on, a dot appears at the selected edge as you drag and becomes larger when the object is close to a guideline it can snap to, as shown in Figure 7-10. It is not advisable to use the Snap to Guides option and Snap to Grid option at the same time because the object will have too many targets to snap to, and you won't be sure whether Flash is locking the object to a guideline or the grid.

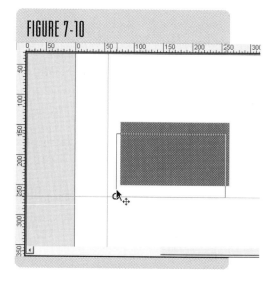

FIGURE 7-10

Using the Edit Guides Command

The Edit Guides command is a convenient way of setting guideline properties in one fell swoop. In addition to applying the guide commands just discussed, you can use the Edit Guides command to change the color of objects that you use as guides and to adjust snapping precision.

To Set PROPERTIES FOR OBJECTS ON A GUIDE LAYER WITH THE EDIT GUIDES COMMAND

1 Choose Guides from the View menu, and then choose Edit Guides. The Guides dialog box appears, as shown in Figure 7-11.

FIGURE 7-11

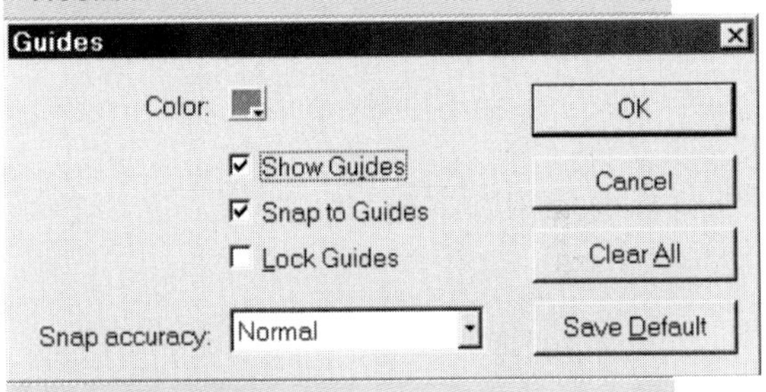

2 To change guideline color, click the Color swatch, and then select a color from the palette. Choose a color that contrasts with your background for maximum guideline visibility.

3 Show Guides toggles the visibility of guidelines. This option is selected by default.

4 Snap to Guides causes objects to snap to guidelines. This option is selected by default.

5 Enable the Lock Guides option to lock the position of guidelines.

6 In the Snap Accuracy field, click the arrow, and then select an option from the menu. Choose from Must be Close, Normal, or Distant. The effects of this option depend upon how many guidelines you are using and how closely they are spaced. The default Normal setting works well in most instances.

7 To clear all guidelines, click Clear All.

8 Click OK.

Creating a Mask Layer

Mask layers generate special effects by creating a window to one or more layers underneath the mask layer. The shape and size of the window are determined by filled objects that you create and position on the mask layer. The only objects revealed on linked layers underneath are those directly under the shapes on the mask layer. Sophisticated special effects can be achieved by animating mask layer objects, a technique you will learn in Chapter 9. Figure 7-12 shows a mask layer in action. Figure 7-13 shows the results of the mask layer when the movie is published.

FIGURE 7-12

By placing a shape on a mask layer, you can reveal objects on linked layers underneath.

FIGURE 7-13

The mask layer in Figure 7-7 produces this result when the movie is published.

To Create A MASK LAYER

1 Create a new layer above the objects that you want to mask.

> **note** You can use multiple editable objects to create the mask layer's window. However, if you are using text objects or symbols to create the mask layer shape, you can use only one.

continues

continued

2 Right-click (Windows) or Control-click (Macintosh) the layer that you just created, and then choose Mask from the context menu. Alternately, choose Layers from the Modify menu, and then choose the Mask option from the Layer Properties dialog box. The Mask Layer icon appears to the left of the layer's name, as shown in Figure 7-14. The Masked Layer icon appears on the layer underneath.

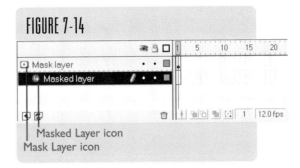

FIGURE 7-14

Masked Layer icon
Mask Layer icon

3 Initially, both the mask layer and the masked layer are locked. Unlock the layers, and then use the drawing tools to create the shape that will mask objects on the layer underneath, or use an instance of a symbol to create the mask.

To Link AN ADDITIONAL LAYER TO THE MASK LAYER, DO ONE OF THE FOLLOWING:

■ ....Drag a layer and position it directly below the mask layer or directly underneath a masked layer. Remember that objects on masked layers obscure those of masked layers underneath. Rearrange the hierarchy of multiple masked layers by dragging each layer to the desired position.

■ ....Select a layer directly underneath a masked layer, choose Layer from the Modify menu, and then choose Masked.

■ ....Right-click (Windows) or Control-click (Macintosh) a layer, choose Properties from the context menu, and then choose Masked from the Layer Properties dialog box.

To Unlink A MASKED LAYER, DO ONE OF THE FOLLOWING:

■ ....Drag the masked layer above the mask layer.

■ ....Right-click (Windows) or Control-click (Macintosh) a layer, choose Properties from the context menu, and then choose Masked from the Layer Properties dialog box.

Creating Frame-by- Frame Animations

In previous chapters, you learned how to create graphic objects with Flash 5 drawing tools, how to convert the objects into reusable symbols, and how to organize them with layers. Now comes the part that you have been waiting for: putting graphic objects into motion. Motion is what sets Flash Web sites apart from their static HTML brethren. Motion and other Flash features that you will learn about in future chapters are also what keep visitors returning to Flash sites on a regular basis. In this chapter, you will learn to use keyframes and frames to create frame-by-frame animations.

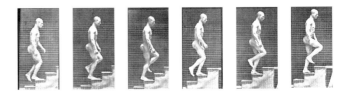

Understanding the Timeline

Frame-by-frame animations are what cartoon animators use to bring characters to life. To make a cartoon character appear to run towards an object, the animator draws a different image for each frame of the animation. When the drawings are compiled and played, smooth motion occurs. If you have ever taken a pad, scribbled a stick figure in slightly different poses on each consecutive page, and then flipped the pages to make the figure move, you have created a basic frame-by-frame animation. To animate objects in Flash movies, you use the Timeline, shown in Figure 8-1. Major events in an animation, such as an object's changing position, shape, or color, take place in keyframes. The amount of time that lapses between key events is determined by the number of frames between keyframes and the movie's frame rate. If you place more frames between keyframes, the time lapse is longer; fewer frames make the time lapse shorter. The Timeline consists of frames, layers, and the playhead. At the top of the Timeline is a time ruler that is divided into frames. Each small vertical mark represents a single frame in the animation. The red rectangle with a vertical line extending from its center is the playhead. The playhead indicates the current frame of the movie. You can use the playhead to navigate from frame to frame by clicking and dragging it.

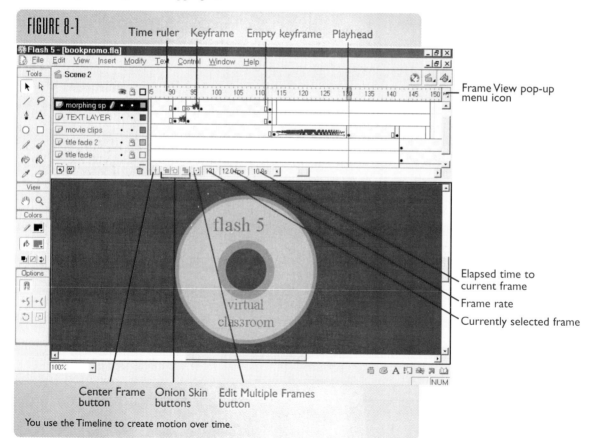

FIGURE 8-1

You use the Timeline to create motion over time.

Adjusting the Frame Rate

A movie's frame rate is measured in frames per second (fps). Flash's default frame rate is 12 fps, which works well for most movies. If you are packing a lot of action into a short time span, the default rate may result in jerky motion. Increasing the frame rate creates smoother motion but increases file size, an important consideration if you plan to display your Flash production at a Web site.

To Change THE MOVIE'S FRAME RATE

1 Choose Movie from the Modify menu. The Movie Properties dialog box appears, as shown in Figure 8-2.

2 In the Frame Rate field, enter a value. This value determines the number of frames that play in one second.

3 Click OK.

> **TIP** To quickly access the Movie Properties dialog box, double-click the movie's frame rate box in the Timeline window.

FIGURE 8-2

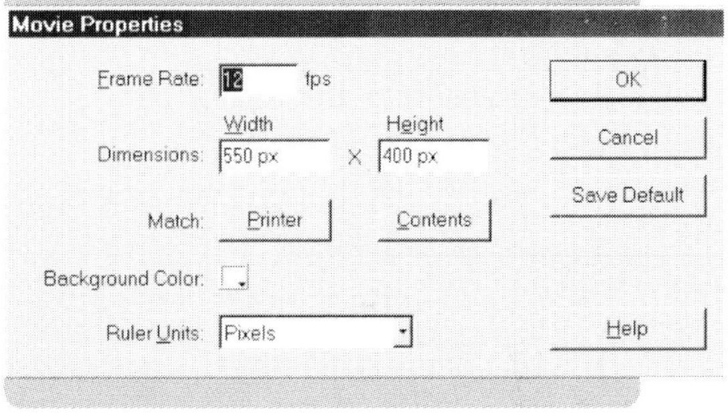

Movie Properties

Frame Rate:	12 fps	OK
Dimensions:	Width 550 px X Height 400 px	Cancel
Match:	Printer Contents	Save Default
Background Color:		
Ruler Units:	Pixels	Help

Changing Frame View

To suit your working preference, you can change the way that frames on the Timeline are displayed. You can modify the number of frames that are displayed, change the height of the frames, or create a preview of keyframe contents.

1 Click the Frame View button to reveal the menu shown in Figure 8-2.

2 Select from the following options:

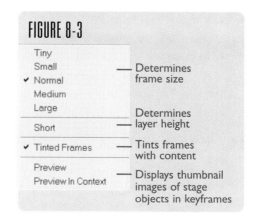

FIGURE 8-3

Tiny
Small
✔ Normal
Medium
Large
— Determines frame size

Short
— Determines layer height

✔ Tinted Frames
— Tints frames with content

Preview
Preview In Context
— Displays thumbnail images of stage objects in keyframes

The top section of the menu determines how many frames are displayed in the Timeline window. Select Tiny to display many frames. Note that if you select Tiny, frames will be difficult to select. Select Medium or Large to display fewer frames and have better control when selecting individual frames.

Short shrinks the height of the Timeline and displays more layers in the Timeline window.

Tinted Frames tints frames with content gray, tints frames with motion tweening applied to them blue, and tints frames with shape tweening applied to them light green. Motion tweening and shape tweening are discussed in Chapter 9.

Preview creates a thumbnail preview of shapes in keyframes.

Preview in Context creates a thumbnail preview of a keyframe's shapes relative to the way that they appear on the Stage.

When displaying frames in Preview or Preview in Context mode, Flash updates the thumbnails when you edit the shapes on the Stage.

Viewing Frame Status

At the bottom of the Timeline, three windows display information about the movie and the currently selected frame. If a frame is not selected, the windows display information about the frame that the playhead is parked on. As you create longer and more complex movies, these windows will be your road map to exactly which frame of the movie is selected along the Timeline. The windows, as shown in Figure 8-4, display the currently selected frame, the movie's frame rate, and the elapsed time to the current frame.

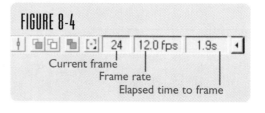

FIGURE 8-4

Current frame
Frame rate
Elapsed time to frame

Working with Frames

When you create a new movie in Flash, you have a single empty keyframe to work with. To create action, you need to add frames and keyframes and manipulate their positions on the Timeline. If you are working with multiple layers, you need to coordinate the position of the frames on each layer, synchronizing the finale of one object's motion with the beginning of another's.

Creating Frames

Frames are placeholders along the Timeline. When you add a frame to a layer's Timeline, you create a virtual copy of the previous keyframe's content along with it. You also use frames to fine-tune an animation's timing, as you will learn in the upcoming sections.

To Create A FRAME

1 Click a spot on the Timeline.

2 Choose Frame from the Insert menu.

To Create MULTIPLE FRAMES

1 Click a spot on the Timeline.

2 Drag to the left or right to increase the size of the selection.

3 Choose Frame from the Insert menu, and Flash adds the exact number of frames that you have selected to the Timeline. Alternately, press F5.

Deleting Frames

Deleting a single frame or a selection of frames from the Timeline allows you to remove an unwanted sequence of events from your movie or to speed up a sequence of events.

To Delete A SELECTED FRAME OR A SELECTED RANGE OF FRAMES, DO ONE OF THE FOLLOWING:

■ ....Press the Delete key.

■ ....Choose Remove Frames from the Insert menu. Alternately, hold down the Shift key, and then press F5.

Working with Keyframes

Keyframes are the very lifeblood of any animation. You create keyframes where you want major changes or events to occur in your movie. You can use keyframes to change an object's position on the Stage, introduce another object into the movie, add a sound event to the movie, or add an action to a movie.

Creating Keyframes

When you add a keyframe to the Timeline, it is blank unless there is already something in the keyframe that precedes it. You can create either a keyframe, which will carry over the content from the previous keyframe, or a blank keyframe, which is a placeholder for an object yet to be created or an event yet to occur. When you create a blank keyframe, a single vertical bar appears at the frame's left border. A filled keyframe is signified by a circular dot between the frame's boundaries, as shown in Figure 8-5.

To Create A KEYFRAME

1 Select a frame.

2 Choose Keyframe from the Insert menu.

FIGURE 8-5

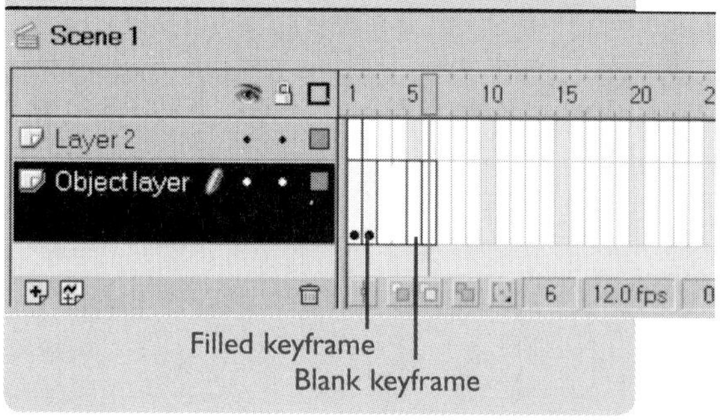

Scene 1

	1	5	10	15	20
Layer 2					
Object layer					

6   12.0 fps   0

Filled keyframe
Blank keyframe

Creating Blank Keyframes

You can create a blank keyframe as a placeholder for a future major change. Creating a blank keyframe is also a convenient way to empty a frame prior to introducing a new symbol, sound, or action. Inserting a blank keyframe in a sequence of frames clears all objects on a layer's frames from that point forward or until the next keyframe.

To Create A BLANK KEYFRAME

1 Select a frame.

2 Choose Blank Keyframe from the Insert menu. A blank keyframe appears on the Timeline. A rectangular icon appears on the frame before, signifying that a keyframe follows.

Creating Multiple Keyframes

Create multiple keyframes when you need a sequence of events to occur in which the object in the first frame changes in subsequent frames. When you create multiple keyframes, you are converting existing frames.

To Create MULTIPLE KEYFRAMES

1 Select the range of frames that you want to convert to keyframes.

2 Choose Frames from the Modify menu, and then choose Convert to Keyframes.

Flash converts the selected frames to keyframes, signified by the dot in each frame. You can now edit the contents of the selected frames to create changes or key events in your movie. If the range of frames that you selected has no objects in it, the converted frames are displayed as blank keyframes.

You can also convert a range of frames to blank keyframes. Use this command when you need to create several placeholders for future objects.

To Create MULTIPLE BLANK KEYFRAMES

1 Select a range of frames that you need to convert to blank keyframes.

2 Choose Frames from the Modify menu, and then choose Convert to Blank Keyframes. Flash creates a range of blank keyframes, designated by the bar at each frame's left border.

3 Select each blank keyframe, and then fill it with the desired symbol, object, or action.

Converting Keyframes

You can convert a keyframe into a normal frame. When a keyframe is converted to a normal frame, its contents are replaced with the contents of the prior keyframe. Use this option when you no longer need a keyframe's event in your movie but still need a frame to maintain the timing of your movie.

To Convert A KEYFRAME INTO A REGULAR FRAME

1 Select the keyframe that you want to convert.

continues

145

continued

2 Choose Clear Frame from the Insert menu.

Labeling Keyframes

You can label keyframes for easy identification. Label keyframes when you introduce ActionScript into your movies. For example, you can use ActionScript to advance a movie to a particular frame. Actions recognize frame numbers, but remembering specific frame numbers can be an arduous task when you are creating a complex movie. Furthermore, if you move a frame that is referred to in an ActionScript by its frame number, the link to the frame with the action or objects that you want the script to refer to is lost; Flash links to the frame number referred to in the action, and the movie will not play properly. However, if you specify a frame label when programming an action, the link remains intact when you move the labeled frame.

To Label A FRAME

1 Select the keyframe that you want to reference with a label.

2 Choose Panels from the Window menu, and then choose Frame. Alternately, click the Instance button on the Launcher bar, and then click the Frame tab after the Instance panel opens.

3 Enter a name in the Label field, and then press Enter or Return. The frame's label is displayed on the Timeline, as shown in Figure 8-6.

Warning Only keyframes can have labels. If you select a regular frame and apply a label to it, the Frame panel accepts the label but applies it to the previous keyframe.

FIGURE 8-6

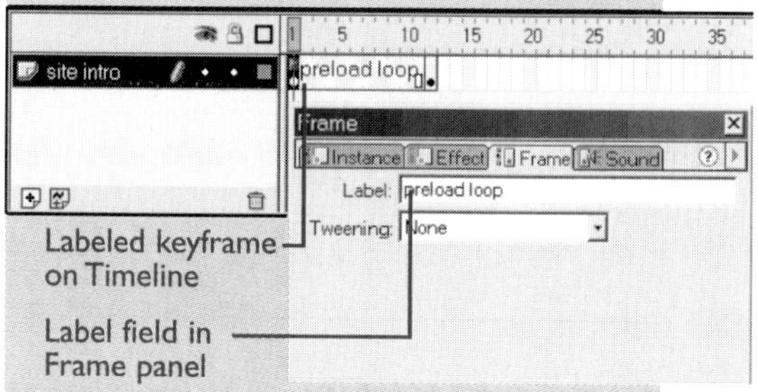

Labeled keyframe on Timeline

Label field in Frame panel

chapter 8: creating frame-by-frame animations

In addition to having their names displayed on the Timeline, labeled keyframes also display a tiny red icon near the top of the frame bounding box. This makes it possible to identify labeled keyframes when you have several keyframes next to each other and a label is totally or partially hidden. To reveal a keyframe's obscured label, place your cursor directly beneath the keyframe, as shown in Figure 8-7.

see also For more information on ActionScript, refer to Chapters 12 and 14.

FIGURE 8-7

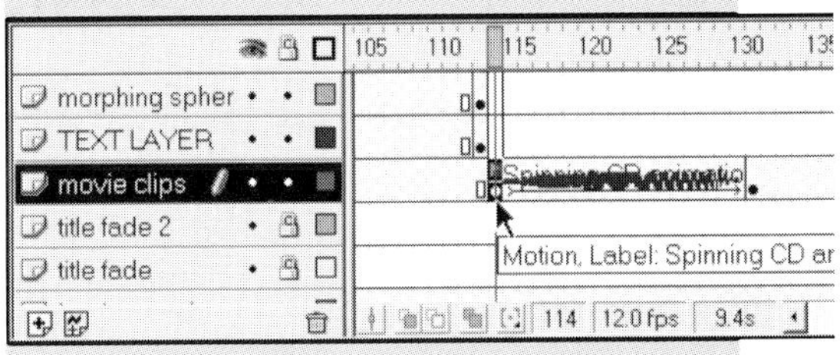

Editing Frames

To fine-tune a movie, you may have to edit individual frames or selections of frames. When you edit frames, you can change the location of keyframes, paste frame selections to another location on the Timeline, or extend the number of frames between keyframes. Additionally, you may end up placing a selection of keyframes in another layer or in another movie.

Selecting Frames

When editing a Flash movie, you often need to select a specific frame or a range of frames. After you select the frames, you can move, copy, cut, or paste them. These operations can take place on the same layer, or you can move the selected frames to another layer. As you move your cursor towards a single frame, a single angled arrow designates its position.

To Select A FRAME

▶ Click it. The frame becomes highlighted in black.

To Add ADJACENT FRAMES TO THE SELECTION

▶ **Drag left or right. Alternately, click another frame on the Timeline. All frames between the two frames that you clicked are now selected.**

As you move your cursor towards a range of frames between two filled keyframes, the cursor changes from an angled arrow to a hand. Click to select the range of frames. The frames become highlighted in black, as shown in Figure 8-8

note If you select and drag a single keyframe and adjacent frames, Flash moves only the keyframe and not the adjacent keyframes. If you need to increase the time span between filled keyframes, press the Ctrl key, click an individual frame to select it, and then drag left or right to increase the selection. Press F5 to add the exact number of frames selected to the Timeline.

FIGURE 8-8

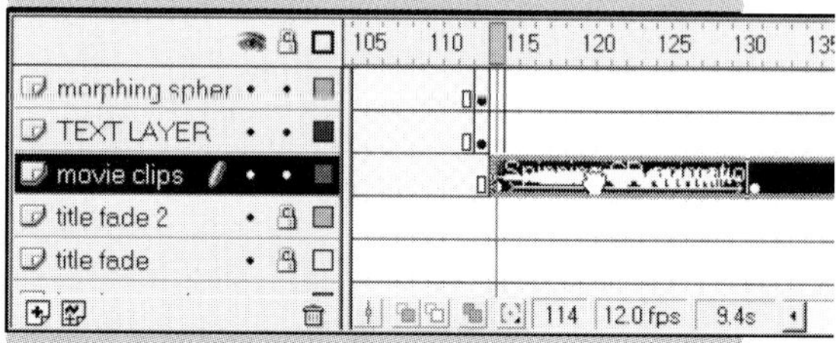

Copying and Pasting Frames

You can copy a selected frame or range of frames and paste them to another part of the current layer's Timeline, another layer's Timeline, or a Timeline in another document.

To Copy A FRAME OR A RANGE OF FRAMES

1 Select a frame or a range of frames as outlined in the preceding steps.

2 Choose Copy Frames from the Edit menu. The selected frames are pasted to the clipboard.

3 Click a frame on the current layer or another layer where you want to paste the frame or range of frames.

4 Choose Paste Frames from the Edit menu, and the frame or range of frames is pasted at the location that you selected.

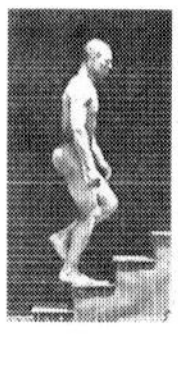

Moving a Frame or Selection of Frames

In addition to copying, cutting, and pasting frames to different locations, you can also move them manually. You can move selected frames within their layer's Timeline, or you can move them to another layer's Timeline.

To Manually MOVE A SINGLE KEYFRAME

1 Select the keyframe that you want to move.

2 Click the keyframe, and then drag it to a new location. As you drag the keyframe, the cursor becomes a closed fist. A preview of the keyframe's new location appears as you drag, as shown in Figure 8-9.

3 Release the mouse button to place the keyframe in its new location.

To Manually MOVE A RANGE OF FRAMES BETWEEN TWO KEYFRAMES

1 Move your cursor towards the range of frames that you want to select. The cursor becomes a hand as you near the selection.

2 Click the selection to select it. Unless the objects have been animated with tweening, all frames are selected except the last keyframe in the group.

3 Hold down the Shift key, and then click the ending keyframe to add it to the selection. The selection is highlighted in black.

n°te If the keyframe that you are moving is at the end of a series of frames, moving it to a new location places empty frames between the keyframe and the series of frames to which it was once linked. To maintain the link with the previous keyframe, select the keyframe, and then hold down the Shift key and click the frame with the rectangle icon before the selected keyframe. Drag both frames, and the link with the previous keyframe remains.

FIGURE 8-9

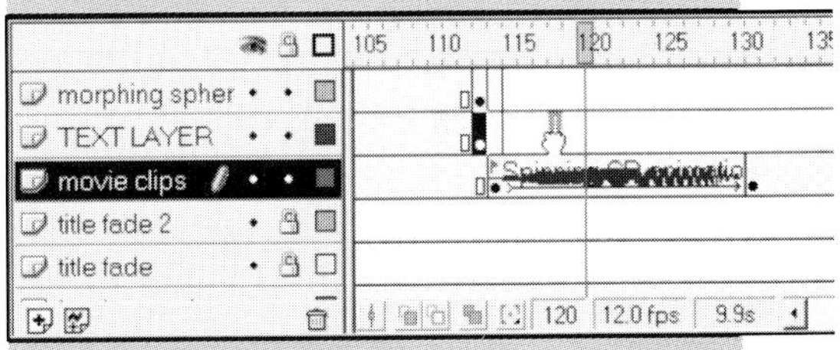

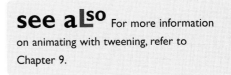

see a[so For more information on animating with tweening, refer to Chapter 9.

continues

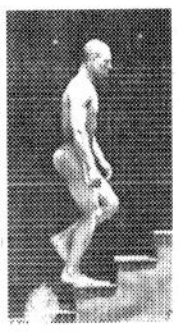

continued

4 Drag the selection to another location on the Timeline. As you drag the selection, a bounding box appears, giving you a preview of the selection's location, as shown in Figure 8-10.

5 Release the mouse button to place the selection at its new location.

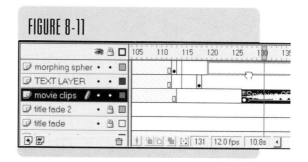

FIGURE 8-10

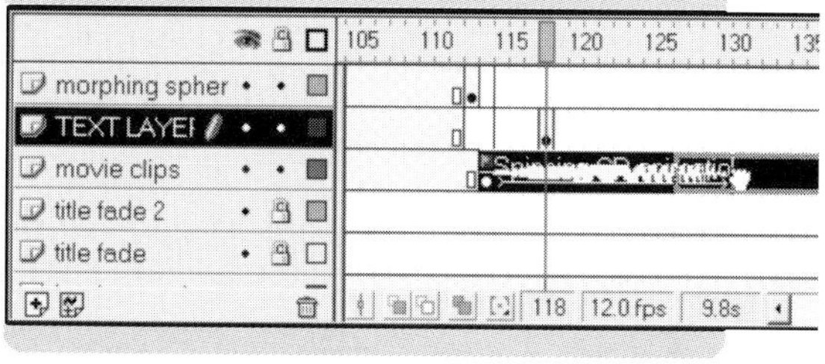

To Manually MOVE A FRAME OR SELECTION OF FRAMES TO ANOTHER LAYER

1 Select a frame or range of frames.

2 Drag the frame or selection of frames to its new location on another layer. As you drag, a bounding box appears, showing you a preview of the selection's location, as shown in Figure 8-11.

3 Release the mouse button when the frames are at the desired location.

FIGURE 8-11

Reversing Frames

Reversing the order in which frames appear on the Timeline is a convenient way to reverse a sequence of events. You can also reverse frames to conclude an introduction sequence. For example, in a movie, text is paraded onto the Stage to display the name of a Web site. You add a single frame further down the Timeline to display the name for a second or two. Copy the frames that you created to parade the text onto the Stage, and then paste them to the frame after the text stops displaying. You then reverse the pasted frames. When the movie is published, the Web site's name enters the Stage, remains stationary, and then reverses off of the Stage.

To Reverse THE ORDER OF SELECTED FRAMES

▶ Choose Frames from the Modify menu, and then choose Reverse.

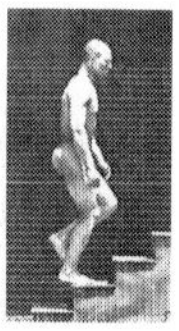

Using the Frames Context Menu

You can quickly access many frame creation and editing commands through the Frames context menu.

To Access THE FRAMES CONTEXT MENU

 Right-click (Windows) or Control-click (Macintosh) a frame, and then click the desired command to select it from the menu, as shown in Figure 8-12.

FIGURE 8-12

Creating a Frame-by-Frame Animation

Now that you know how to create and edit frames, it's time to use this knowledge to create motion in Flash. The following example shows how to create a frame-by-frame animation of a basketball arcing through the air and swishing through a hoop. Three layers are used for this animation: two for the basketball hoop and one for the basketball. It's a good idea to create a separate layer any time that you animate an object. In fact, with tweened animations, this is essential. You learn how to create tweened animations in the next chapter.

To Create A FRAME-BY-FRAME ANIMATION

1 Create a new document in Flash.

2 Determine the frame rate of the animation. In the case of the basketball animation, accept Flash's default frame rate of 12 fps.

3 Determine how long it will take for the action to occur. For the basketball animation, it was predetermined that the ball would take one second to reach the backboard and another second to go through the hoop and fall to the ground.

continues

continued

4 Create the backdrop for the scene, and then create a separate layer for the basketball and the hoops. Place the basketball layer between the hoop layers.

5 Using the Oval tool, create the basketball, and then position it at its starting position.

6 Click frame 24 (two seconds of elapsed time at 12 fps) to select it, and then choose Frame from the Insert menu.

7 On each hoop's layer, click frame 24, and then choose Frame from the Insert menu. If you neglect this step, the hoop and background for the scene will not appear after frame 1.

8 On the basketball layer, click frame 24, and then drag left to select all of the frames.

9 Choose Frames from the Modify menu, and then choose Convert to Keyframes. The contents of frame 1 are copied into the new keyframes, as shown in Figure 8-13.

TIP To make the basketball appear as though it is going through a hoop, create an oval with no fill on the first hoop layer. Create a straight line, and then position it over the hoop to cut it in two. (Remember, placing a line over another shape bisects the shape.) Select the top half of the hoop, and then choose Cut from the Edit menu. Select the top hoop layer, and then choose Paste in Place from the Edit menu. Delete the line, group the hoop halves, and then position them on the backboard. By placing the basketball layer between each hoop layer, the basketball appears to be going through a three-dimensional hoop.

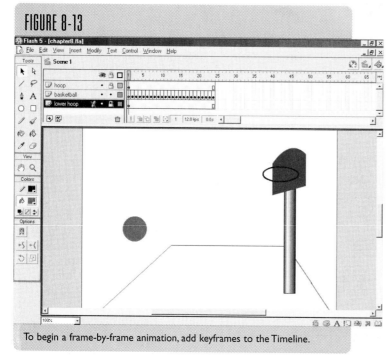

FIGURE 8-13

To begin a frame-by-frame animation, add keyframes to the Timeline.

continues

continued

10 Advance to each consecutive keyframe and move the basketball to a new position, gradually advancing the ball towards the backboard, through the hoop, and to the ground, as shown in Figure 8-14.

To see frame-by-frame animation in action, watch **A Virtual Typewriter** lesson on the **Virtual Classroom CD-ROM.**

TIP To quickly center a frame on the Timeline, press the Center Frame button. Note that if the frame is between the first frame on the Timeline and the center of the Timeline, it will not be centered.

Accurately positioning the basketball in each frame is difficult because you see only one keyframe at a time. To view more than one keyframe at a time, you need to use the onion skin feature.

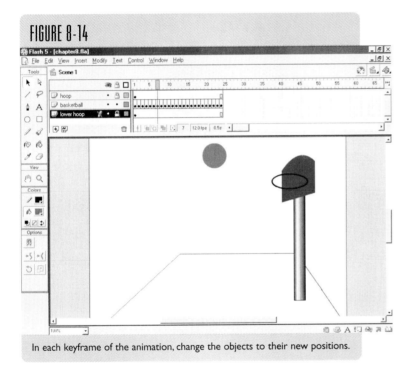

FIGURE 8-14

In each keyframe of the animation, change the objects to their new positions.

Working with Onion Skins

Onion skins make it possible for you to preview several frames of an animation at once. When you enable onion skins, the object on the current frame is displayed normally; the objects on other keyframes are displayed dimmed or as outlines. When you enable onion skins, you can specify the range of frames on which they are displayed.

To Preview KEYFRAMES USING ONION SKINS

1 To enable onion skins, click the Onion Skin button below the Timeline. A marker appears over the frames, as shown in Figure 8-15. The dots on each end of the onion skin marker are used to specify the range of frames on which onion skins are displayed.

2 Drag the Start Onion Skin and End Onion Skin anchors to specify the range of frames. As you move the playhead from frame to frame, the onion skin marker follows it, and Flash displays the specified number of frames on either side of the current frame as onion skins. Figure 8-16 shows the shapes in all frames of the basketball animation displayed as onion skins.

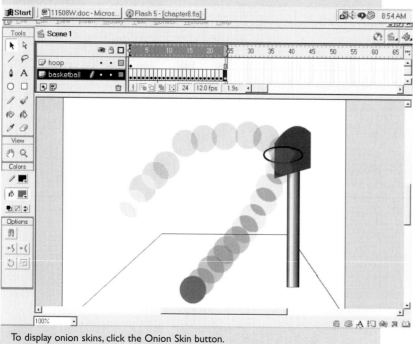

FIGURE 8-15

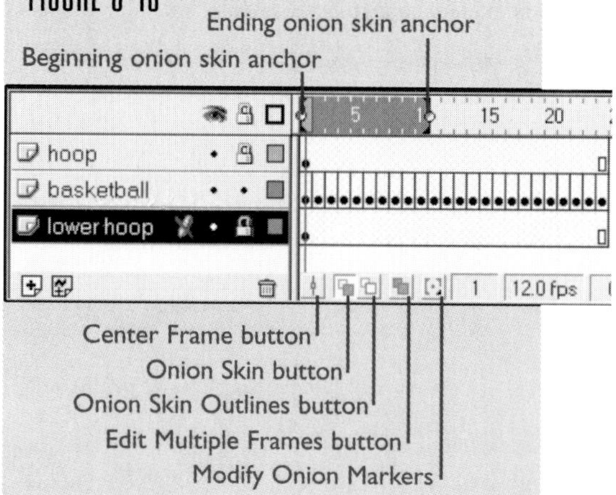

Ending onion skin anchor
Beginning onion skin anchor

Center Frame button
Onion Skin button
Onion Skin Outlines button
Edit Multiple Frames button
Modify Onion Markers

FIGURE 8-16

To display onion skins, click the Onion Skin button.

To Modify THE NUMBER OF ONION SKINS DISPLAYED

▶ Manually drag onion skin markers or click the **Modify Onion Markers** button, and then choose one of the following options from the drop-down menu:

Anchor Onion anchors onion skins to the selected frames and does not move the marker or display onion skins when you move the playhead beyond the selected frames.

Anchor 2 displays two frames on either side of the current frame.

Anchor 5 displays five frames on either side of the current frame.

Onion All displays all frames in the movie.

Editing Multiple Frames

Another option at your disposal is the ability to edit multiple frames. In this mode, you can select and edit objects on every keyframe between onion skin markers, regardless of whether they are on the currently selected frame. When you are editing multiple frames, objects are displayed normally, not dimmed as they appear in onion-skin mode. In the edit-multiple-frames mode, you can select objects on several frames at once. Make sure that you have selected the intended objects before performing an edit. Figure 8-17 shows the completed basketball animation displayed as onion skins after the ball was repositioned using the Edit Multiple Frames option.

FIGURE 8-17

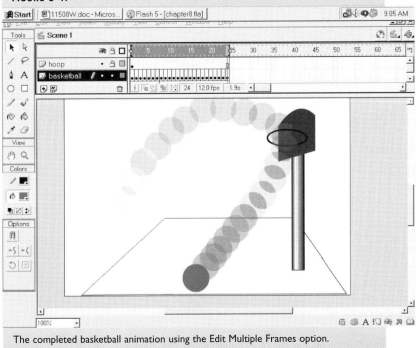

The completed basketball animation using the Edit Multiple Frames option.

To Edit MULTIPLE FRAMES

1 Click the Edit Multiple Frames button. The onion skin marker is displayed, as shown in Figure 8-18.

2 Drag the Start Onion Skin and End Onion Skin markers to specify the range of frames that you can edit.

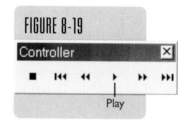

FIGURE 8-18   Onion skin marker

Edit Multiple Frames button

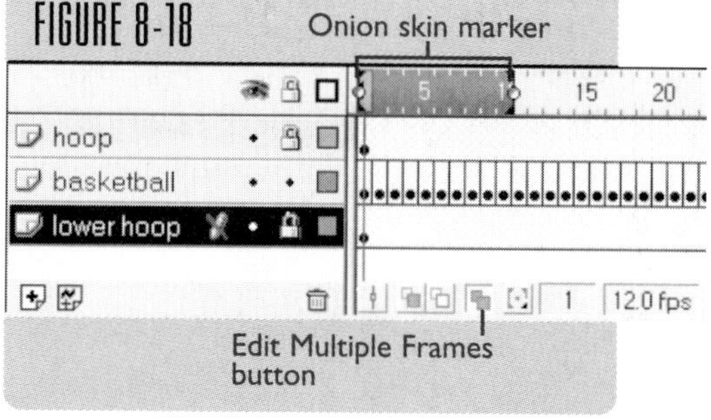

All objects in the specified range of frames are now available for editing. If your movie has multiple layers, be sure to lock all layers except the one that you are editing. This will prevent you from inadvertently selecting an object on another layer.

Previewing the Animation

After setting up a frame-by-frame animation, you can preview it in the movie-editing environment by using either the playhead or the Controller.

To Preview THE ANIMATION USING THE PLAYHEAD

▶ Click the playhead and drag it from frame to frame to advance the movie.

> **note** You may find that it suits your working habits to dock the Controller just above the Timeline window.

To Preview THE ANIMATION USING THE CONTROLLER

1 Choose Toolbar from the Window menu, and then choose Controller.

2 Press the Controller's Play button, as shown in Figure 8-19. You can also preview the animation by pressing Enter or Return.

FIGURE 8-19

Controller

Play

Frame-by-frame animations have their place: they work well for animating text and sequences of images. A frame-by-frame animation is not always the best choice for animating objects because frame-by-frame animation can be tedious work. For example, in the basketball animation, every change in motion had to be choreographed in a keyframe. Fortunately, there is an easier way to animate motion, as you will learn in the next chapter.

Animating Objects with Tweening

9

As you learned in the previous chapter, frame-by-frame animations are tedious work. Fortunately, in Flash 5 there is an easier way to create animations: tweening. When you use tweening to animate an object, Flash redraws the object on frames in between keyframes (also known as in-between frames). When you play back the animation, there are no gaps, and smooth action occurs. There are two types of tweening: shape tweening, which transforms an object's shape from one keyframe to the next; and motion tweening, which interpolates an object's position between keyframes. In this chapter, you will learn how to create sophisticated animations using both forms of tweening.

Creating Motion Tween Animations

To create a few seconds of animation, a cartoonist would have to draw dozens of pictures, one for each frame, a technique similar to creating a frame-by-frame animation. To create a refined animation in Flash, you need to create only a few keyframes, change the shape in each keyframe, and then apply motion tweening. Flash completes the animation by redrawing the shape on each of the in-between frames. Note that you cannot create a motion tween animation using editable objects; you can apply motion tweening only to symbols.

To Create A MOTION TWEEN ANIMATION

1 Create a shape in a keyframe, and then convert it to a symbol by pressing **F8**. Alternately, select a symbol from the Library.

2 Determine how long the animation will be, advance to the final frame, and then insert a keyframe by pressing **F6**.

3 Change the object's position in the final keyframe.

4 Click a frame between the keyframes that you just created, and then choose **Create Motion Tween** from the **Insert** menu. Alternately, right-click (**Windows**) or Control-click (**Macintosh**), and then choose **Create Motion Tween** from the context menu. The background of the in-between frames is tinted a light blue with an arrow connecting the beginning and ending keyframes, indicating that motion tweening has been applied. In Figure 9-1, motion tweening has been applied to create an animation of a jet airplane taking off.

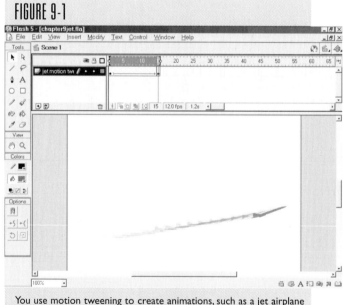

FIGURE 9-1

You use motion tweening to create animations, such as a jet airplane lifting off.

continues

continued

5 To preview the animation, click the Controller's play button. Alternately, press Enter or Return. An alternate method of creating a motion tween is to open the Frames panel in Step 4 and then choose Motion from the panel's Tweening menu, as shown in Figure 9-2.

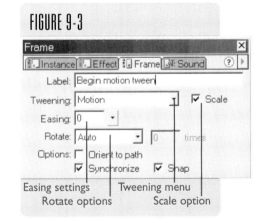

FIGURE 9-2

To Remove A MOTION TWEEN THAT HAS AN ERROR OR IS NO LONGER NEEDED

1 Select the first frame in the motion tween sequence or any of the in-between frames.

2 Choose Panels from the Window menu, and then choose Frame to open the Frame panel. Choose None from the panel's Tweening menu.

Warning Although it will not work, you can apply motion tweening to frames containing editable objects. When you apply motion tweening to an editable object, a broken line connects the keyframes, indicating that there is a problem with the tween.

Setting Motion Tween Options

In addition to creating smooth motion between keyframes, you can use motion tweening to scale a symbol, rotate a symbol, or orient a symbol to a path. You can also specify how the transition between keyframes starts and ends.

To Modify A MOTION TWEEN

▶ Select a frame that the motion tween property has been applied to, right-click (Windows) or Control-click (Macintosh), choose Panels, and then choose Frame from the context menu. Alternately, you can choose Panels from the Window menu, and then choose Frame.

Figure 9-3 shows the Frame panel and the options available for a motion tween.

FIGURE 9-3

Scaling an Object

When you create a motion tween animation, you are working with instances of symbols. As you know, you can modify instances. If the scale of an instance differs from one keyframe to the next in a motion tween animation, selecting the Scale option (see Figure 9-3) causes the object to change size incrementally between keyframes.

Rotating an Object

You can also use motion tweening to make an object rotate between keyframes. This option works well for creating swirling text and other special effects.

To Rotate A TWEENED OBJECT

1 Set up a motion tween animation as outlined previously.

2 Click the first keyframe or one of the in-between frames, choose Panels from the Window menu, and then choose Frame. Alternately, right-click (Windows) or Control-click (Macintosh) the first keyframe or one of the in-between frames, choose Panels, and then choose Frames from the context menu.

3 Click the triangle to the right of the Rotate field, as shown previously in Figure 9-3, and then select one of the following options:

>   **None:** Select this option and the object does not rotate.

>   **Auto:** Select this option if you manually rotated the object in either the first or the last keyframe. When the animation is played, the object rotates in the direction requiring the least motion.

>   **CW:** Select this option to rotate the object in a clockwise direction between keyframes.

>   **CCW:** Select this option and the object rotates in a counterclockwise direction between keyframes.

4 If you select **CW** or **CCW,** the Times option becomes available. Enter the number of times that you want the object to rotate between keyframes. You must enter a whole integer in this field.

Editing the Tween's Transition

A motion tween's default transition between one keyframe and the next is linear. Objects in real life don't exhibit a linear transition when changing states. Take a car accelerating from rest, for example. Motion starts slowly and builds as the car overcomes inertia. Use the motion tween's easing controls to control how the transition starts and stops.

To Edit THE TWEEN'S TRANSITION, DO ONE OF THE FOLLOWING:

■ .... To change how a motion tween animation eases from one keyframe to the next, click the triangle to the right of the easing control, and then drag the slider up or down. Alternately, enter a value between -100 and 100. Drag the slider closer to either value to exaggerate acceleration or deceleration.

■ .... To have a motion tween animation begin slowly and end quickly, drag the Easing slider towards In, or enter a negative value in the Easing field.

■ .... To begin the motion tween animation quickly and end it slowly, drag the Easing slider towards Out, or enter a positive value in the Easing field.

FIGURE 9-4

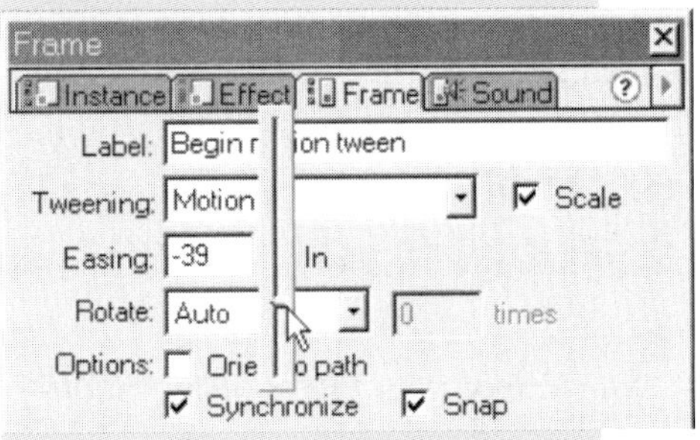

Editing Motion Tween Animations

Easing is used to control how an animation starts and stops. However, you may also need to adjust the time span of the animation and add events to a motion tween animation. Preview the animation with the Controller to learn what you must do to fine-tune the animation.

To Speed UP A MOTION TWEEN ANIMATION

▶ Delete one or more frames between the starting and ending keyframes.

To Slow DOWN THE SEQUENCE OF EVENTS IN A MOTION TWEEN ANIMATION

▶ Add one or more frames between the beginning and ending keyframes.

see also For more information on adding and deleting frames, refer to the Working with Frames section in Chapter 8.

Inserting Keyframes

You can also insert a keyframe in the middle of a motion tween. The new keyframe will have an instance of the symbol as it appears at that point in the animation. For example, look at the motion tween animation illustrated in Figure 9-1 on page 158. The airplane is rising at a steady angle, something very few airplanes are capable of. To create a more realistic animation, add a keyframe or two, and then modify the airplane's instance at each keyframe, as shown in Figure 9-5. Motion tweening is also an excellent way to introduce special effects in a Flash movie. By applying an effect to an instance in one keyframe and then modifying the effect in another keyframe, you can animate objects while making them become brighter, change colors, become visible, or disappear.

FIGURE 9-5

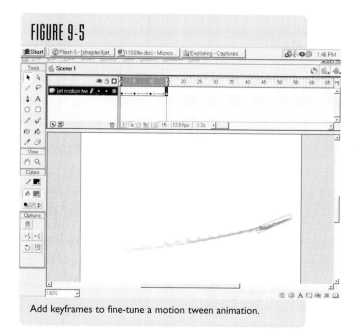

Add keyframes to fine-tune a motion tween animation.

TIP To make a message seem as though it is magically materializing from thin air, create a block of text with the Text tool, and then convert it to a symbol. In the keyframe where animation begins and the text is invisible, drag an instance of the text symbol onto the Stage, and then center it. Create another keyframe at the point where you want the text to be fully visible. Select the keyframe with the first instance of the text. Use the Arrow tool to scale the symbol to a smaller size, and then apply the Tint effect to it. Click the Tint Color swatch, and the cursor becomes an eyedropper. Drag the eyedropper over the movie background, and then click to sample the background color. The text now blends in perfectly with the background. Apply a motion tween to the in-between frames. When you play back the animation, the text gradually appears from nowhere while increasing in size.

see also For more information on applying effects, refer to Chapter 6.

chapter 9: animating objects with tweening

Animating with Motion Paths

Motion paths are guides that symbols follow in motion tween animations. Motion guides have their own layers. You can create motion guides with any of the drawing tools, or you can use an imported .ai or .eps file as a guide. You need to ungroup imported files before you can use them as paths.

Creating a Motion Guide Layer

On a motion guide layer you create the motion path that you want a symbol to follow. When the movie is published, the motion guide layer and its path are not visible.

To Create A MOTION GUIDE LAYER

1 Create a tweened animation as outlined previously, but do not move the second instance of the symbol.

2 Right-click (Windows) or Control-click (Macintosh) the animation layer, and then choose **Add Motion Guide** from the context menu. A new layer appears above the animation layer. The animation layer is now a guided layer and is linked to the motion guide layer.

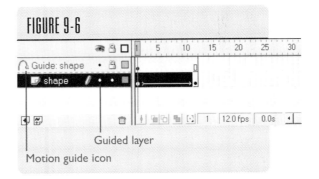

FIGURE 9-6

Guided layer

Motion guide icon

Motion guide layers are given the default name of Guide: followed by the name of the layer that you selected when you created the motion guide layer. A motion guide layer is identified by an icon that looks like the Gateway Arch in St. Louis, as shown in Figure 9-6. The icon for a guided layer is indented to differentiate it from normal layers.

Creating the Motion Path

You can create a motion path with any of the drawing tools; you do not have to limit yourself to the Line tool or the Pencil tool. You can create interesting motion paths using the Pen, Oval, or Rectangle tool. Using the Pen tool to draw a path gives you point-to-point control. A path that you create with either the Oval or Rectangle tool will be closed, but you can open it with the Eraser tool. After creating the motion path, you should lock the motion guide layer to prevent accidentally altering the path.

Aligning and Orienting Objects to the Motion Path

To complete a motion path animation, you align the object being animated to the start of the path at the beginning keyframe of the motion tween animation and to the end of the path at the ending keyframe of the motion tween animation. Turn on the Snap option in the Frame panel's Options section to aid in aligning the symbol to the path. When you align the instance to the path, remember to drag it by its center or one of the reference points along the side or corner. As you drag the instance towards the motion path, the black circle becomes larger, signifying that you can align it precisely to the path.

To Align THE SYMBOL INSTANCE TO THE MOTION PATH

1 Switch to the animation layer, and then select the first frame of the motion tween.

2 Right-click (Windows) or Control-click (Macintosh), choose Frame from the Panels menu, and then make sure that Snap is checked in the Options section.

3 Select the instance, and then align it to the start of the motion path.

4 Select the last keyframe of the motion tween.

5 Drag the instance until it aligns to the end of the motion path. Figure 9-7 shows a symbol instance properly aligned to a motion path.

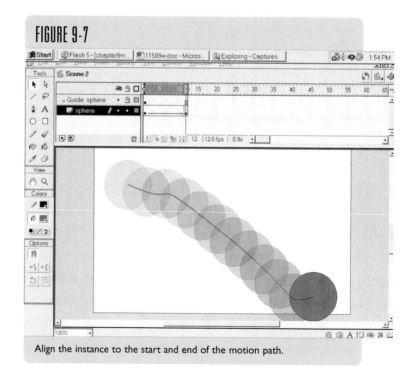

FIGURE 9-7

Align the instance to the start and end of the motion path.

Another motion tweening option available to you is orienting the instance to the path. Enabling this option causes an object to change its orientation as it travels along a path. In Figure 9-8, the plane on the left is not oriented to its path; the plane on the right is.

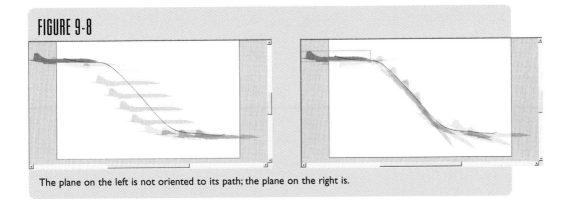

FIGURE 9-8

The plane on the left is not oriented to its path; the plane on the right is.

To Orient AN OBJECT TO ITS MOTION PATH

1 Create a motion tween animation in which an object follows a motion path.

2 Align the object to the path in the first and last keyframes.

3 Choose Panels from the Window menu, and then choose Frame.

4 Check the Orient to Path option, as shown in Figure 9-9.

FIGURE 9-9

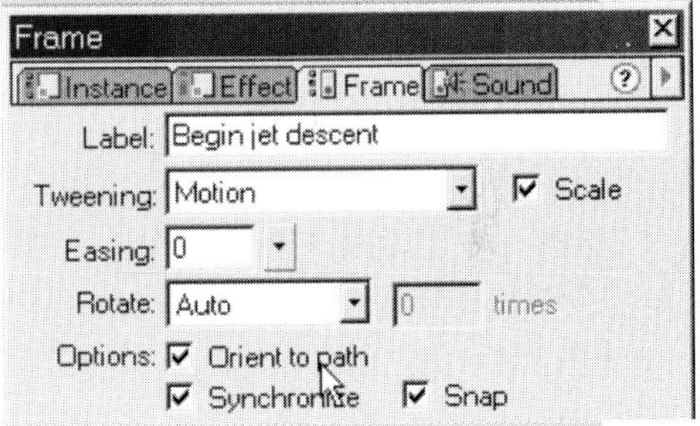

Frame

Instance | Effect | Frame | Sound

Label: Begin jet descent

Tweening: Motion ▼ ☑ Scale

Easing: 0 ▼

Rotate: Auto ▼ 0 times

Options: ☑ Orient to path
☑ Synchronize ☑ Snap

Linking Additional Layers to the Motion Guide Layer

You use an existing motion path to animate objects on other layers by linking other layers to the motion guide layer. A layer that is linked to a motion guide layer is guided. If objects in your movie will follow different paths, you need to create additional motion guide layers for the differently shaped paths.

To Create AN ADDITIONAL GUIDED LAYER, DO ONE OF THE FOLLOWING:

■ ....If the layer that you want to link to the motion guide layer is above it, select the layer, and then drag it directly beneath the motion guide layer.

■ ....If the layer that you want to be guided by the motion guide layer is below it, select the layer, and then drag it directly below the motion guide layer.

■ ....Right-click (Windows) or Control-click (Macintosh) a layer directly beneath a guided layer, choose Properties from the context menu, and then select Guided in the Layer Properties dialog box.

 To learn an easier method for animating the basketball scene in the last chapter, watch the **Motion Paths** lesson on the Virtual Classroom CD-ROM.

Creating Shape Tween Animations

A shape tween animation morphs one shape into another. As in motion tweening, you create the starting and ending shapes in keyframes, and Flash fills in the blanks by redrawing the object on the in-between frames. With shape tweening, you transform editable shapes instead of symbols because symbols cannot be edited and therefore will not work in this type of animation. Shape tweening does not restrict you to transforming an object's shape. You can also change an object's color, size, and location. Shape tweening has slightly different options than motion tweening. With shape tweening, you cannot automatically rotate a shape or make it follow a motion path. Another limitation is the inability to apply effects to editable objects.

To Create A SHAPE TWEEN ANIMATION

1 Select the beginning frame for the animation, and then use any of the drawing tools to create a shape.

continues

chapter 9: animating objects with tweening

continued

2 Determine how long the animation will be, select the ending frame for the animation, and then insert a keyframe by pressing **F6**.

3 The shape from the first keyframe is copied into the new keyframe. Modify the size, shape, location, color, or any combination of these parameters to create the shape that you want the first shape to change into. You can also delete the shape and create an entirely new shape.

4 Right-click (Windows) or Control-click (Macintosh) either the first frame or one of the in-between frames, choose **Panels**, and then choose **Frame** from the context menu.

5 Click the triangle to the right of the Tweening window, and then select **Shape** from the menu. The shape tween frames are tinted green, and an arrow appears, connecting the starting and ending keyframes, as shown in Figure 9-10.

6 Press Enter or Return to preview the animation. Figure 9-11 shows a typical shape tween animation.

To Remove SHAPE TWEENING

1 Right-click (Windows) or Control-click (Macintosh) either the first frame or one of the in-between frames, choose **Panels**, and then choose **Frame** from the context menu.

2 Click the triangle to the right of the Tweening field, and then select **None**.

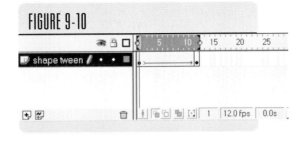

FIGURE 9-10

TIP To shape tween a text object, you must first convert it into an editable shape by choosing Break Apart from the Modify menu.

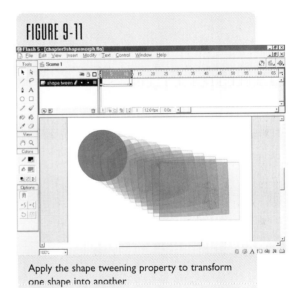

FIGURE 9-11

Apply the shape tweening property to transform one shape into another.

Warning Although it will not work, it is possible to apply a shape tween to a symbol. When this happens, a broken line appears between the keyframes to which you applied the tween, indicating that there is a problem with the tween.

Setting Shape Tween Options

Shape tweening has options that you can modify and that affect the final animation. You can change the way that the transition starts and stops, and you can modify the way that Flash redraws the shapes on the in-between frames.

To Edit A SHAPE TWEEN

1 Right-click (Windows) or Control-click (Macintosh) either the first keyframe or one of the in-between frames in the animation, choose Panels, and then choose Frame from the context menu.

2 In the Easing section, drag the slider to determine how the transition begins and ends.

To have the transition begin slowly and end quickly, drag the slider down (towards In). Alternately, enter a value between 0 and -100.

To have the transition begin quickly and end slowly, drag the slider up (towards Out). Alternately, enter a value between 0 and 100.

3 The option that you choose in the Blend section determines how one shape blends into the next. Choose from the following options:

Distributive blends one shape into another using smooth, flowing curves.

Angular preserves pointy corners and straight lines when Flash draws the shapes on the in-between frames.

Animating Multiple Objects with Shape Tweening

With shape tweening, it is possible to morph several shapes on a single layer. The results, however, are unpredictable, especially when the shapes that you are tweening change positions. Flash can't read your mind and determine when you want shapes to cross paths instead of going in a straight line. When you apply shape tweening to multiple objects, it's always best to create each animation on its own layer.

Shape Tween Complex Objects with Shape Hints

Flash uses the cold, hard logic of mathematics to determine how one shape morphs into another. This works well in most instances. However, when you use shape tweening to transform a simple shape like an oval into a complex shape like a flower, Flash does not always take into account the way that humans perceive things. When you create a shape tween and do not get the expected results, you need to give Flash a helping hand with shape hints. Shape hints are markers that you use to designate key points on the first shape that need to match up with key points on the second shape. Previewing the animation gives you your first clue that shape hints are necessary. You can also use onion skins to identify a shape tween animation gone awry. Figure 9-12 shows a shape tween animation in need of shape hints.

FIGURE 9-12

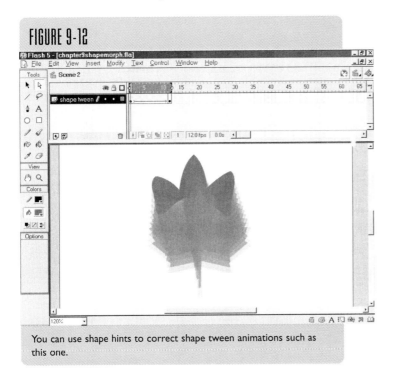

You can use shape hints to correct shape tween animations such as this one.

Applying Shape Hints

After you determine that shape hints are needed, the next step is to decide where to place the hints on each shape. You can drag the playhead from frame to frame and examine each in-between shape as Flash redraws it, or you can turn on onion skins to view the in-between shapes of several frames at once. If you notice any jarring or unnatural transitions, you will know exactly where to place each shape hint. When a shape tween animation plays, your viewer should have an idea of what the new shape will look like as Flash redraws the shape on the in-between frames.

To Apply SHAPE HINTS

1 Create a shape tween animation where a simple shape transforms into a complex one.

2 Preview the animation to determine the problem areas on each shape.

3 Click the Onion Skin button to enable onion skins.

4 Click the first frame of the animation, choose Transform from the Modify menu, and then choose **Add Shape Hint**. A shape hint appears in the middle of the shape. Shape hints are round circles surrounding a letter of the alphabet. A shape hint's letter is how you determine which shape hints on the first shape correspond to the shape hints on the last shape. For example, if you are morphing a circle into a cartoon character's head, you might place a shape hint with the letter a on a point on the circle that you want to transform into the character's nose. When you position the shape hints on the character's head (the last shape in the animation), you would place the shape hint with the letter a on the character's nose. Shape hints on beginning shapes become green after they are positioned, yellow on ending shapes.

5 Select the shape hint, and then drag it to a trouble area on the first shape.

6 Repeat steps 4 and 5 for each problematic area on the first shape. Apply shape hints counterclockwise in alphabetical order.

7 Select the last keyframe in your animation. The shape hints that you applied in the first frame are stacked in a neat little pile.

8 Click a shape hint to select it, and then drag it to its corresponding position on the animation's ending shape. Remember to apply the shape hints in alphabetical order with counterclockwise rotation as you did on the first shape in the animation. **Figure 9-13** shows the animation in Figure 9-12 with shape hints applied.

As you position the shape hints, the onion skins update, giving you a preview of how Flash will redraw the shape with the aid of shape hints. If the onion skins don't update, click anywhere on the Stage to refresh the view.

FIGURE 9-13

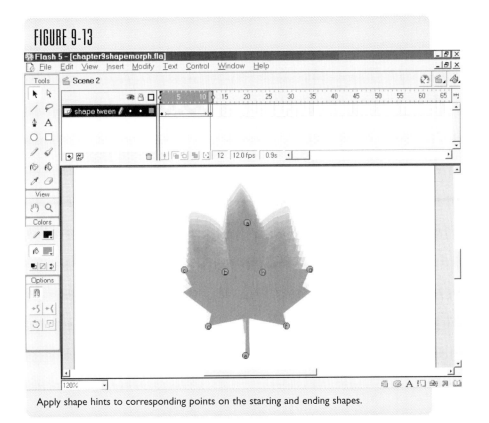

Apply shape hints to corresponding points on the starting and ending shapes.

Editing Shape Hints

After applying the shape hints, preview the animation by using the Controller or by pressing Enter or Return. If you are still not satisfied with the animation, reposition the shape hints on either or both shapes. You may have to add additional shape hints or delete a shape hint or two.

To Delete A SHAPE HINT

Select it, and then drag it off of the Stage. The shape hint is removed from both shapes.

To Delete ALL SHAPE HINTS

Choose Transform from the Modify menu, and then choose Remove All Hints.

To see how you can use shape tweening to transform simple shapes into complex ones, watch the Morphing II lesson on the Virtual Classroom CD-ROM.

Combining Motion with Shape Tweening

You combine motion with shape tweening by moving the ending shape to a different position than the first shape. When you play the shape tween animation, the shape transforms and moves at the same time. To create an animation more sophisticated than a shape morphing as it moves in a straight line from point A to point B, add additional keyframes, and then move the shape to the desired position on each keyframe. Turn on onion skins and the Edit Multiple Frames feature to work more efficiently. With enough keyframes, you can create an animation that looks like a shape morphing while following a motion path. Figure 9-14 shows a shape morphing while moving along a complex path.

With motion tweening, you can automatically rotate an object during an animation. To rotate an object in a shape tween animation requires adding keyframes and rotating the object in each keyframe either manually with the Arrow tool or mathematically with the Transform panel. Figure 9-15 shows a shape tween animation with rotation applied at intermediate keyframes.

FIGURE 9-14

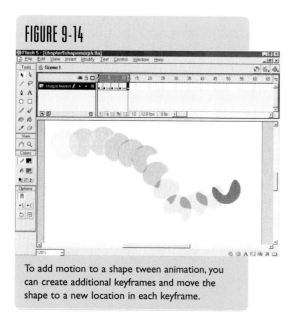

To add motion to a shape tween animation, you can create additional keyframes and move the shape to a new location in each keyframe.

FIGURE 9-15

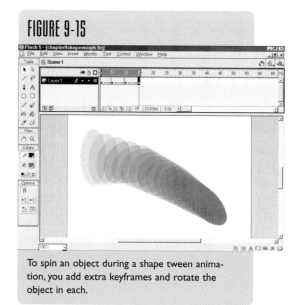

To spin an object during a shape tween animation, you add extra keyframes and rotate the object in each.

Combining Shape and Motion Tweening in an Animation

You can also combine motion tweening and shape tweening in the same animation by creating a symbol with a shape tween animation within it and then applying motion tweening to the symbol.

To Combine SHAPE TWEENING AND MOTION TWEENING IN A SINGLE ANIMATION

see also For more information on motion tweening and motion paths, refer to the Creating Motion Tween Animations section earlier in this chapter. For more information on creating movie clips, refer to chapter 10.

1 Choose **New Symbol** from the **Insert** menu to access the **Symbol Properties** dialog box.

2 Enter a name for the symbol, and then assign the **Movie Clip** behavior to the symbol. Click **OK** to enter symbol-editing mode.

3 Create a shape tween animation as outlined previously.

4 Click the **Current Scene** button to exit symbol-editing mode.

5 Create a keyframe where you want the animation to begin.

6 Open the document **Library**, select the symbol that you just created, and then drag it onto the **Stage**.

7 Create a keyframe further down the Timeline. If your shape tween movie clip is five frames long, position the new keyframe exactly five frames down the Timeline.

8 Apply motion tweening to the in-between frames.

9 Create a motion guide layer, and then draw the motion path that you want the shape tween movie clip to follow.

10 Align the movie clip symbol with the shape tween animation to the start of the motion path at the beginning keyframe and to the end of the motion path at the ending keyframe.

Observe First, Animate Later!

Animators are students of motion. They observe how objects move in the world around them and apply their observations to their work. For example, when an object accelerates from rest, it overcomes inertia before coming up to speed. And when an object stops moving, it almost never stops on a dime. You can use the tweening easing controls to simulate these natural phenomena.

Secondary motion is another trait that you notice about natural movement. A car traveling down the highway sways sideways when a truck hurtles past in the opposite direction. Your pet cat almost always arches its back before leaping onto your canary's cage. Apply secondary motion to your Flash movies for that extra dose of realism.

Believe it or not, television commercials are one of the better sources for Flash inspiration. Advertisers are using interesting text effects and sophisticated motion to sell their products. You can duplicate many of these effects in Flash by using motion and shape tweens or by applying effects to tweened instances of symbols. The next time that a commercial plays, resist the urge to jump up and get your favorite snack. Watch the commercial instead, and then figure out how to use Flash to duplicate an effect that you find appealing. Your Web sites will look better for the effort.

Creating Complex Animations

In the previous two chapters, you learned to animate objects on single layers. To realize the full power of Flash 5, in this chapter you will learn to create complex animations that involve several objects and span many layers. You will also learn to break a movie down into scenes, create reusable animations, and choreograph animated objects with layers.

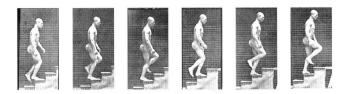

Managing Complex Animations with Scenes

Complex movies with a lot of animation have Timelines of equal complexity. If you don't like scrolling through what seems like an endless procession of frames to edit a Flash production, you can break the movie down into scenes. Scenes play in the order in which they were created, just like in a three-act play: scene one ends, scene two begins, scene two ends, and scene three begins, etc. In Flash, however, you can use ActionScript to halt a scene while waiting for user input. Another difference is that there is no intermission between the scenes that you create in Flash unless, of course, you create one.

Warning If a movie with multiple scenes and extensive use of ActionScript does not play properly, use Flash's Debug Movie command to trace actions, objects, and variables. If you are unable to successfully debug the movie, Flash may have problems interpreting actions between scenes. Consider converting each scene to an individual movie and using the *loadMovie* action to navigate from one movie to the next.

You use the Scene panel to create, delete, and manage scenes in your movie. A Flash movie has one scene by default. You can break a movie down into scenes whenever it becomes too cumbersome to manage. If your movie has a discernable beginning, middle, and end, break it down into three scenes.

Creating Scenes

You can create a scene on the fly as needed when a movie gets to the point where it is logical to create new content in its own scene, or you can create a scene when you have so many frames in a movie that editing it as a single scene would be a logistical nightmare. You can also create a scene and then paste frames and layers from another scene into it. You use this technique when you create a new scene and decide that frames from a previous scene should be in it.

To Create A SCENE

1 Choose Panels from the Window menu, and then choose Scene.

2 Click the Add Scene button.

continues

chapter 10: creating complex animations

continued

3 A new scene appears in the Scene panel, as shown in Figure 10-1. Flash opens the scene in a new window for the scene with a blank Timeline and one layer.

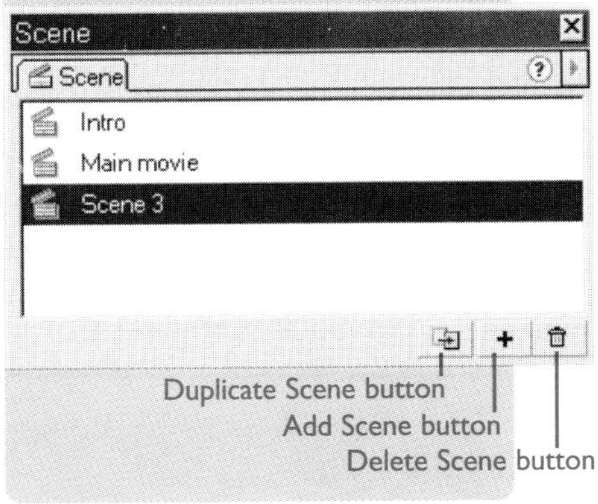

To Create A NEW SCENE USING EXISTING LAYERS AND FRAMES

1 Select the frames with which you want to start the new scene. Remember to select the frames on all layers.

2 Choose Cut Frames from the Edit menu.

3 Choose Panels from the Window menu, and then choose Scene to open the Scene panel.

4 Click the Add Scene button. A new scene is added to the movie. The new scene becomes the current scene and opens up in its own window.

5 Click the first frame on the Timeline, and then choose Paste Frames from the Edit menu. Flash pastes the frames that you cut into the new scene and creates layers if the frames appear on multiple layers in the other scene. The layers are in the same order as in the other scene; however, you need to rename them.

FIGURE 10-1

Scene ☒

Scene ⑦ ▶

🎬 Intro
🎬 Main movie
🎬 Scene 3

Duplicate Scene button
Add Scene button
Delete Scene button

Deleting Scenes

You can delete scenes when they are no longer needed. Note that this action cannot be undone.

To Delete A SCENE

1 Choose Panels from the Window menu, and then select Scene to access the Scene panel.

2 Select the scene that you want to delete, and then click the Delete Scene button (which looks like a trashcan) in the lower-right corner of the panel.

3 Flash displays a warning dialog box, telling you that the action cannot be undone.

4 Click OK to close the warning dialog box and delete the scene.

TIP Press Ctrl, and then click the Delete Scene button to bypass the Delete Scene Warning dialog box.

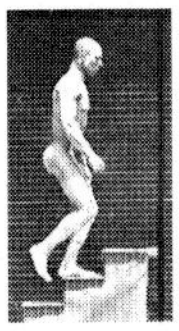

Duplicating Scenes

You can duplicate an existing scene and use all or part of it as a new scene. When you opt to duplicate a scene, Flash creates a carbon copy. All layer names, frame names, and actions are preserved in the duplicate.

To Duplicate A SCENE

1 Open the Scene panel by choosing Panels from the Window menu and then choosing Scene.

2 Select the scene that you want to duplicate.

3 Click the Duplicate Scene button.

An exact duplicate of the original scene is created. The default name for a duplicated scene is the scene's name, followed by the word "copy," as shown in Figure 10-2.

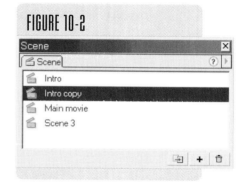

FIGURE 10-2

Naming Scenes

Flash gives a scene the default name of Scene, followed by the next available scene number. It's a good idea to get in the habit of naming scenes, especially if you are going to use ActionScript. When you name a scene, the scene name appears on the Actions panel's Scene window menu, and you can reference it when assigning an action to an object, frame, or button. Remembering a scene name is considerably easier than remembering in which scene number an event occurs.

To Name A SCENE

1 If the scene that you want to name is an existing scene, choose Panels from the Window menu, and then choose Scene to open the Scene panel. If you are naming a scene that you just created, skip to step 2.

2 Double-click the scene's name. A text field surrounds the scene's current name.

continues

chapter 10: creating complex animations

continued

3 Type a new name for the scene, as shown
in Figure 10-3, and then press Enter
or Return.

FIGURE 10-3

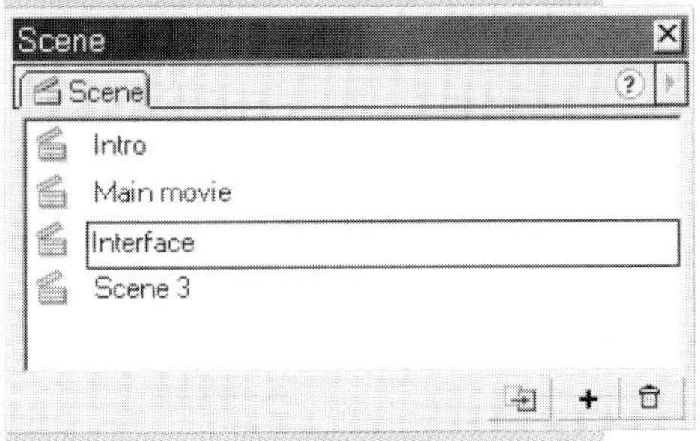

Scene

Scene

🎬 Intro
🎬 Main movie
🎬 Interface
🎬 Scene 3

Selecting Scenes

When editing a Flash movie with multiple scenes, you navigate from scene to scene to
add elements and to fine-tune the content of your movie. There are three ways to select a
scene in Flash.

To Select A SCENE, DO ONE OF THE FOLLOWING:

■ .... Choose Goto from the View menu, and then
choose the name of the scene that you wish
to select, as shown in Figure 10-4.

■ .... Choose Panels from the Window menu, and
then choose Scene. Select the name of the
scene that you want to select from the panel's
window.

FIGURE 10-4

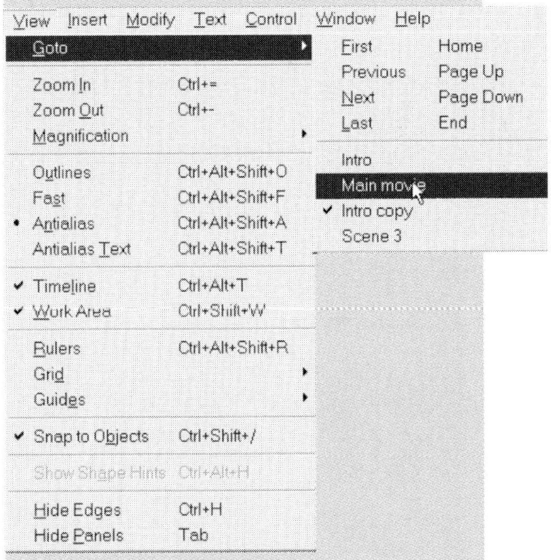

View Insert Modify Text Control Window Help

Goto	▶	First	Home
		Previous	Page Up
Zoom In	Ctrl+=	Next	Page Down
Zoom Out	Ctrl+-	Last	End
Magnification	▶		
Outlines	Ctrl+Alt+Shift+O	Intro	
Fast	Ctrl+Alt+Shift+F	Main movie	
• Antialias	Ctrl+Alt+Shift+A	✔ Intro copy	
Antialias Text	Ctrl+Alt+Shift+T	Scene 3	

✔ Timeline   Ctrl+Alt+T
✔ Work Area   Ctrl+Shift+W

Rulers   Ctrl+Alt+Shift+R
Grid   ▶
Guides   ▶

✔ Snap to Objects   Ctrl+Shift+/

Show Shape Hints   Ctrl+Alt+H

Hide Edges   Ctrl+H
Hide Panels   Tab

continues

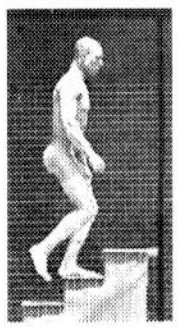

continued

........**Click the Edit Scene button located to the upper-right of the Timeline, as shown in Figure 10-5, and then click the name of the scene that you want to select.**

After you select a scene, it is displayed in its own window, and all of its elements are available for editing.

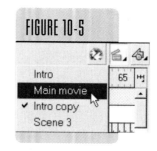

FIGURE 10-5

Intro
Main movie
✓ Intro copy
Scene 3

Changing the Order of Scenes

Scenes play in the order in which they were created. When you view scenes in the Scene panel, the last scene that you created appears at the bottom of the list.

To Change THE ORDER IN WHICH A SCENE PLAYS

▶ **Click the scene's name, and then drag it to a new position in the Scene panel.**

Animating a Mask Layer

As you learned in Chapter 7, a mask layer is a window to linked layers beneath it. You can achieve some unique effects in Flash by animating the objects that you used to create the mask. For example, you could have a message scroll across the screen one letter at a time. You can achieve other interesting effects by creating animated layers beneath the animated mask layer. Or you could copy the frames in the animated mask layer to a masked layer beneath it, apply an effect to each instance of the symbol, and then change the effect in subsequent keyframes. The possibilities are limited only by your imagination.

To Create AN ANIMATED MASK LAYER USING A SYMBOL

1 **Create a new layer directly above the layer that you want the mask layer to reveal.**

2 **Right-click (Windows) or Control-click (Macintosh) the new layer, and then select Mask from the context menu. The selected layer is converted to a mask layer, and the layer beneath it becomes a masked layer.**

continues

3 Click the mask layer's padlock to unlock it.

4 Select the first frame, and then drag onto the Stage an instance of the symbol that you are using as a mask.

5 Determine how long the mask layer animation will be, advance to the animation's final frame, and then create a keyframe by pressing F6.

6 Reposition and reshape the symbol's instance in the final keyframe.

7 Right-click (Windows) or Control-click (Macintosh) any frame between the keyframes, and then select **Create Motion Tween** from the context menu.

8 Choose **Panels** from the Window menu, and then choose **Frame** to access the Frame panel.

9 Adjust the motion tween's properties.

 Shape tweening is another excellent way to animate a mask layer. For a close-up look at creating an animated mask layer using shape tweening, watch the **Animating a Mask Layer** lesson on the **Virtual Classroom CD-ROM.**

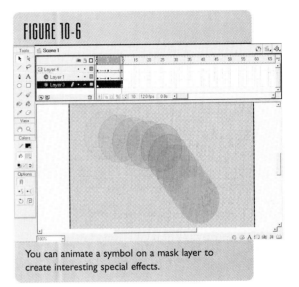

FIGURE 10-6

You can animate a symbol on a mask layer to create interesting special effects.

When the movie is published, the animated mask layer reveals the masked layer Figure 10-6 shows an animated mask layer with two masked layers linked to it. You can use only one symbol or text object on a mask layer. However, you can animate a mask layer's text object, revealing one letter per keyframe.

Creating a Movie Clip

A movie clip symbol is a reusable animation. A movie clip has its own Timeline and plays independently of the main movie. When the playhead reaches a frame with a movie clip, the movie clip begins to play at its first frame. You can use as many layers as you need and any animation method to create a movie clip.

To Create A MOVIE CLIP

1 Choose **New Symbol** from the **Insert** menu to open the Symbol Properties dialog box.

continues

continued

2 Enter a name for the movie clip, select the Movie Clip behavior, and then click **OK.** Flash enters symbol-editing mode.

3 Use any of the animation methods to create the movie clip. Remember that you can use as many layers and frames as needed for the movie clip animation.

4 After creating the movie clip, click the **Current Scene** button to return to movie-editing mode. The movie clip symbol is stored in the document Library for future use.

see also You can also use actions in the movie clip. For more information on using actions, refer to Chapters 12 and 14.

To Create AN INSTANCE OF A MOVIE CLIP SYMBOL

1 Select the frame where you want the movie clip to play, and then press F6 to create a keyframe.

2 Open the document Library by clicking the Library button on the Launcher bar.

3 Select the desired movie clip, and then drag it onto the Stage.

4 If action occurs further down the Timeline, be sure to leave enough frames for the clip to play in its entirety. If you introduce another symbol or movie clip before sufficient frames have elapsed to play the clip, it will end prematurely.

Converting an Animation into a Movie Clip

After creating an animation on the Stage, you may decide that you want to use it in other parts of your movie. You can convert any selection of frames and layers into a movie clip symbol.

To Convert AN ANIMATION INTO A MOVIE CLIP

1 Select all of the frames and layers that you used to create the animation.

2 Choose Copy Frames from the Edit menu.

3 Click anywhere on the Stage to deselect the frames.

continues

continued

4 Choose New Symbol from the Insert menu to open the Symbol Properties dialog box.

5 Enter a name for the movie clip, select the Movie Clip behavior, and then click OK. Flash enters symbol-editing mode.

6 Select the first frame on the Timeline, and then choose Paste Frames from the Edit menu. The copied frames and layers are pasted into the new movie symbol.

7 To exit symbol-editing mode, click the Current Scene button above the Timeline.

8 Delete the frames that you used to create the animation and that you just converted into a symbol, and then replace them with an instance of the new movie clip.

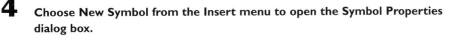

Previewing a Movie Clip Within the Main Movie

You can preview a movie clip in symbol-editing mode by using the Controller or by pressing Enter or Return. However, once a movie clip is in the main movie, it occupies only one frame on the Timeline, and one frame is all that you see if you try to preview it in movie-editing mode. You use the Test Movie command to preview a movie clip as it will play in the main movie. The Test Movie command publishes the movie and plays it in another window, giving you a preview of how the movie clip looks in the finished movie.

To Preview A MOVIE

1 Choose Test Movie from the Control menu.

2 The Exporting Flash Player dialog box appears.

3 Flash publishes the movie and plays it in another window, as shown in Figure 10-7.

4 After previewing the movie, close the window to return to movie-editing mode.

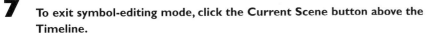

FIGURE 10-7

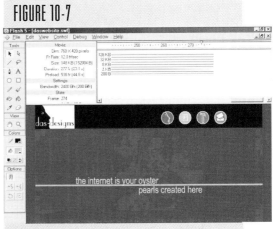

The Test Movie command publishes a movie and displays it in another window.

Synchronizing Symbols

When you synchronize symbols, you ensure that a movie clip plays correctly within the main movie. This command will force the clip to play properly even if the number of frames in the clip is not an even multiple of the main movie's frames.

To Synchronize SYMBOLS, DO ONE OF THE FOLLOWING:

■ ....If the movie clip animation uses shape tweening, select one of the in-between frames, open the Frames panel, and then select the Synchronize option.

■ ....If you used motion tweening to create the movie clip animation, select one of the in-between frames, open the Frames panel, and then in the Options section, select Synchronize.

■ ....If you used the frame-by-frame animation technique to create the movie clip, select all of the clip's frames, choose Frames from the Modify menu, and then choose Synchronize Symbols.

Naming Movie Clip Instances

When you have several instances of a movie clip in a movie, you can use actions to have the clip play in conjunction with another action, such as a mouse event action. In order for the action to locate the proper instance of the movie clip, a movie clip must have a unique name.

To Name A MOVIE CLIP INSTANCE

1 Select an instance of a movie clip on the Timeline.

2 Open the Instance panel by choosing Panels from the Window menu and then choosing Instance or by clicking the Instance button on the Launcher bar.

3 In the Name field, enter a name for the instance, and then press Enter or Return. The instance's name appears on the Insert a Target Path dialog box, which is associated with certain actions.

> **see also** For more information on ActionScript, refer to Chapter 14.

Controlling Animation with Layers

To create a movie in which you animate several objects, the only way to keep your content organized is to create multiple layers. When creating a movie of this magnitude, you end up working with frames on several layers at once to properly coordinate the timing of each individual animation.

Selecting Frames Across Multiple Layers

One of the more common tasks that you face when editing a multiple layer animation is selecting frames across several layers. After creating a selection of frames, you can then move the frames to a different place on the Timeline, copy them to another layer, or paste them into another scene or document.

To Select FRAMES ACROSS SEVERAL LAYERS

1 Press Ctrl, and then click a frame that will be either the first or last frame in the selection that you are creating.

2 While holding down the Ctrl key, drag down to add frames from a lower layer or up to add frames from an upper layer, and then drag right or left to complete the selection. Flash highlights the selected frames in black, as shown in Figure 10-8.

note You can create a selection of frames only from contiguous layers.

FIGURE 10-8

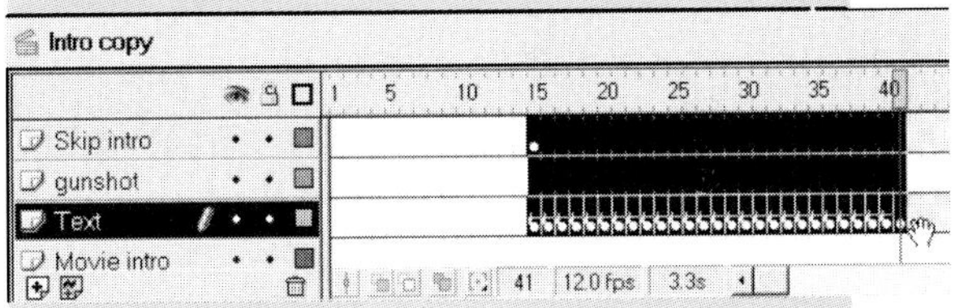

To Move A SELECTION OF FRAMES TO A NEW POSITION ON THE TIMELINE

1 Select the frames as outlined in the preceding section.

continues

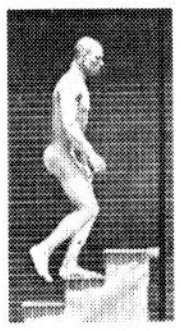

continued

2 Drag the selection to a new position on the Timeline. As you drag, a bounding box appears, giving you a preview of the frame selection's new location, as shown in Figure 10-9.

3 Release the mouse button when the frames are in the desired position.

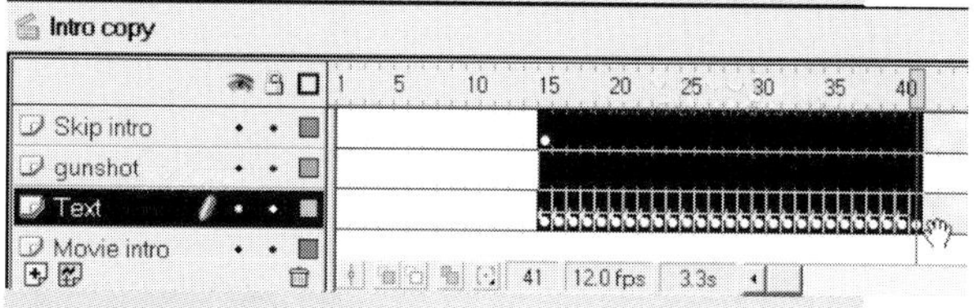

To Copy FRAMES TO ANOTHER LAYER

1 Create a selection of frames on a single layer or across multiple layers, as shown in Figure 10-10.

2 Choose Copy Frames from the Edit menu. To completely remove the selected frames from their current layers prior to pasting them to another layer, choose Cut Frames from the Edit menu.

3 Create a new layer, or select an existing layer.

4 Select the frame where you want the copied or cut selection of frames to begin, and then choose Paste Frames from the Edit menu. The frames are pasted beginning at the frame that you selected on the new layer. If you pasted a selection from several layers, Flash creates additional layers, as shown in Figure 10-11.

FIGURE 10-9

FIGURE 10-10

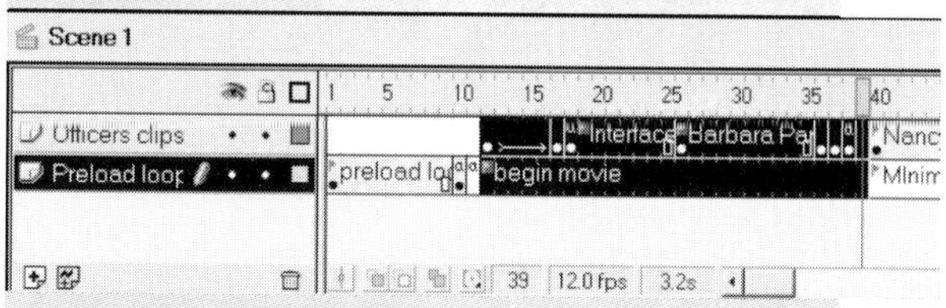

FIGURE 10-11

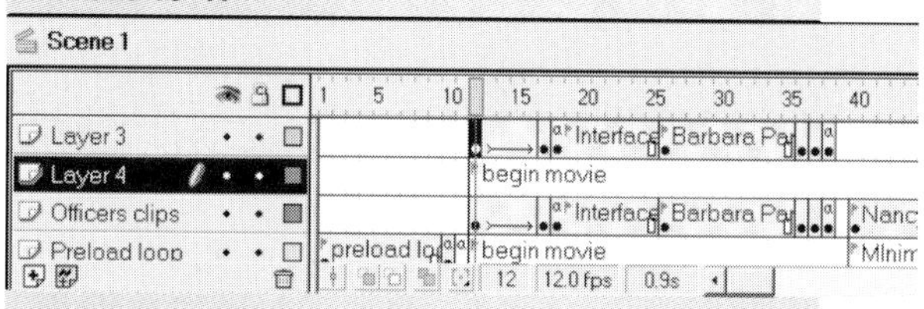

Adding and Deleting Frames Across Multiple Layers

To edit the timing of a complex animation, you often need to add or delete the same number of frames across several layers. Adding frames speeds up a sequence of events; deleting frames slows down the sequence.

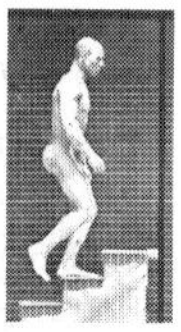

To Add OR DELETE FRAMES ACROSS MULTIPLE LAYERS

1 Press Ctrl, and then click a frame to select it.

2 Drag down or up and left or right to add frames from other layers to the selection.

3 To add the exact number of frames in the selection to the Timeline, choose Insert Frames from the Insert menu, or press **F5**.

4 To delete the selected frames from the Timeline, choose Remove Frames from the Insert menu, or hold down the Shift key and press **F5**.

Creating a Multiple Layer Animation

Creating multiple layers is the only way to produce a sophisticated Flash movie. In fact, it's the only way to predictably animate multiple objects with motion tweening. When you animate objects with multiple layers, you have the freedom to determine which objects appear in front of others by arranging the order of layers. With multiple layers, you can edit the sequence of events by manipulating individual frames or a selection of frames. To see how multiple layer animation works, perform the following steps to create an animation in which a small sphere orbits a larger sphere.

To Create AN ORBITING SPHERE ANIMATION

 To learn more about using layers in movies, watch the Morphing II lesson on the Virtual Classroom CD-ROM.

1 Create a new document in Flash, and then add two layers to the Timeline.

2 Name the bottom layer Motion Path 1, the middle layer Sphere, and the top layer Motion Path 2.

3 Right-click (Windows) or Control-click (Macintosh) the Motion Path 1 layer, and then select Motion Guide from the context menu. A new layer named Guide: Motion Path 1 appears.

4 Create a motion guide layer for the Motion Path 2 layer as outlined in step 3. A new layer named Guide: Motion Path 2 appears. The two motion guide layers are where you create the motion paths that the orbiting sphere will follow. Your Timeline should resemble Figure 10-12.

FIGURE 10-12

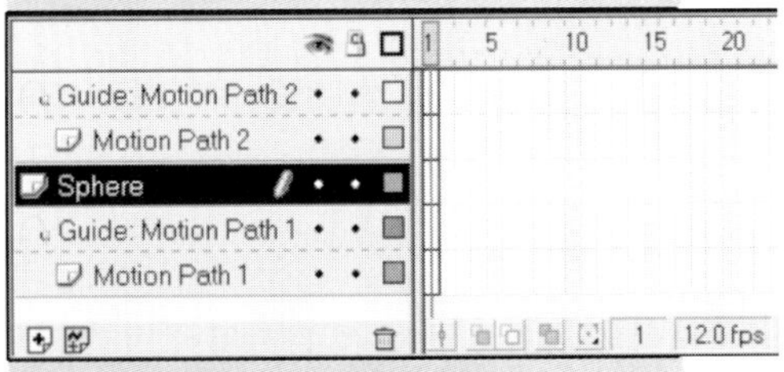

	🐦 🔒 □	1	5	10	15	20
Guide: Motion Path 2	• • □					
Motion Path 2	• • □					
Sphere	🖉 • • ■					
Guide: Motion Path 1	• • ■					
Motion Path 1	• • ■					

Create separate layers for each major part of the animation.

continues

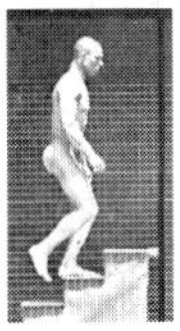

continued

5 Select the first frame in the Sphere layer, and then use the Oval tool to create a large sphere. Use a gradient fill to make the sphere appear three-dimensional.

6 Press F8 to convert the sphere to a symbol. After the Symbol Properties dialog box opens, assign the Graphic behavior to the sphere, and then click OK to add the symbol to the document Library.

7 Use the Align panel to center the sphere on the Stage, and then lock the Sphere layer.

8 Select the Guide: Motion Path 2 layer, and then, using the Oval tool, create an unfilled oval. The unfilled oval is the basis for the motion path that the small sphere will follow. Align the unfilled oval to the larger sphere, and then use the Eraser tool to open the path, as shown in Figure 10-13.

9 Select frame 12 on the Sphere layer, and then press F5 to add a frame.

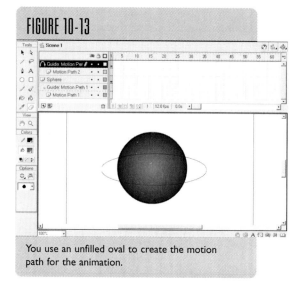

FIGURE 10-13

You use an unfilled oval to create the motion path for the animation.

If you were to align a small sphere to the motion path as it appears, the small sphere would never orbit behind the large sphere. To solve this problem, you cut the motion path in two and put half of it on the Guide: Motion Path 1 layer. Placing half of the motion path on a layer beneath the Sphere layer causes it to appear behind the sphere. When the smaller sphere follows this half of the path, it momentarily disappears behind the sphere before popping out on the other side.

10 To cut the motion path in two, return to the Guide: Motion Path 2 layer and select the Line tool. Hold down the Shift key to constrain the line horizontally, and then draw a line through the middle of the motion path. The motion path is now cut in two.

11 Click the top half of the motion path to select it, as shown in Figure10-14.

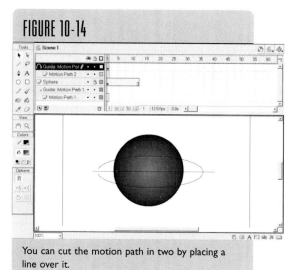

FIGURE 10-14

You can cut the motion path in two by placing a line over it.

continues

continued

12 Choose Cut from the Edit menu.

13 Click the first frame in the Guide: Motion Path 1 layer, and then choose Paste in Place. Notice that the motion path now circumnavigates the sphere.

14 Delete the line that you used to bisect the motion path.

15 Select frame 12 on the Guide: Motion Path 1 layer, and then press F5 to create a frame. Repeat for Guide: Motion Path 2 layer.

 To learn more about using multiple layers to create animations, watch the Creating a Site Intro lesson on the Virtual Classroom CD-ROM.

16 Lock the Guide: Motion Path 1 and Guide:Motion Path 2 layers by clicking the dot in each layer's Lock/Unlock column. Locking each layer will prevent you from accidentally moving their motion paths.

17 Select Frame 1 in the Motion Path 2 layer, and then Press F6 to create a keyframe.

18 Hide the motion path on the Guide: Motion Path 1 layer by clicking the dot in the layer's Show/Hide column.

19 Open the document Library. Select the sphere symbol that you created in Step 6, and then drag an instance of it onto the Stage.

20 Resize the sphere with the Arrow tool, and then align it to the beginning of the motion path on Guide: Motion Path 2.

21 Select frame 6 on the Motion Path 2 layer, and then press F6 to create a keyframe.

22 Align the small sphere to the end of the motion path on the Guide: Motion Path 2 layer, as shown in Figure 10-15. This is where the first sphere will end up in Frame 6.

23 Right-click (Windows) or Control-click (Macintosh) one of the in-between frames on the Motion Path 2 layer, and then choose Create Motion Tween from the context menu.

24 Select the instance of the sphere symbol in frame 6, and then choose Copy from the Edit menu.

continues

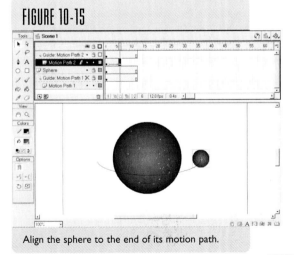

FIGURE 10-15

Align the sphere to the end of its motion path.

continued

25 Lock the Guide: Motion Path 2 layer.

26 Hide the motion path on the Guide: Motion Path 2 layer.

27 Click the dot in the Guide: Motion Path 1 layer's Show/Hide column to reveal the motion path.

28 Select frame 7 on the Motion Path 1 layer, and then insert a keyframe by pressing F6.

29 Choose Paste in Place from the Edit menu. The sphere that you copied from the Motion Path 2 layer is now perfectly aligned with the start of the motion path on the Guide: Motion Path 1 layer.

30 Select frame 12 on the Motion Path 1 layer, and then insert a keyframe by pressing F6.

31 Align the sphere with the end of the motion path on the Guide: Motion Path 1 layer.

32 Right-click (Windows) or Control-click (Macintosh) one of the in-between frames on the Motion Path 1 layer, and then choose Create Motion Tween from the context menu. Figure 10-16 shows the completed movie in movie-editing mode.

33 Preview the animation by pressing Enter or Return, or use the Test Movie command to publish the movie and preview it in another window.

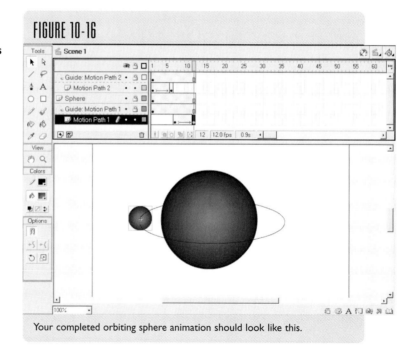

FIGURE 10-16

Your completed orbiting sphere animation should look like this.

Creating Buttons

Buttons are an essential part of any Web site. They give the user the power to navigate within the site and follow links to other Web sites. Buttons in Flash 5 can run the gamut from a simple button that a user clicks to multi-state buttons that react differently depending upon the location of the user's mouse and the action that the user is performing with the mouse. In Flash, you can create buttons that swap images, morph into different shapes, or become animated when interacting with a user's mouse. Buttons can also have sounds associated with them. In this chapter, you will learn to create reusable button symbols for your Flash movies.

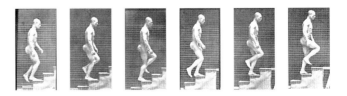

Creating a Rollover Button

When you create a button symbol in Flash, you have a Timeline with four frames: Up, Over, Down, and Hit. The simplest button that you can create uses just one frame, the Up frame. When you create a multi-state button, you place a different image in each frame. The image that you place in the Up frame is displayed whenever the user's mouse is beyond the active area of the button. The image in the Over frame appears when the user's mouse is over the button. When the user clicks the button, the image in the Down frame is displayed. The Hit frame designates the active area of the button. If you are creating a particularly dainty button with a small target area, placing an oval or rectangle in the Hit frame that is larger than the graphic in the Up frame gives the user a larger target area.

Creating a Button

The most basic buttons are simple shapes, such as ovals or rounded rectangles. When you use a common shape as the basis for a button, you can create a graphic symbol to use as a template for all of the buttons in the movie. Remember, using symbols helps reduce the file size of your movie. Create an instance of the symbol in each of a button symbol's frames, and then apply an effect to the instance to make it appear different when the user rolls a mouse over it and clicks the button. Like any other animation in Flash, buttons can have as many layers as needed. For example, you can use one layer for the button's basic shape, another layer for a text message, and yet another layer for a sound event that occurs when the button is rolled over or clicked. In the following example, you learn how to create a basic rollover button.

To Create A ROLLOVER BUTTON

1 Open the Symbol Properties dialog box by choosing New Symbol from the Insert menu. Alternately, hold down Ctrl and press F8.

2 Enter a name for the button, select the Button behavior, and then click OK. Flash enters symbol-editing mode. Figure 11-1 shows the Timeline for a button.

FIGURE 11-1

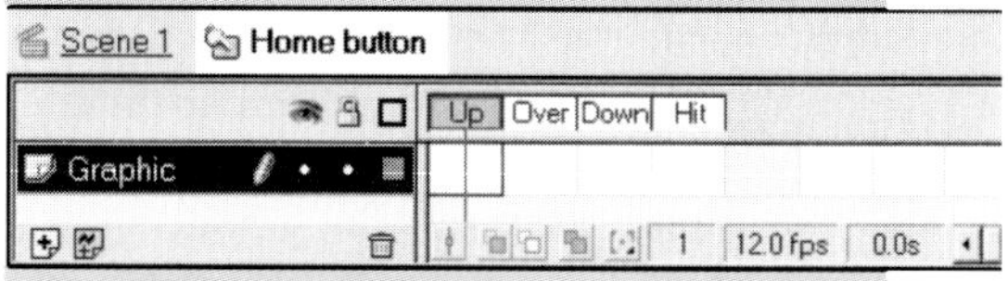

Scene 1 Home button

| | | | Up | Over | Down | Hit |
| Graphic | | | | | | |

A button symbol's Timeline has four frames

continues

chapter 11: creating buttons

continued

3 Click the Up frame, and use any of the drawing tools to create an object or use a symbol from the document Library. As soon as the shape is created, a dot fills the frame, signifying that it is a keyframe. Align the object to the center of the Stage, as shown in Figure 11-2.

4 Click the Over frame, choose Insert, and then choose Blank Keyframe. Alternately, right-click (Windows) or Control-click (Macintosh), and then select Insert Blank Keyframe from the context menu. Remember that when you create a blank keyframe, you are creating a placeholder for an item yet to be created.

5 Use any of the drawing tools to create an object for the Over frame, or select a symbol from the document Library. To copy the graphic from the Up frame to the Over frame, create a keyframe instead of a blank keyframe. The graphic in the Over frame in Figure 11-3 is the same image used in the Up frame in Figure 11-2. The graphic was then rotated to give it a different appearance when the user's mouse rolls over the button.

6 Click the Down frame, and then choose Blank Keyframe from the Insert menu, or press F7.

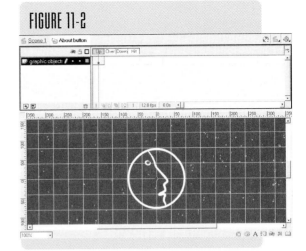

FIGURE 11-2

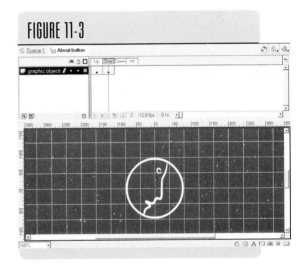

FIGURE 11-3

continues

continued

7 Create the graphic that the user will see when clicking the button, and then center it to the Stage. The graphic used in the Down frame in Figure 11-4 was copied from the button's Up frame, as shown in Figure 11-2, pasted in place, and then flipped and rotated to give it a different look.

8 Click the Hit frame, and then insert a keyframe by pressing F6.

9 Create a graphic for the Hit frame. The shape that you use for the Hit frame will not be visible in the final movie. Its sole function is to increase the target area of the button. The object that you create for the Hit frame should be slightly larger than the biggest shape in the button's preceding frames but not so large that it will interfere with the target areas of other buttons that will be in close proximity in the final movie.

10 Turn on onion skins to see how the shapes in each frame relate to each other, as shown in Figure 11-5.

11 To return to movie-editing mode, click the Current Scene button to the left of the button's name.

After you create a button, Flash adds it to the document Library for future use. To add a button symbol to a scene, you select a frame on the Timeline and then drag an instance of the symbol onto the Stage from the document Library. Remember that you can animate a button symbol just like any other symbol. Instead of having the button appear on the Stage in its final position, you can use motion tweening to animate it as it moves into place. Apply an effect to the button for even more visual interest. When you animate a button, you leave no doubt in the user's mind that clicking it will reveal something very interesting.

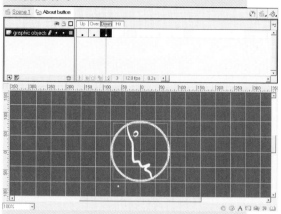

FIGURE 11-4

TIP To create the ever-present pill shape for a button, use the Rectangle tool with the Round Rectangle Radius modifier enabled. Enter a value of about 50 points for the Corner Radius, and then drag the tool onto the Stage to create the pill.

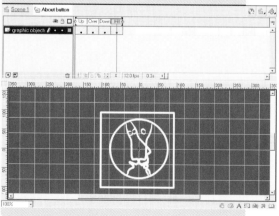

FIGURE 11-5

chapter 11: creating buttons

Creating Complex Buttons with Layers

As you gain more experience with Flash, you will come up with new and more interesting ways to dazzle your viewers with buttons. Just like any other graphic object in your movies, complex buttons require more than one layer. Consider, for example, a button that opens a character's eyes when the user's cursor moves over the button. The button creates a point of visual interest, and the user will click it out of curiosity, just to find out what is linked to it. Icons make excellent buttons. You can create an icon for the button's basic shape and then have a message appear when the user's cursor passes over it. Figure 11-6 shows a multi-state icon button comprised of six layers.

The button in Figure 11-6 uses three frames: Up, Over, and Down. When the movie first loads, the button appears, and the graphic in the Up frame is displayed, as shown in Figure 11-7.

When the user's cursor moves over the button, the image in the Over state is displayed, as shown in Figure 11-8.

When the button is clicked, a sound plays, and the icon in the Up state moves, as shown in Figure 11-9.

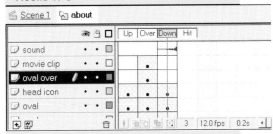

FIGURE 11-6

A button symbol's Timeline has four frames

FIGURE 11-7

FIGURE 11-8

FIGURE 11-9

Previewing the Button in Movie-Editing Mode

When you create a button, you see all of the graphic elements and can preview them a frame at a time; however, you cannot see how the button will react to a mouse-over or click. You can preview other animations—except movie clips—in movie-editing mode, but by default Flash disables all buttons in this mode. If buttons were active, they would be difficult to select and move because they would act like buttons every time you moved your mouse close to them. However, you can enable buttons in movie-editing mode as needed to preview them.

To Preview BUTTONS IN MOVIE-EDITING MODE

 Choose Enable Simple Buttons from the Control menu.

After you enable this command, buttons react to your cursor, just as they do when the movie is published. After you preview the buttons, apply the command again, and you will be able to move buttons around the Stage just like symbols.

note The Enable Simple Buttons command will not work with an animated button created with a movie clip. The button will change from one frame to the next, but the movie clip will not play. To preview these types of buttons, you need to use the Test Movie command.

Creating Morphing Buttons

A button that morphs changes its basic shape from one button frame to the next. To create a morphing button, you start out with a basic shape and then modify the shape in each of the button's frames. Create a shape for the Hit frame that is slightly bigger than the largest shape in the other frames. Morphing buttons work well as clues in games. Create a button that blends in with the scenery and changes when the user's cursor moves over it. For example, you could have a road sign morph into an arrow, pointing the user toward another clue.

To Create A MORPHING BUTTON

1 Choose Symbol from the Insert menu to open the Symbol Properties dialog box.

2 Type a name for the button, choose the Button behavior, and then click OK to enter symbol-editing mode.

continues

continued

3 Click the Up frame, and then choose Keyframe from the Insert menu.

4 Use any of the drawing tools to create the base shape for the button, as shown in Figure 11-10.

5 Select the Over frame, and then press F6 to create a keyframe. The shape created in the Up frame is copied into the Over frame.

6 Modify the shape as desired using the Subselect tool or the Arrow tool, as shown in Figure 11-11.

7 Select the Down frame, and then insert a keyframe. The shape from the Over frame is copied to the Down frame.

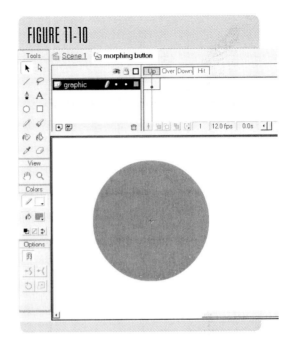

FIGURE 11-10

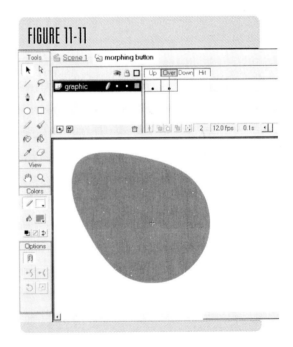

FIGURE 11-11

continues

continued

8 Use the **Arrow** tool or **Subselect** tool to modify the shape, as shown in Figure 11-12.

9 Select the **Hit** frame, and then choose **Blank Keyframe** from the **Insert** menu.

10 Use any of the drawing tools to define a target area for the button. Make sure that the target area is large enough to encompass the largest shape used in the button. Turn on onion skins to size and align the shape in the Hit frame to the shapes in the other frames.

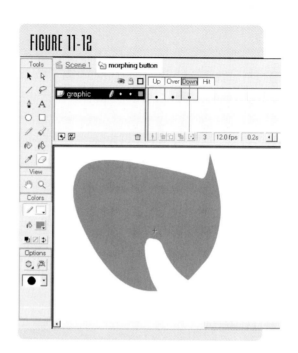

FIGURE 11-12

Creating Animated Buttons

By nature, a rollover button is animated; it does something when the cursor passes over it. However, with Flash you can take animated buttons to the next level with the use of movie clips. A fully animated button uses movie clips in one or more of the button's frames to create the action. When the user's mouse interacts with the button, full motion occurs.

To Create AN ANIMATED BUTTON

1 Choose **New Symbol** from the **Insert** menu to open the **Symbol Properties** dialog box. Enter **Button Template** for the symbol's name, choose **Graphic** for the behavior, and then click **OK** to enter symbol-editing mode.

2 Create a circle with the fill color of your choice and no stroke. Using the **Align** panel, center the circle to the **Stage**.

3 Choose **Panels** from the **Window** menu, and then choose **Info** to open the **Info** panel. Enter a value of 80 for the sphere's width (**W**) and Height (**H**).

4 Click the **Current Scene** button to exit symbol-editing mode.

continues

continued

5 Choose New Symbol from the Insert menu to open the Symbol Properties dialog box. Enter Glowing Sphere for the symbol's name, and then choose the Movie Clip behavior. Click OK to enter symbol-editing mode.

6 Open the document Library, and then drag an instance of the Button Template symbol onto the Stage. Center the instance to the Stage using the Align panel.

7 Select frame 7, and then press F6 to insert a keyframe.

8 Select one of the in-between frames, and then choose Create Motion Tween from the Insert menu.

9 Press Ctrl, click frame 4, and then choose Keyframe from the Insert menu.

10 With frame 4 still selected, choose Panels from the Window menu, and then choose Effect.

11 Select the Alpha effect, and then drag the slider to a setting of about 50, as shown in Figure 11-13.

FIGURE 11-13

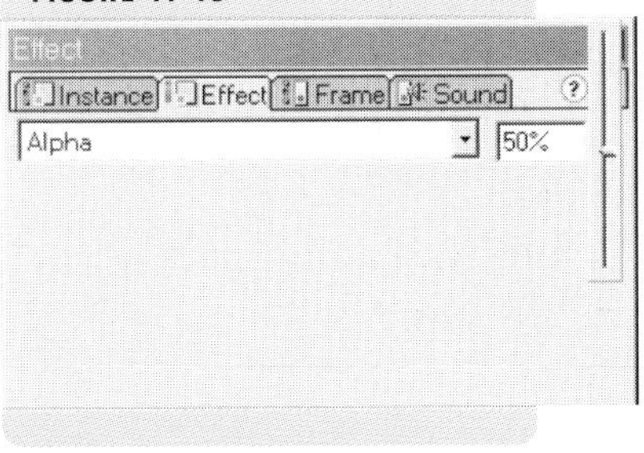

12 Click the Current Scene button to exit symbol-editing mode.

13 Choose Symbol from the Insert menu to open the Symbol Properties dialog box.

14 Enter Glowing Button for the symbol's name, and then apply the Button behavior. Click OK to enter symbol-editing mode.

15 Click the Up frame to select it, and then drag an instance of the Button Template symbol onto the Stage. Center it to the Stage with the Align panel.

16 Click the Over frame, and then choose Blank Keyframe from the Insert menu.

17 Open the Character panel by choosing Panels from the Window menu and then choosing character. Select a font style, and then drag the Size slider to 40.

18 Select the Text tool, and then type the word *Illuminating*.

19 Turn on onion skins to view the Button Template instance in the Up frame.

continues

continued

20 Select the text in the Over frame, center the text to the Stage vertically, and then move it to the right of the Button Template instance, as shown in Figure 11-14.

21 Select the Down frame, and then choose Blank Keyframe from the Insert menu.

22 Drag an instance of the Button Template onto the Stage, and then center it with the Align panel.

23 Right-click (Windows) or Control-click (Macintosh) Layer 1, and then choose Insert Layer from the context menu. Name the new layer *Movie Clip*.

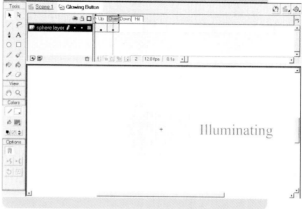

FIGURE 11-14

24 Select the Over frame in the Movie Clip layer, and then choose Blank Keyframe from the Insert menu.

25 Open the document Library, drag an instance of the Glowing Sphere movie clip onto the Stage, and then center it to the Stage with the Align panel. Your finished button should look like Figure 11-15.

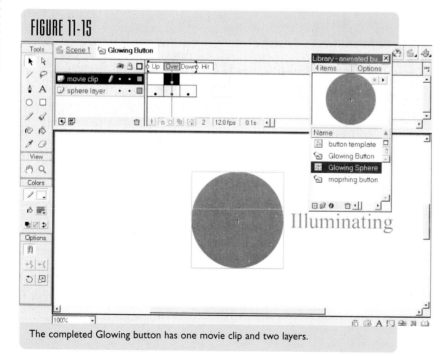

FIGURE 11-15

The completed Glowing button has one movie clip and two layers.

continues

26 Click the **Current Scene** button to exit symbol-editing mode. Flash saves the button in the document **Library** for future use.

27 Drag an instance of the button that you just created onto the Stage, and then choose Test Movie from the Control menu. When you place your cursor over the button, the movie clip animation plays, the word "Illuminating" appears, and the button glows on and off. Click the button, and the glowing stops.

Creating an Invisible Button

As the name implies, an invisible button cannot be seen. You use invisible buttons to designate a hot spot on the Stage. The most common use for an invisible button is to advance a movie to the next frame after the movie has been stopped in order to display a large block of text. To do this, you create an invisible button larger than the block of text, place it on a separate layer, and then align it to the block of text. After the user reads the message, clicking the text activates the invisible button and advances the movie to the next frame. You can also use invisible buttons to good effect when creating games.

To Create AN INVISIBLE BUTTON

1 Choose Symbol from the Insert menu to open the Symbol Properties dialog box.

2 Enter a name for the symbol, and then select the Button behavior.

3 Select the Hit frame, and then choose Blank Keyframe from the Insert menu.

4 Select one of the drawing tools.

5 Drag the selected tool onto the Stage to create the invisible button.

6 Click the Current Scene button to exit symbol-editing mode. The invisible button is now stored in the document Library.

TIP If you are creating an irregular hotspot, use the Pen tool for point-to-point control over the final shape of the invisible button.

note You are advised to put all buttons on one layer and then lock the layer to prevent accidentally moving buttons after they are aligned. Creating a button layer keeps your movie organized and simplifies the editing task.

Figure 11-16 shows an invisible button behind a block of text. Although the button is readily visible in movie-editing mode, it will not be seen when the movie is published.

FIGURE 11-16

The Flash 5 Virtual Classroom, combines text and multimedia to create the ultimate learning experience

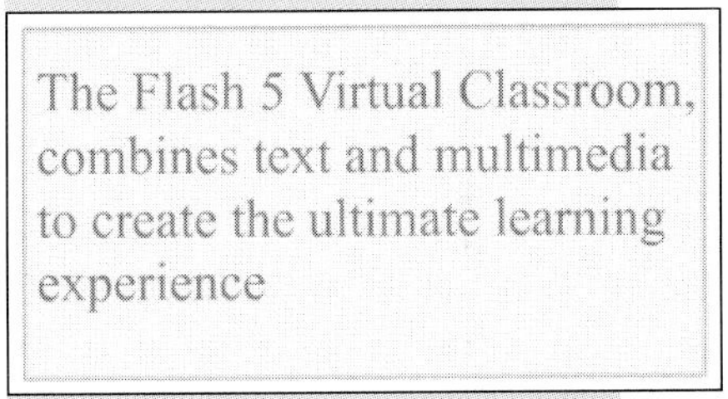

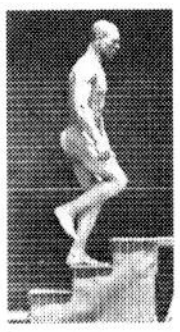

Assigning Actions to Buttons

Flash literally has enough actions to warrant a book on the subject. In this section, you will learn about actions commonly used for buttons. Actions are covered in greater detail in Chapters 12 and 14. Actions applied to buttons occur when the user's mouse interacts with the button's active (Hit frame) area. Actions commonly used with buttons transport the user to another part of the movie or to another Web site. You apply actions to a button's instance. As you will learn, you can also apply actions to frames on the Timeline. The exception to this rule is with buttons. Although they have a Timeline of four frames, you cannot apply actions to them.

To Assign AN ACTION TO A BUTTON

1 Create an instance of a button symbol by selecting it in the document Library and dragging it onto the Stage.

2 Select the button on the Stage, and then choose Actions from the Window menu. The Object Actions window appears, as shown in Figure 11-17.

3 Assign an action to the button by doing one of the following:

Select an action, and then drag it into the right column.

Double-click an action.

see aLso You can apply multiple actions to a button. For more information on working with actions, refer to Chapters 12 and 14.

FIGURE 11-17

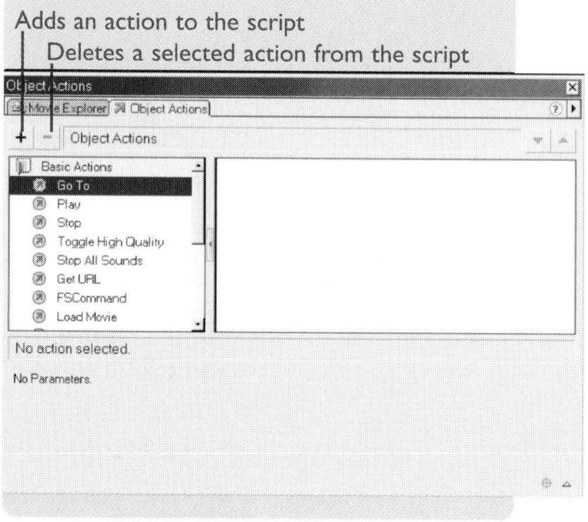

Adds an action to the script

Deletes a selected action from the script

When you assign an action to a button, the On Mouse Event action precedes it. In Figure 11-18 the Go To action was assigned to the button. Notice that the On Mouse Event action's Release event precedes it. In this case, when the user clicks the button and then releases the mouse button, the movie will go to and play a frame named Interface.

To Delete AN ACTION FROM A BUTTON

▶ Select the action in the right column, and then click the - button.

Using the *On Mouse Event* Action

Flash automatically assigns the *On Mouse Event* action to a button whenever you assign an action to a button. The default *On Mouse Event* action, Release, performs the action when the mouse button is released, the mouse button's up stroke after a click. However, you can modify the *On Mouse Event* action to have an action occur when the user's mouse interacts outside of the button's target range, when it rolls over the button, or when the user makes a keyboard entry.

To Modify AN *On Mouse Event* ACTION ALREADY ASSIGNED TO A BUTTON

1 Select the button that the action is applied to.

2 Choose Actions from the Window menu to open the Actions panel.

continues

continued

3 In the right-hand (ActionScript) column, click the *On Mouse Event* action currently applied to the button. The Events section opens, as shown in Figure 11-19.

4 In the Events section, click the currently applied event to deselect it.

5 Click the desired event to apply it.

Warning It is possible to apply multiple events to a single *On Mouse Event* action. Be sure to delete unwanted events to prevent scripting errors.

FIGURE 11-19

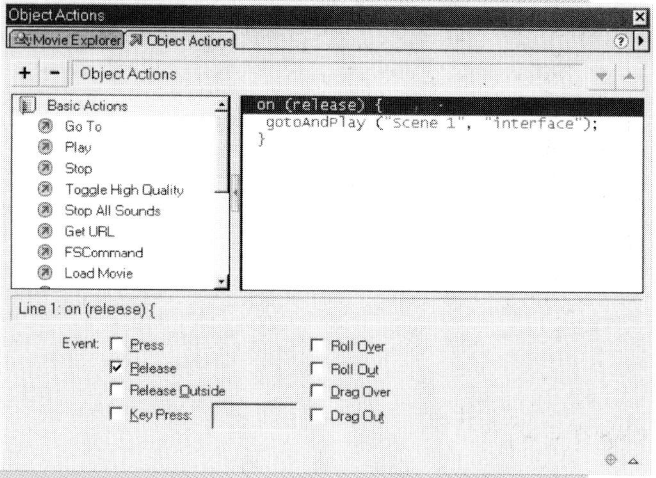

To Assign THE ON MOUSE EVENT ACTION TO A BUTTON

1 Create an instance of a button symbol on the Stage.

2 Select the button, and then choose Actions from the Window menu to open the Actions panel. Alternately, right-click (Windows) or Control-click (Macintosh) the instance, and then choose Actions from the context menu.

3 Double-click the *On Mouse Event* action to add it to the script. The default Release event appears in the ActionScript column, as shown in Figure 11-20.

FIGURE 11-20

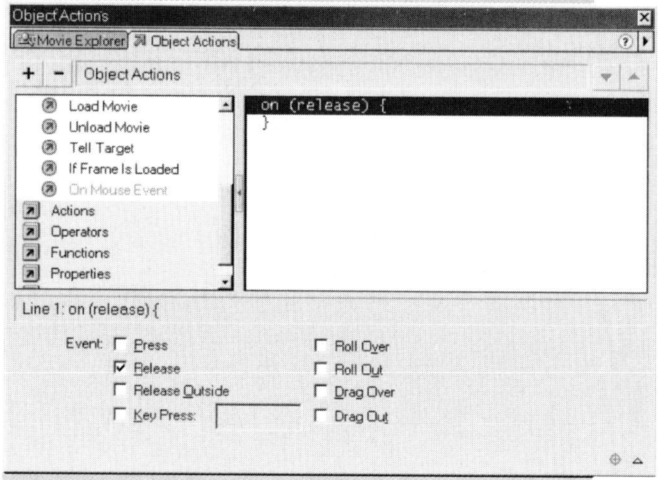

continues

continued

4 Accept the Release event, or choose one of the following from the Events section of the window:

> **Press:** This event triggers an action on the down stroke of a user's mouse click.

> **Release:** The default event applies an action on the upstroke of a user's mouse click.

> **Release Outside:** Choose this event to have an action occur when the user releases the mouse outside of the button's target area.

> **Key Press:** Select this event to have an action occur when the user makes a keyboard entry. If you select the Key Press event, a text field appears. On your computer's keyboard, press the key that you want to activate the button.

> **Roll Over:** This event triggers an action when the user's mouse is over the button.

> **Roll Out:** This event causes an action to occur when the user's cursor rolls outside of the button's target area.

> **Drag Over:** This event triggers an action when the user's mouse is clicked while over a button, and with the mouse button still held down, moves the mouse outside of the button's target area and then back over the button.

> **Drag Out:** This event triggers an action when the user's mouse is clicked while over the button and then rolls outside of the button's target area.

5 After you choose the event, it appears in the right window, followed by an empty bracket.

6 With the *On Mouse Event* action still selected, add the desired action by double-clicking the action's name in the left-hand column.

7 The selected action appears between the brackets, as shown in Figure 11-21.

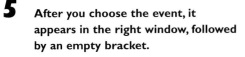

FIGURE 11-21

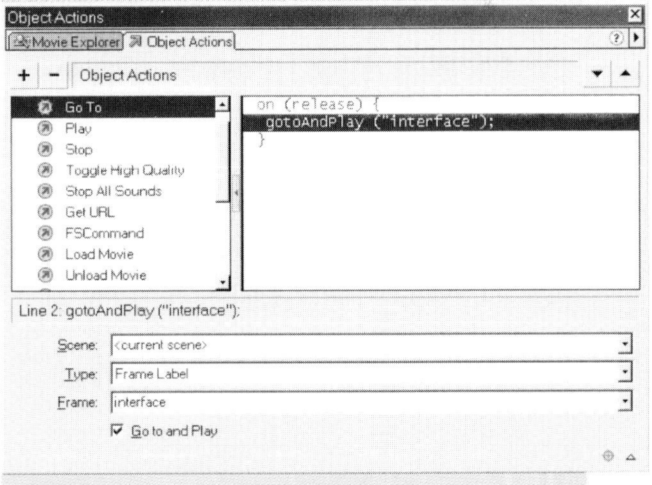

Creating a Multi-State Rollover Button

You can apply multiple *On Mouse Event* actions to a button to create a multi-state rollover button. For example, when the user's mouse rolls over the button, a movie clip begins to play and stops immediately when the mouse is beyond the button's target area. When the user clicks the button, the movie advances to another frame and plays.

To Assign MULTIPLE ON MOUSE EVENT ACTIONS TO A BUTTON

1 Follow the preceding steps to assign a mouse event and action to a button.

2 Select the last line in the Actions List (right-hand) window.

3 Double-click the *On Mouse Event* action.

 To see how a multi-state rollover button is built, watch the Rollover Buttons lesson on the Virtual Classroom CD-ROM.

4 In the Parameters panel, select the event that will trigger another action.

5 Double-click the action that you want the mouse event to trigger. Figure 11-22 shows an ActionScript for a multi-state rollover button.

FIGURE 11-22

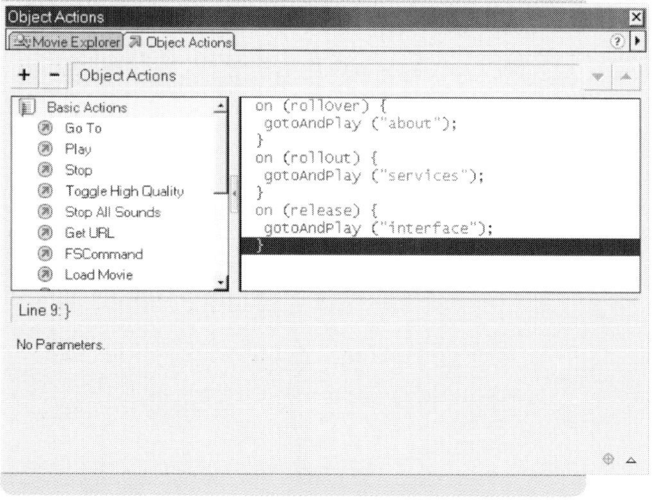

```
Object Actions                                                    [X]
[Movie Explorer] [Object Actions]                             [?] [▶]
[+] [-]  Object Actions                                        [▼] [▲]
Basic Actions           ▲   on (rollover) {
  Go To                       gotoAndPlay ("about");
  Play                      }
  Stop                      on (rollout) {
  Toggle High Quality         gotoAndPlay ("services");
  Stop All Sounds           }
  Get URL                   on (release) {
  FSCommand                   gotoAndPlay ("interface");
  Load Movie            ▼   }
Line 9: }

No Parameters.

                                                          ⊕ ▲
```

Creating Interactive Movies

In previous chapters, you learned to create objects and animate them for your movies. When a published movie is played, the Flash 5 Player rolls it in sequence, frame by frame, scene by scene. You can control the sequence in which a movie plays by adding actions to frames. You can use actions to halt a movie while awaiting input from the viewer. You add actions to a movie through the Actions panel. Creating ActionScript in Flash is much like creating Javascript, with one notable exception: when you select a Flash action, Flash automatically generates the script. In this chapter, you will learn how to use the most common actions to create your own ActionScripts.

Using the Actions Panel

You use the Actions panel to generate ActionScript in your movies. The panel, as shown in Figure 12-1, is comprised of two windows. Flash displays the Actions panel as Frame Actions if you select a frame when the panel is opened, as Object Actions if you select a button or movie clip. The left-hand window houses the ActionScript elements that you assign to a frame or object. The actions are broken down into groups. To open an action group, you click the arrow to left of the group's name to display the group's available actions. When you open the Actions panel and start opening individual groups, you notice that some of the choices are grayed out and others are highlighted. You cannot apply the grayed out choices to the current selection. If an action is highlighted in green, that means that, while fully functional, the action is deprecated in Flash 5. Deprecated actions will be replaced with other actions in future versions of Flash. To find the equivalent for a deprecated action, refer to the Flash ActionScript Reference Guide. Unfortunately, there are so many Flash actions that posting the equivalent of each deprecated action is beyond the scope of this book. If you publish your movies in earlier versions of Flash, certain actions are yellowed out. This means that they do not work with the version of Flash that you have specified with the Publish Settings command.

FIGURE 12-1

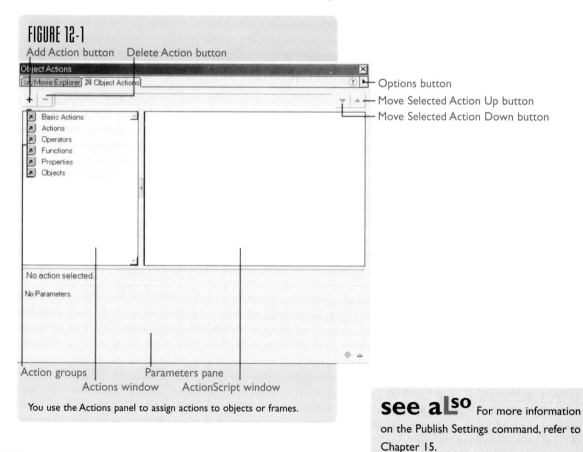

Add Action button   Delete Action button

Options button
Move Selected Action Up button
Move Selected Action Down button

Basic Actions
Actions
Operators
Functions
Properties
Objects

No action selected.
No Parameters.

Action groups | Parameters pane
Actions window   ActionScript window

You use the Actions panel to assign actions to objects or frames.

see also For more information on the Publish Settings command, refer to Chapter 15.

chapter 12: creating interactive movies

Assigning Actions

You can apply actions to frames and objects. For example, you apply the *Stop* action to a frame to tell Flash to stop playing the movie when the frame is reached. In concert with the *Stop* action on a frame, you might assign the *Go To* action to a button. The *Go To* action tells Flash to go to and play a certain frame when the button is clicked, thereby resuming the movie.

To Assign AN ACTION, DO ONE OF THE FOLLOWING:

■ ....Select an action by clicking its name, and then drag it from the left window to the right.

■ ....Click the + button atop the window to reveal a drop-down menu for each action group, click an action group to open it, and then choose an action from the submenu.

■ ....Double-click an action's name.

After an action is assigned to a frame or object, it appears in the right window as part of the ActionScript. You can assign as many actions as needed to create the desired effect.

Assigning Actions to Frames and Objects

You assign an action to an object or frame when you need to add interactivity to a movie, for example moving from one frame to the next or one scene to the next. When you apply an action to an object, Flash executes the applied action when the object occurs in the movie. Frame actions are executed when a frame is reached.

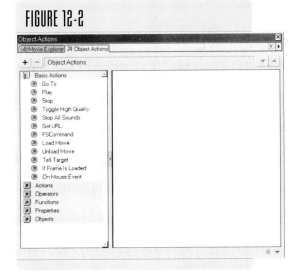

FIGURE 12-2

To Add AN ACTION TO A FRAME OR OBJECT

1 Select the object or frame to which you want to assign the action.

2 Choose Actions from the Window menu to open the Actions panel.

3 Open the desired group of actions by clicking the arrow to the left of its name. A menu appears, as shown in Figure 12-2.

continues

continued

4 Select an action, and then add it to the ActionScript, using one of the methods previously described.

5 Add additional actions as needed to complete the ActionScript. Figure 12-3 shows a multi-line ActionScript assigned to a button.

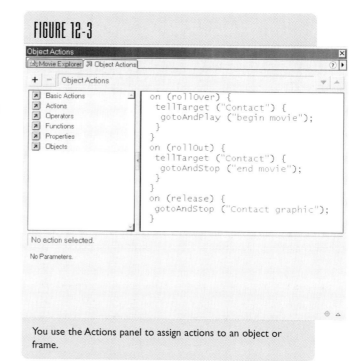

FIGURE 12-3

You use the Actions panel to assign actions to an object or frame.

Deleting an Action from an ActionScript

After you create a few ActionScripts in Flash, you gain confidence and have a tendency to experiment. Some experiments are successful; others are not. Fortunately, you can delete an action from the script when one or more lines of code are not giving you the expected results.

To Delete ONE OR MORE LINES OF CODE FROM AN ACTIONSCRIPT

1 Select the frame or object to which the dubious script is applied.

2 Choose Actions from the Window menu to open the Actions panel.

3 In the right-hand window, select the line of script that you want to remove. To add additional lines of code to the selection, hold down the **Shift** key while clicking an adjacent line of code. Hold down the **Ctrl** key, and then click to add a non-contiguous line of code to the selection. The selected actions become highlighted in blue.

4 Click the Delete Action button to remove the unwanted lines of code.

Arranging the Hierarchy of Actions

When you assign multiple actions to an object or frame, the actions execute in the order that you added them to the script. If upon testing the movie you decide that you need to change the order in which the actions execute, you can easily edit the list.

To Rearrange THE ORDER IN WHICH FLASH EXECUTES A MULTI-LINE ACTIONSCRIPT

1 Select the object or frame to which the actions are applied.

2 Choose Actions from the Window menu. The Actions panel opens, as shown previously in Figure 12-1.

3 Select the line of ActionScript that you want to rearrange. To add to the selection, press the Shift key and click adjacent lines of code.

> **note** Although you can select non-contiguous lines of ActionScript, you cannot rearrange their order in the script's hierarchy.

4 To move selected actions up, click the Move Selected Action Up button in the upper right-hand corner of the panel.

5 To move selected actions lower in the hierarchy, click the Move Selected Action Down button.

Using the Parameters Pane

Many actions have parameters that you can apply to them. Parameters are similar to a tool's modifiers; when you modify a parameter, the action behaves accordingly. If an action has no parameters, the panel is blank, and the No Parameters dialog is displayed in the pane. Figure 12-4 shows an action with its Parameters pane displayed.

FIGURE 12-4

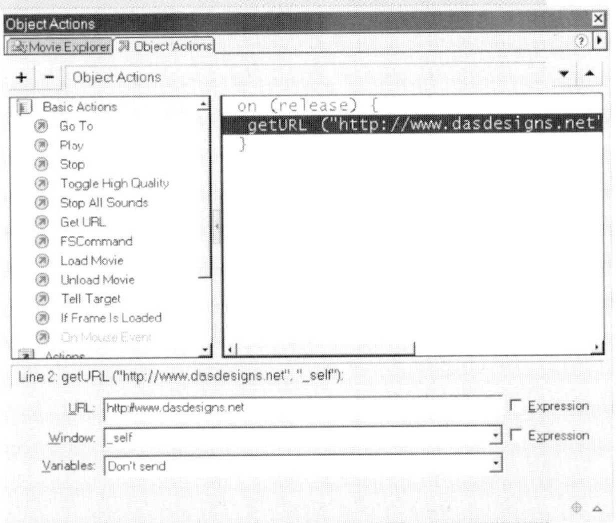

You modify an action's parameters to execute a line of script in a desired manner.

To Display A MENU OF AVAILABLE OPTIONS

 Click the triangle to the right of a parameter window, as shown in Figure 12-5.

To Expand OR COLLAPSE THE PARAMETERS PANE AREA

 Click the small triangle at the lower-right corner of the Actions panel.

Collapsing the Parameters pane area is useful when you are editing ActionScript with multiple lines.

FIGURE 12-5

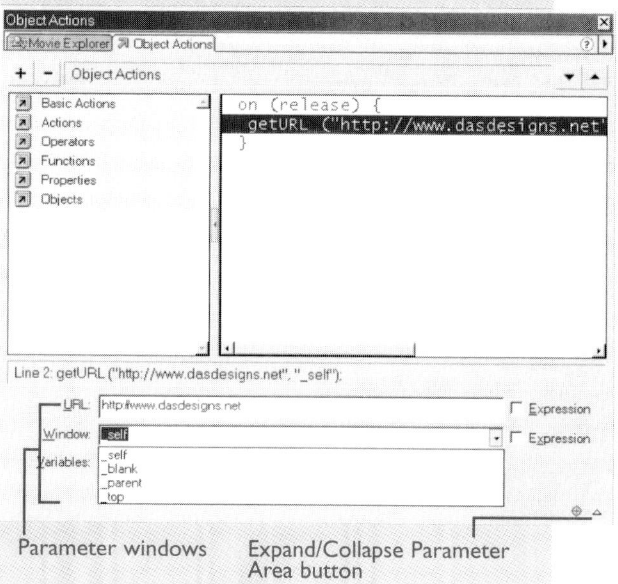

Parameter windows   Expand/Collapse Parameter Area button

Labeling Frames

You learned how to label frames in Chapter 8. When you begin to create interactive movies with actions, labeling frames is especially important. You can instruct Flash to execute an action that will end on or jump to a numbered frame. However, if you add, delete, or move frames, Flash still links the action to the numbered frame, and the ActionScript does not execute as you had planned. If you label a frame and instruct Flash to execute an action based on the frame's label then rearrange the frames along the Timeline, the script still plays properly because Flash searches for the labeled frame. When an action's parameters involve frames, labeled frames are noted in the drop-down menu, as shown in Figure 12-6.

FIGURE 12-6

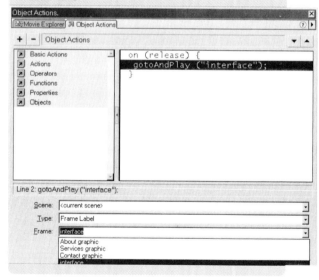

chapter 12: creating interactive movies

Using the Actions Panel's Options Menu

In the upper right-hand corner of the Actions panel is a triangle that you click to reveal the menu, shown in Figure 12-7. The various options in this menu allow you to modify the way that ActionScript is displayed and edited. The first two options in the menu let you switch between Normal mode and Expert mode.

FIGURE 12-7

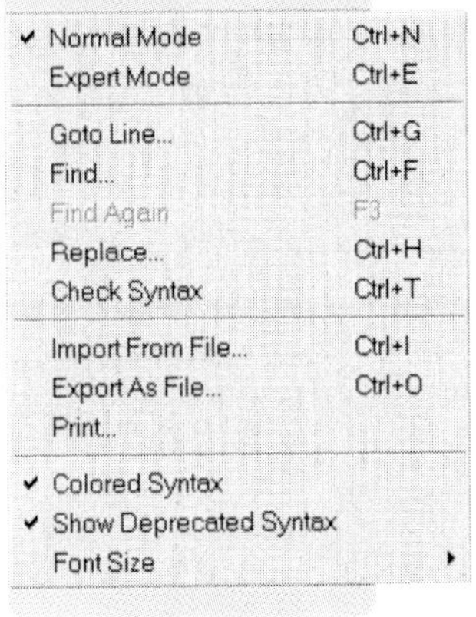

✔ Normal Mode	Ctrl+N
Expert Mode	Ctrl+E
Goto Line...	Ctrl+G
Find...	Ctrl+F
Find Again	F3
Replace...	Ctrl+H
Check Syntax	Ctrl+T
Import From File...	Ctrl+I
Export As File...	Ctrl+O
Print...	
✔ Colored Syntax	
✔ Show Deprecated Syntax	
Font Size	▶

Using Expert Mode

Up to this point, you have learned how to create ActionScript using Normal mode. In Expert mode, you can enter script by typing code directly into the right-hand window of the Actions panel. This option may be useful if you are experienced with ActionScript from earlier versions of Flash.

In Expert mode:

When you choose an action from one of the groups, it is inserted at the cursor's position in the text-editing window on the right-hand side of the Actions panel.

The Parameters pane does not appear.

Only the Add Actions button is functional.

The Up and Down Arrow buttons, which rearrange the hierarchy of actions, are disabled.

You can still double-click an action's name to add it to the script.

The Remaining options on this menu allow you to do the following:

Navigate to a specific line of the ActionScript.

Find and replace specific items in an ActionScript.

Check the syntax of the ActionScript for errors.

Import previously saved ActionScript.

Export the ActionScript.

Print a hard copy of the ActionScript.

Change the appearance of the ActionScript in the window.

Using Basic Actions

Basic Actions, the first group of actions in the panel, allows you to control navigation within a Flash movie and add a degree of user interaction. In the upcoming sections, you will learn how to use the most common actions in your movies.

Using the *Go To* Action

You use the *Go To* action to jump to a specific frame or scene within your movie. You can add this action to a button's *On Mouse Event* action to have the movie advance to a specific scene or frame in conjunction with input from the user's mouse. You also use the *Go To* action to create movie clips that loop back to a specific frame in conjunction with other actions.

To Assign THE *Go To* ACTION TO A FRAME

1 Select the frame to which you want to apply the action.

2 Choose Actions from the Window menu to open the Actions panel.

3 Click the arrow to the left of the Basic Actions group.

4 Double-click the *Go To* action to add it to the script.

continues

214

continued

5 In the Parameters pane, adjust the following parameters:

> Click the triangle to the right of the Scene window, and then choose a scene from the menu. This parameter tells Flash which scene to advance to when the action is executed.

> Click the triangle to the right of the Type window, and then choose an option from the drop-down menu. The most common choices are Frame Number and Frame Label.

> Click the triangle to the right of the Frame window, and then select a labeled frame from the drop-down menu. If you have no labeled frames in your movie, enter a frame number in the text field.

FIGURE 12-8

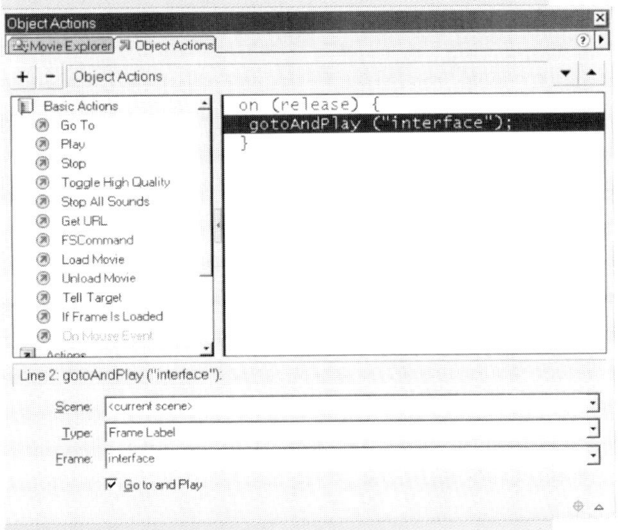

You use the *Go To and Play* action to advance to a specific frame in a movie and play it.

The action's Go To and Play parameter is enabled by default. Disable this parameter to have Flash stop the movie at the frame that the movie advances to when the action is executed. Figure 12-8 shows a typical use of the Go To and Play action.

Using the *Play* and *Stop* Actions

By default, Flash plays a movie from start to finish with no pauses. You use the *Stop* and *Play* actions to control how the Flash Player shows the published movie. You would typically use the *Stop* action to halt a movie while displaying a large block of text or at the beginning of a new scene. You would then assign the *Play* action to a button that the user would click to advance the movie.

To Stop A MOVIE AT A SELECTED FRAME

1 Select the frame where you want the movie to stop, and then press F6 to convert it to a keyframe.

2 Choose Actions from the Window menu to access the Actions panel.

3 Click the arrow to the left of Basic Actions, and then double-click *Stop* to add the action to the script. The *Stop* action has no parameters. Flash halts the movie when this frame is reached.

To Play A MOVIE AT A SPECIFIED FRAME

1 Select the frame where you want the movie to play, and then press **F6** to convert it to a keyframe.

2 Choose Actions from the Window menu to access the Actions panel.

3 Click the arrow to the left of Basic Actions, and then choose *Play*. The *Play* action has no parameters. Flash begins playing the movie when this frame is reached.

In many instances, you use the *Stop* and *Play* actions in conjunction with each other. For example, if you create a movie clip that appears in the same frame as other objects, you do not want it to play until it is summoned by another action. Assign the *Stop* action to frame 1 of the movie clip, and then assign the *Play* action to frame 2 of the movie clip. Assign the *Stop* action to the last frame of the movie clip to halt it. When you create ActionScript for a button or other object that calls the movie clip, specify the proper frames, and the Flash Player runs the movie clip when prompted.

Stopping Sounds in a Movie

You use the *Stop All Sounds* action to stop all sounds from playing in a movie. When the Flash Player reaches the frame to which the action is assigned, all attached sounds stop. Assign the *Stop All Sounds* action to a button when you want to give the user the option of turning off all sounds in a movie.

To Assign THE *STOP ALL SOUNDS* ACTION TO A FRAME

1 Select the frame where you want all sounds to stop, and then convert it to a keyframe by pressing **F6**.

2 Choose Actions from the Window menu to access the panel.

3 Click the arrow to the left of Basic Actions to expand the group, and then double-click the *Stop All Sounds* action to add it to the script. The Flash Player stops all sounds when this frame is reached.

To Create A BUTTON THAT STOPS ALL SOUNDS

1 Create a simple button, and then add it to the document Library.

continues

chapter 12: creating interactive movies

continued

2 Drag an instance of the button onto the Stage.

3 Choose Actions from the Window menu to access the Actions panel.

4 Click the arrow to the left of Basic Actions, and then double-click *Stop All Sounds*. Flash automatically includes the *On Mouse Event* action to the script. Accept the default Release event. When viewing the movie, the user can stop all sounds by clicking the button. The ActionScript for the button is shown in Figure 12-9.

FIGURE 12-9

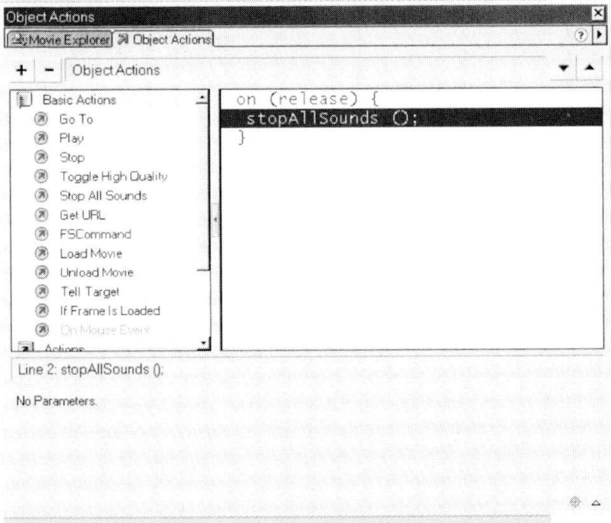

Using the *Get URL* Action

You use the *Get URL* action to jump the movie to a specified URL. In most instances, you use the *Get URL* action in conjunction with a button, giving the user the option to jump to a specified URL. Use the *Get URL* action to create a Links page for a Flash Web site. You can also assign the *Get URL* action to a frame. When you assign the *Get URL* action to a frame, the Flash Player jumps to the specified URL. Assign the *Get URL* action to a frame when you want to end a Flash introduction and jump to a static HTML page.

To Assign THE *GET URL* ACTION TO A BUTTON OR FRAME

1 Select the keyframe or button to which you want to apply the action.

2 Choose Actions from the Window menu to open the Actions panel.

3 Click the arrow to the left of the Basic Actions group, and then double-click *Get URL* to add the action to the script.

see also When you assign the Get URL action to a button, Flash automatically includes the Release event of the On Mouse Event action. The On Mouse Event action is covered in detail in Chapter 11.

continues

217

continued

4 In the Parameters pane, select one of the following parameters:

Self: Opens the specified URL in the same browser window.

Blank: Opens the URL in another window.

Parent: Opens the specified URL in the current frame.

Top: Opens the specified URL in the top-level frame of the current browser window.

When the script is executed, the Flash Player opens to the specified URL in the user's browser when the frame is reached or when the user clicks a button to which the action is assigned.

Opening a URL in a Different Size Browser Window

When you open a URL in another window, the Flash Player opens the URL in a browser window that is the same size as the current browser. To open a URL in a window that is a different size, open the Actions panel, click the arrow at the top-right corner of the panel, and then choose Expert from the menu. Add the *On Mouse Event* action to the script, accept the default Release event, and then enter the following Javascript between the brackets:

```
on (release) {
getURL ("Javascript:newwin1 ()");
}
```

Enter the following Javascript in the head section of the HTML document in which the Flash movie is embedded:

```
<script language="Javascript">
function newwin1() {
window.open(http://www.yourURL.htm', 'links'
'scrollbars=yes,width=640,height=480')
}
</script>
```

Testing an ActionScript in Movie-Editing Mode

You can test simple frame actions in movie-editing mode by using the Enable Simple Frame Actions command. When you enable this command, Flash executes simple actions in movie-editing mode when you use the Controller or when you press Enter or Return to preview the movie.

To Test SIMPLE ACTIONS IN MOVIE-EDITING MODE

1 Choose Enable Simple Frame Actions from the Control menu.

2 Choose Toolbars from the Window menu, choose Controller, and then click the Controller's Play button. Alternately, press Enter or Return to play the movie.

Previewing ActionScripts

If your ActionScript is embedded within movie clips, or if you are using a combination of complex actions, the only way to accurately preview your handiwork is to use the Test Movie command. When you use the Test Movie command, Flash publishes the movie and plays it in another window. The Test Movie command has other powerful functions that enable you to preview the movie's streaming. These advanced features are covered in Chapter 15.

To Test ACTIONSCRIPT WITH THE TEST MOVIE COMMAND

 Choose Test Movie from the Control menu.

When the command is executed, Flash publishes the movie and plays it in another window.

Adding Sound to Flash Movies

Adding sound to a Flash 5 movie creates a more compelling experience for the viewer by involving another sense. Sounds in Flash can be incorporated as ongoing background music loops, or they can be tied to an event, for example a short fanfare playing when a new scene begins. In this chapter, you will learn to use sound to create polished Flash productions.

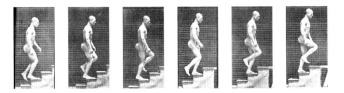

Using Sound in Flash

In Flash, there are event sounds and streaming sounds. Event sounds play independently of the Timeline. An event sound is synchronized to a frame or button and plays until it is finished. Streaming sounds are linked to the Timeline for playback on a Web site. Streaming sounds begin to play when enough data has downloaded for the first few frames to play. You can also assign sounds to buttons. You can add a sound to the Over frame of a button to alert the user that their cursor is over an active button, or you can add it to the Down frame to notify the user that they have successfully clicked the button.

Importing Sounds

Flash has an impressive library of sound effects that you can add to a frame or a button. However, if you want to add a music loop or custom sound effect to a movie, you need to import it. Flash recognizes the following sound formats: WAV (Windows only), AIFF (Macintosh only), and MP3 (both platforms). If you have QuickTime 4 installed on your system, you can import these additional formats:

Sound Designer 2 (Macintosh)

Audio track only QuickTime movies (Windows and Macintosh)

Sun AU (Windows or Macintosh)

System 7 Sounds (Macintosh only)

WAV (Windows & Macintosh)

To Import A SOUND INTO FLASH

1 Choose Import from the File menu. The Import dialog box opens.

2 Click the triangle to the right of the Files of Type window, and then choose **All Sound Formats**.

3 Navigate to the location of the sound file that you want to import, as shown in Figure 13-1.

4 Click Open to import the sound.

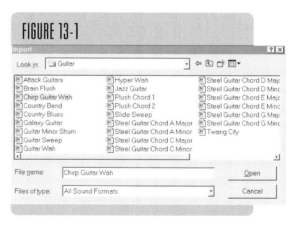

FIGURE 13-1

chapter 13: adding sound to Flash

The imported sound is added to the document Library. A small speaker icon designates a sound in the Library. When selected, the sound's waveform appears in the Library window. To preview the sound, click the Play button, as shown in Figure 13-2.

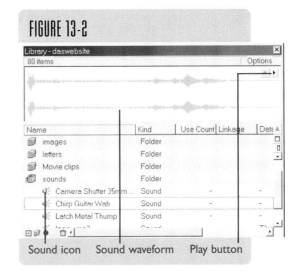

FIGURE 13-2

Sound icon   Sound waveform   Play button

Creating a Soundtrack

Background music can set the tone for a Flash movie. Use dramatic music to urge a viewer to take action at a commercial Web site, rock music to drive the movie with a heavy backbeat, jazz or new age music to create a subdued, mellow mood. When choosing background music for a movie, consider the audience and the message that you want to deliver, and then choose a loop that will satisfy both parameters.

To Add A SOUNDTRACK TO A FLASH MOVIE

1 Import a sound as outlined in the preceding steps.

2 Choose Layer from the Insert menu. Name the layer Soundtrack.

3 Determine when you want the soundtrack to begin playing, and then insert a keyframe at that point in the movie. To begin the soundtrack on the first frame, click the first frame on the Soundtrack layer that you just created.

4 Choose Panels from the Window menu, and then choose Sound to open the Sound panel.

note When you use sound in a Flash movie, assign it to its own layer. If you use multiple sounds in your movie, it is advisable to create one layer for each sound. You can add sounds to layers with other objects; however, it will be easier to select and edit sounds if they have their own unique layers.

continues

continued

5 Click the triangle to the right of the Sound field to reveal a menu of all sounds currently stored in the document Library, as shown in Figure 13-3. Click a sound to select it. The sound's waveform appears on the Timeline.

6 Click the triangle to the right of the Effects window, and then choose one of the following:

> **None** is the default setting for this option. Choose None to remove a previously applied effect.

> **Left Channel** plays the sound in the left channel only.

> **Right Channel** plays the sound in the right channel only. Use either of the channel options when you want a different sound playing or silence in the other channel.

> **Fade Left to Right** fades the sound from the left channel to the right.

> **Fade Right to Left** fades the sound from the right channel to the left.

> **Fade In** gradually increases the amplitude of the sound as it plays. If you loop the sound, it fades in the first time that it plays.

> **Fade Out** causes the sound to gradually decrease its amplitude as it plays.

> **Custom** lets you create a custom effect, something that you will learn to do in the Creating Custom Sound Effects section of this chapter.

7 Click the triangle to the right of the Synch window, and then choose Start from the menu.

8 To play the soundtrack loop more than once, enter a value in the Loops field. Settings for a movie soundtrack are shown in Figure 13-4.

FIGURE 13-3

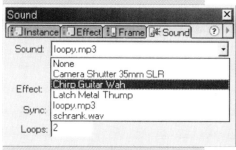

Warning Do not apply the Fade Out effect to a sound if you loop it to play more than once. The sound will fade out during its first repetition, and additional loops will not be heard.

FIGURE 13-4

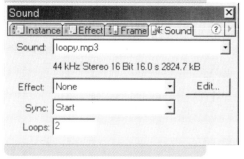

chapter 13: adding sound to flash

To Stop A MOVIE SOUNDTRACK

1 Select the frame where you want the soundtrack to stop playing, and then choose Keyframe from the Insert menu.

2 Choose Panels from the Window menu, and then choose Sound to access the Sound panel.

3 Click the triangle to the right of the Sound window, and then select the sound file that you are using for the movie's soundtrack.

4 Click the triangle to the right of the Synch window, and then select Stop. When the movie is published, the soundtrack stops when this frame is reached.

n°te You can apply the Stop Synch option on a different layer than the sound it is stopping is on. When you apply the Stop option to a sound, all instances of the sound are stopped at the frame where the option is invoked.

Adding a Sound to a Movie

Assign sounds to keyframes to synchronize sound effects with key events in your movie. For example, when creating a Flash movie for a photographer's Web site, you can have the sound of a camera shutter clicking play every time an image flashes across the screen. A sound that is assigned to a keyframe is known as an event sound. Create sound effects on their own layers, separate from the movie's soundtrack layer. If you are using several sound effects in a movie, create one layer for each sound effect.

Sound layers are not organized like object layers. A sound plays when the movie reaches its keyframe, no matter how many other sounds are playing at the same time, no matter where the sound's layer appears in the hierarchy of layers. Flash mixes all sounds when the movie is published. To help organize the sound layers, place them next to each other, either above or below the other layers in your movie.

To Assign A SOUND TO A FRAME

1 Choose Layer from the Insert menu, and then name the new layer *Sound Effects*.

2 Select the frame where you want to add the sound effect, and then choose Keyframe from the Insert menu.

3 Click the Library button on the Launcher bar to open the document Library.

4 Select a sound from the Library, and then drag it onto the Stage.

If no sounds are stored in the document Library, import a sound as described in the preceding steps, or insert a sound from Flash's Sounds Library.

To Use A SOUND FROM THE SOUNDS LIBRARY

1 Choose Common Libraries from the Window menu, and then choose Sounds to open the Sounds Library.

2 Select a sound by clicking its name.

3 Preview the sound by pressing the Play button in the Library's window, as shown in Figure 13-5.

4 Add the sound to your movie by dragging it from the Sounds Library to the Stage. The sound that you selected is added to the document Library for future use, as shown in Figure 13-6.

note When you place several sounds on a layer's Timeline, their waveforms become truncated where they overlap. To identify a sound on the Timeline, place your cursor over the keyframe that the sound is assigned to. If you have Show Tooltips enabled in Preferences, the name of the sound is displayed below your cursor.

FIGURE 13-5

Play button

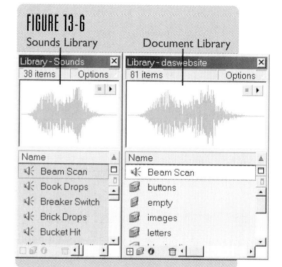

FIGURE 13-6

Sounds Library   Document Library

When you assign a sound to a frame from either the document Library or the Sounds Library, it is synchronized as an event by default. A waveform appears in the keyframe and extends down the Timeline for the exact number of frames that it will play, as shown in Figure 13-7. The sound will play in its entirety. If you add a second sound before enough frames have transpired to play the first sound, the sounds will overlap. Flash mixes the sounds when you publish the movie.

FIGURE 13-7

chapter 13: adding sound to Flash

Starting Different Sounds Simultaneously

When you are working with multiple sound effects, it is advisable but not necessary to set up more than one sound effects layer. The only time that it is absolutely necessary to add additional sound effects layers is when you want different sounds to begin playing at the same time.

To Start DIFFERENT SOUNDS SIMULTANEOUSLY

1 Select the frame in your sound effects layer where you want the sounds to start playing.

2 Choose Keyframe from the Insert menu.

3 Select the first sound from the document Library, and then drag it onto the Stage.

4 Choose Layer from the Insert menu. Give the second sound effects layer a name that you can easily identify when editing the movie.

5 Select the corresponding frame on the new layer, and then choose Keyframe from the Insert menu.

6 Select the second sound from the document Library, and then drag it onto the Stage. When the movie is published, the two sounds start playing at the same time. Figure 13-9 shows two different sounds starting at the same time.

TIP Display the layer height of sound layers at 200% or 300% to see more of a sound's waveform, as shown in Figure 13-8. Seeing more of a sound's waveform makes it easier to synchronize an event to one of the sound's peaks or valleys.

FIGURE 13-8

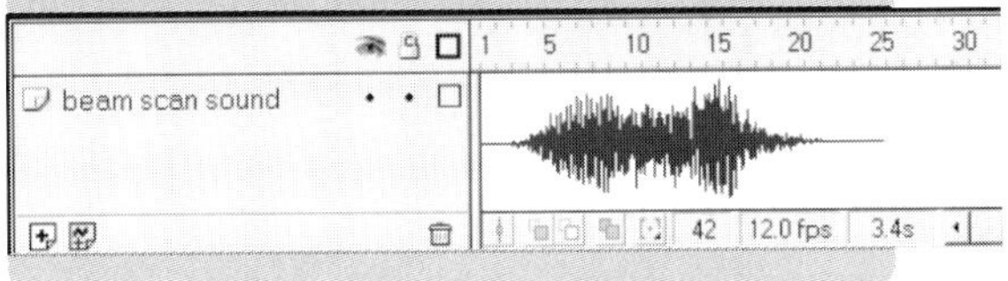

FIGURE 13-9

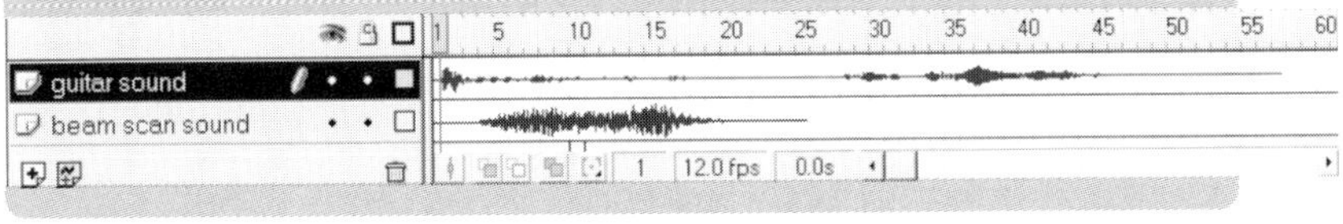

Adding Sound to a Button

Auditory clues enable your viewers to correctly interact with the buttons in your movies. A sound that plays when a cursor is passed over a button tells viewers that the button is active. A sound that plays when a button is clicked adds more realism to your movie, especially if you pattern your buttons after real-life buttons. If you add sounds to buttons that are disguised as parts of the movie's background, your viewers will know they have discovered a button. This is especially useful if you are creating a game with hidden buttons that reveal clues when clicked.

Sounds are commonly added to the Over and Down frames of a button. A sound added to the Over frame plays when a user's cursor passes over the button. A sound added to the Down frame of a button plays when the user clicks the button. A sound added to the Up frame plays when the user's cursor is outside of the button's target area after passing over it. A sound added to a button's Hit frame plays when the user releases the mouse button after clicking.

To Create A BUTTON WITH AUDIO FEEDBACK

1 Double-click a button in the document Library to open the button in symbol-editing mode.

2 Choose Layer from the Insert menu. Name the layer *Button Sounds*.

3 Select the Over frame, and then choose Blank Keyframe from the Insert menu.

4 Select a sound from the document Library, and then drag it onto the Stage. Flash displays the sound's waveform in the frame.

5 Select the Down frame, and then choose Blank Keyframe from the Insert menu.

6 Select a sound from the document Library, and then drag it onto the Stage. A waveform is displayed in the Down frame.

7 Click the Current Scene button to exit symbol-editing mode. All instances of the button used in the movie will now give auditory feedback when the movie is published.

note If you add a sound to a button's Hit frame, make sure that you have a graphic in the Hit frame; otherwise, the button will not work, and the sound will not play.

Synchronizing Movie Sounds

In the sections prior, you learned how to synchronize sounds for soundtracks and sound effects. However, you often need to start and stop sounds on the fly or use streaming sounds to synchronize a sound with frames.

Starting and Stopping Sounds

There will be times when you will need to start and stop a sound during the course of your movie, for example when stopping one soundtrack and starting another.

To Start a sound

1 Select the point in the movie where you want the sound to begin playing, and then choose Keyframe from the Insert menu.

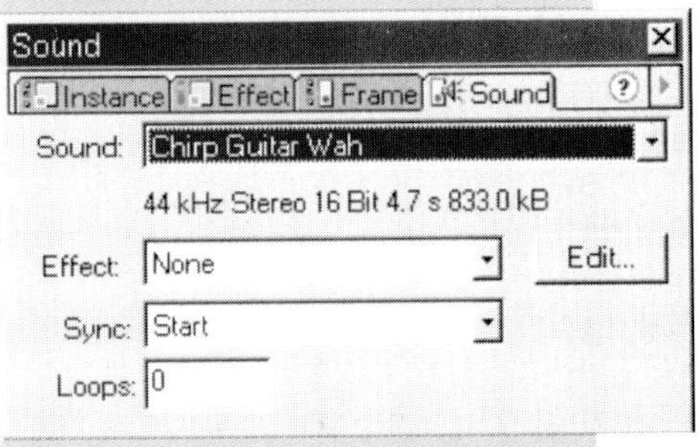

2 Choose Panel from the Window menu, and then choose Sound.

3 Click the triangle to the right of the Sound window, and then select a sound from the menu.

4 Click the triangle to the right of the Effect window, and then choose an option from the menu.

5 Click the triangle to the right of the Event window, and then choose Start, as shown in Figure 13-10.

6 Enter a value in the Loops field to play the sound that you are starting a specific number of times.

FIGURE 13-10

Sound	☒
Instance	Effect	Frame	Sound	⑦ ▶

Sound: Chirp Guitar Wah ▾

44 kHz Stereo 16 Bit 4.7 s 833.0 kB

Effect: None ▾   Edit...

Sync: Start ▾

Loops: 0

To Stop an existing soundtrack or to prevent future instances of a sound in your movie from playing

1 Click the frame where you want the sound to stop playing, and then choose Keyframe from the Insert menu.

2 Choose Panels from the Window menu, and then choose Sound to open the Sound panel.

continues

continued

3 Click the triangle to the right of the Sound window, and then select the sound that you want to stop from the menu.

4 Click the triangle to the right of the Event window, and then select Stop from the drop-down menu, as shown in Figure 13-11.

The selected sound stops playing when this keyframe is reached. Other instances of the sound that appear further down the Timeline will not play unless you start the sound again.

note If you stop a sound that is assigned to a button's frame, all instances of the button will still play the sound. You can stop only a sound that is assigned to a frame.

FIGURE 13-11

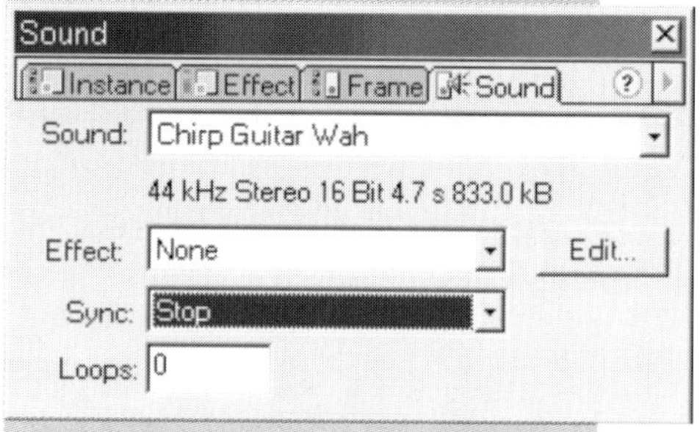

Sound ✕

Instance | Effect | Frame | Sound ⑦ ▶

Sound: Chirp Guitar Wah ▾

44 kHz Stereo 16 Bit 4.7 s 833.0 kB

Effect: None ▾ Edit...

Sync: Stop ▾

Loops: 0

Using Streaming Sound

Streaming sound is divided into smaller clips that are synchronized with individual frames. Streaming sound is specifically designed for playback over the Web. A streaming sound begins playing after a few frames have downloaded. Depending upon a user's connection and computer speed, the Flash Player may drop a few frames in order to synchronize sounds and images as closely as possible. You can use streaming sound to synchronize dialog as a movie narration or character dialog. Streaming sound is not recommended for soundtracks.

To Use STREAMING SOUND IN A MOVIE

1 Select the frame where you want the streaming sound to begin, and then choose Keyframe from the Insert menu.

2 Choose Panels from the Window menu, and then choose Sound.

continues

continued

3 Click the triangle to the right of the Sound window, and then select the sound that you want to stream.

4 Click the triangle to the right of the Synch window, and then select **Stream** from the drop-down menu.

When the published movie is played back over the Web, the sound downloads and plays one frame at a time.

To Get A BETTER UNDERSTANDING OF HOW STREAMING SOUND WORKS

1 Follow the preceding steps to create a streaming sound on the Timeline.

2 Drag the playhead along the Timeline to hear the sound play back one frame at a time.

3 Choose Movie from the Modify menu.

4 Change the movie's frame rate to 24 fps.

5 Drag the playhead across the Timeline to compare each frame's sound to what you heard in step 2.

Creating Custom Sound Effects

You can create custom sound effects by editing instances of a sound clip. You can modify the length of a sound clip, modify the point where the clip starts and stops playing, adjust its volume, and create a custom fade in or fade out. You can edit each channel of a sound independently in the Edit Envelope window.

To Open THE EDIT ENVELOPE WINDOW

1 Select an instance of a sound on the Timeline, choose Panels from the Window menu, and then choose Sound.

continues

continued

2 After the Sound panel appears, click the Edit button, which appears to the right of the Effects window, to open the Edit Envelope dialog box, shown in Figure 13-12.

The Edit Envelope window displays the sound's waveform and the controls that you use to modify the sound. At the lower-left corner of the window are the Stop and Play buttons. To the left of the Help button are controls to zoom in and out on the waveform. Click the Zoom In button to display less of the waveform, Zoom Out to display more of the waveform. To the right of the Zoom Out button are two buttons that you use to display the waveform's Timeline as seconds or as frames. Each channel of the sound is displayed in its own window. Between each channel's window is the Timeline. To the left of the Timeline is the Time In slider; to the right is the Time Out slider. One or more envelope handles are displayed in each channel's window. You use envelope handles to modify the sound's amplitude at a given point on the Timeline.

To Change THE VOLUME OF A SOUND IN A CHANNEL

 Drag the envelope handle down, as shown in Figure 13-13.

To Decrease THE PLAYING TIME OF A SOUND, DO ONE OF THE FOLLOWING:

■ .... Drag the Time In slider to the right. The clip is shorter and starts playing at a different point.

■ .... Drag the Time Out slider to the left. The clip is shorter and finishes playing at a different point.

■ .... Drag the Time In and Time Out sliders towards each other. The clip is shorter and begins and finishes playing at different points than the original.

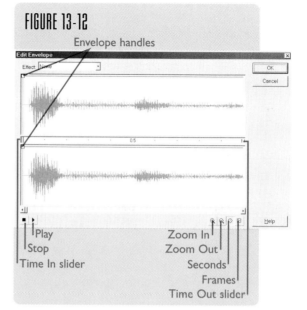

FIGURE 13-12

Envelope handles

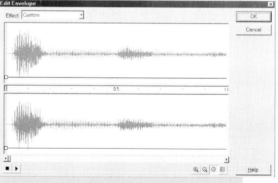

FIGURE 13-13

To Create A CUSTOM FADE IN EFFECT

1 Drag the envelope handle in each of the sound's channels down.

2 Click anywhere inside either channel's window to create a new envelope handle. A corresponding handle appears in the other channel's window.

3 Drag each channel's handle to the desired position to create the fade in, as shown in Figure 13-14.

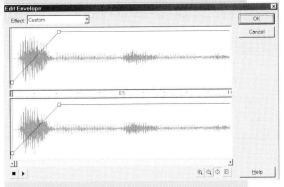

FIGURE 13-14

To Create A CUSTOM FADE OUT EFFECT

1 Click inside either channel's window at the Time Out slider to create a new envelope handle. An identical handle appears in the other channel's window.

2 Drag the new handle in each channel's window down to decrease the sound's volume to zero at the end of the clip.

3 Click inside either channel's window to create a new handle. A corresponding handle appears in the other channel's window.

4 Drag each channel's envelope handle to the point where you want the volume to start fading out, as shown in Figure 13-15.

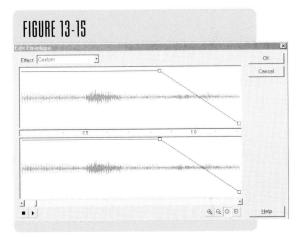

FIGURE 13-15

You can add as many envelope handles as needed to create the effect that you are after. Figure 13-16 shows a sound that gradually fades in, abruptly decreases, and then increases in volume before gradually fading out.

TIP You can use Flash's standard effects as starting points for your custom effects. Open the Edit Envelope window, click the triangle to the left of the Effect window, and then choose an option from the menu. Add envelope handles, and then drag as needed to modify the preset effect.

FIGURE 13-16

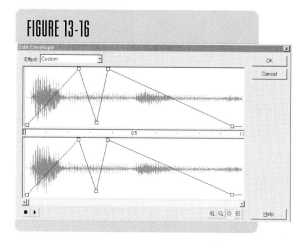

Adjusting Sound Export Settings

When you publish a movie, Flash compresses all sounds to create the smallest possible file size. You can change sound compression settings globally, something that you will learn to do in Chapter 15. You can also change the compression setting for individual sounds in the document Library. When sound files are compressed, sound quality suffers. For simple sounds like button clicks, the loss in quality will be negligible; however, if you are playing music clips as part of a musician's Web site, export the music clips with the least amount of compression possible.

To Change A SOUND'S EXPORT SETTINGS

1 Choose Library from the Window menu to display the document Library.

2 Select the sound whose export settings you want to modify.

continues

continued

3 Click the Options button, and then choose Properties from the drop-down menu. The Sound Properties dialog box appears, as shown in Figure 13-17.

4 Click the triangle to the right of the Compression window, and then choose a compression method. Each compression method uses different options and is covered separately in upcoming sections.

5 Apply the desired export settings.

6 Press the Test button to hear the sound with the new export settings.

7 If the sound quality is acceptable, click **OK** to apply the new settings.

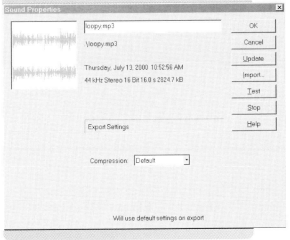

FIGURE 13-17

Exporting a Sound with ADPCM Compression

The ADPCM sound format sets compression for 8 and 16 bit sound data. This format is best suited for sounds such as button clicks.

To Export A SOUND WITH **ADPCM** COMPRESSION

1 Click the sound's name in the document Library, and then choose Properties from the Options menu.

2 Click the triangle to the right of the Compression window, and then choose **ADPCM**, as shown in Figure 13-18.

3 In the Preprocessing section, select Convert Stereo to Mono to convert stereo sounds to monaural. This option is enabled by default and has no effect on monaural sounds.

FIGURE 13-18

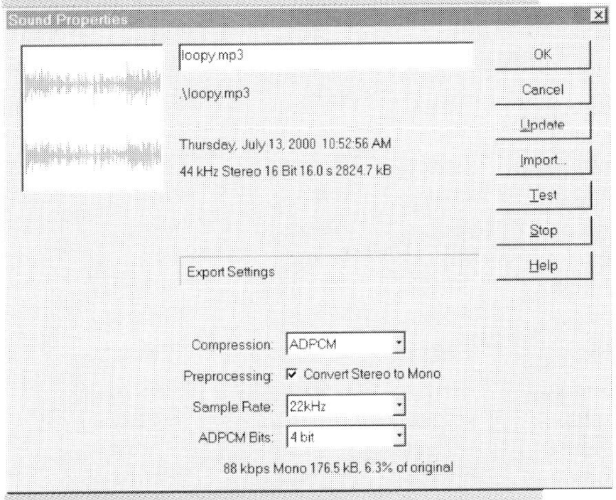

continues

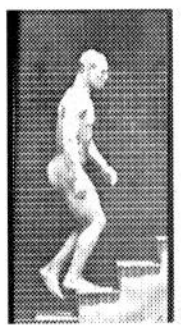

continued

4 Click the triangle to the right of the **Sample Rate** window, and then choose an option from the drop-down menu. Lower rates decrease file size but degrade sound quality. Choose from the following settings:

5KHz is barely acceptable for the spoken word.

11KHz is the lowest acceptable setting for musical passages.

22KHz is a good choice for Web playback.

44KHz is CD quality.

5 Click the triangle to the right of the **ADPCM Bits** section, and then choose an option from the drop-down menu. Choose a lower bit rate to speed up download time. A dialog box appears at the bottom of the window that notes the new compression ratings and compares the file size at the new settings with the original.

6 Click the **Test** button to hear the sound with the new compression options. If the sound is acceptable, click **OK** to apply the new settings.

Exporting a Sound with MP3 Compression

MP3 compression is an excellent choice for a movie soundtrack. The resulting file size of a sound with MP3 compression is small, considering the high quality of the sound.

To Export A SOUND WITH MP3 COMPRESSION

1 Click the sound's name in the document Library, and then choose Properties from the Options menu.

2 Click the triangle to the right of the Compression window, and then choose the MP3 option, as shown in Figure 13-19.

3 Click the triangle to the right of the Bit Rate window, and then select a setting from the drop-down menu. Flash supports settings from 8 kbps through 160 kbps CBR (Constant Bit Rate). For music tracks, select a setting of 16 kbps or higher.

FIGURE 13-19

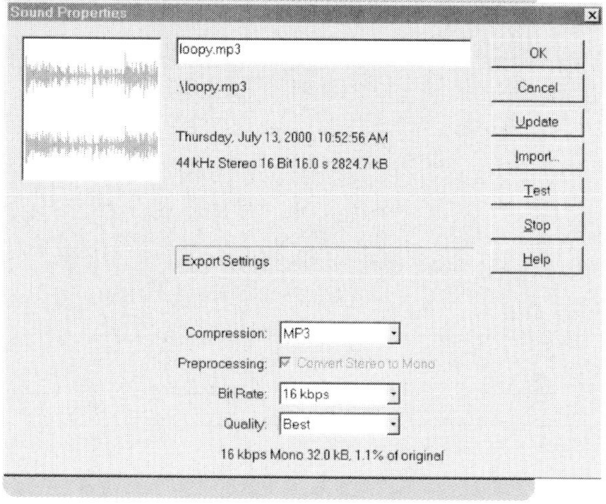

Sound Properties

loopy.mp3

\loopy.mp3

Thursday, July 13, 2000 10:52:56 AM
44 kHz Stereo 16 Bit 16.0 s 2824.7 kB

OK
Cancel
Update
Import...
Test
Stop
Help

Export Settings

Compression: MP3
Preprocessing: ☑ Convert Stereo to Mono
Bit Rate: 16 kbps
Quality: Best

16 kbps Mono 32.0 kB, 1.1% of original

continues

continued

4 Click the triangle to the right of the **Quality** window, and then select an option. This setting determines how quickly the music file is compressed when the movie is published. Choose from **Fast** (quick compression, poorest sound quality), **Medium** (slower compression, better sound quality), or **Best** (slowest compression, highest sound quality). A dialog box appears at the bottom of the window that notes the new compression ratings and compares the file size with the original.

Warning If you are working with a slower machine, selecting Best may result in a long wait while the movie is published.

5 Click the Test button to preview the sound at the new settings.

6 If the sound is acceptable, click the **OK** button to apply the settings.

Exporting a Sound with Raw Compression

If you choose the Raw compression method, Flash exports the sound with no compression.

To Export A SOUND WITH RAW COMPRESSION

1 Select a sound in the document Library, and then choose Properties from the Options menu.

2 Click the triangle to the right of the Compression window, and then choose the Raw option, as shown in Figure 13-20.

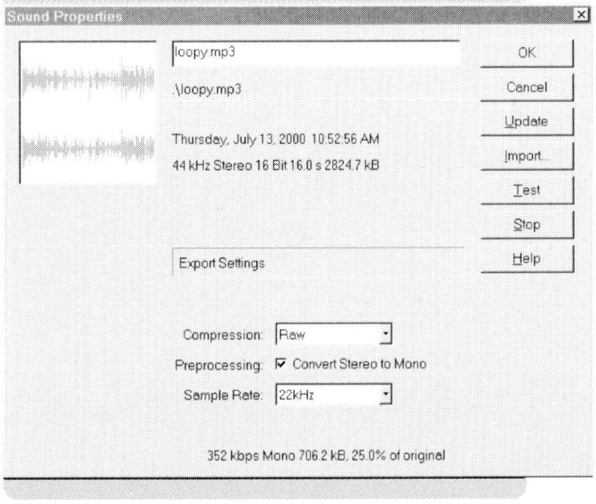

3 Click the triangle to the right of the Sample Rate window, and then choose one of the following:

5KHz is acceptable for button sounds.

11KHz is a good choice for human speech.

22KHz works well for music playback over the Web.

44KHz is CD quality. Use this setting for multi-media presentations where file size is not an issue.

FIGURE 13-20

Sound Properties

loopy.mp3

.\loopy.mp3

Thursday, July 13, 2000 10:52:56 AM
44 kHz Stereo 16 Bit 16.0 s 2824.7 kB

Export Settings

Compression: Raw

Preprocessing: ☑ Convert Stereo to Mono

Sample Rate: 22kHz

352 kbps Mono 706.2 kB, 25.0% of original

OK
Cancel
Update
Import...
Test
Stop
Help

continues

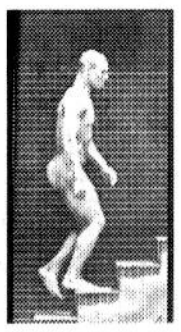

continued

4 Click the Test button to preview the sound at the new settings.

5 If the sound is acceptable, click **OK** to apply the new settings.

n°te None of the compression options can increase the KHz rate of a sound above the rate at which it was imported.

Sources for Flash Sounds

Music adds pizzazz to your Flash movies. Although Flash doesn't ship with music loops, there are many Web sites where you can download royalty-free music loops. You can log on to the Internet and type the keywords **Flash + music** into your favorite search engine. If you explore the search results, you are sure to find many sites offering free music loops.

If music loops are going to be a staple in your Flash movies, consider investing in a sound-editing program with the capability of mixing sampled sound. Mixman (http://www.mixman.com) and Acid Music (http://www.sonicfoundry.com/) are two excellent sound-editing programs that give you the necessary tools to create sophisticated soundtracks from sampled sounds. When you master either of these programs, you can offer your clients custom soundtracks with their Flash Web sites.

Introduction to ActionScript

In Chapter 12, you learned how to use some basic Flash actions to add interactivity to your movies. Flash 5 has enough actions to warrant a book on the subject of ActionScript alone. In this chapter, you will be introduced to other actions that will add even more interactivity to your Flash productions.

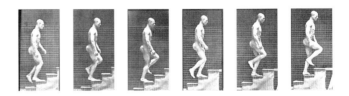

Creating ActionScripts in Flash

When you create an ActionScript in Flash, you combine several actions to achieve a desired result. For example, you can create an ActionScript that programs a button to scroll a block of Dynamic Text one line at a time. Another example of ActionScript at work is when you create a multi-state rollover button by programming several actions in one script. When the movie is published, the button reacts differently, depending upon where the user's mouse is in relation to the button and whether the mouse is dragged over or clicked on the button. In the sections that follow, you will learn to use some of the more popular Flash actions that will become part of your own ActionScripts. You are encouraged to experiment with the other Flash actions to expand your knowledge of ActionScript. Figure 14-1 shows the Actions panel with the Basic Actions group expanded.

FIGURE 14-1

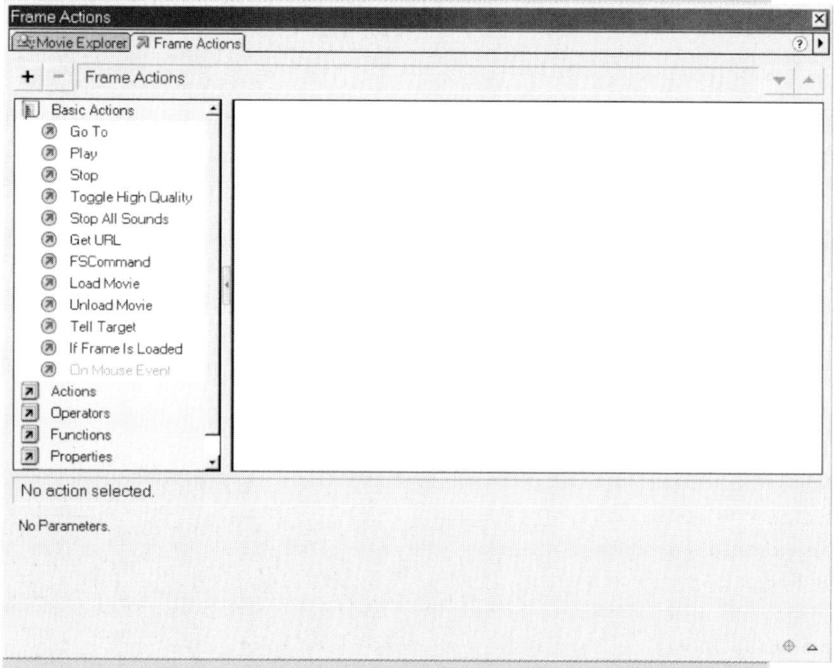

Frame Actions	☒
🎬 Movie Explorer 📃 Frame Actions	⑦ ▶

+ − │ Frame Actions ▼ ▲

- 📘 Basic Actions
  - ⓐ Go To
  - ⓐ Play
  - ⓐ Stop
  - ⓐ Toggle High Quality
  - ⓐ Stop All Sounds
  - ⓐ Get URL
  - ⓐ FSCommand
  - ⓐ Load Movie
  - ⓐ Unload Movie
  - ⓐ Tell Target
  - ⓐ If Frame Is Loaded
  - ⓐ On Mouse Event
- 📄 Actions
- 📄 Operators
- 📄 Functions
- 📄 Properties

No action selected.

No Parameters.

⊕ ▵

You use the Actions panel to create ActionScripts for your movies.

Using the *loadMovie* Action

The *loadMovie* action lets you load another Flash movie and play it within the base movie, also known as the root movie. One excellent use of this action is when you want to break a Web site into bite-sized chunks. You create different movies for each part of the site and then assign the *loadMovie* action to a button that loads and then plays the movie. It is possible for you to load two or more movies at the same time. Flash uses levels to separate loaded movies. You may understand this concept better if you equate levels with layers. The level of the base Flash movie is level 0. A movie loaded into a higher level eclipses items on the level below it. If you load a movie into the same level currently occupied by another movie, the newly loaded movie plays in place of the old movie. The most common use for the *loadMovie* action is to assign it to a button. However, you could also assign it to an object in a game to have another movie load when the user's mouse passes over the object.

To Assign THE *LOADMOVIE* ACTION TO AN OBJECT

 To learn how to use the *loadMovie* action to manage a complex Web site, cue up the Complex Web Sites lesson on the Virtual Classroom CD-ROM.

1 Select the object to which you want to assign the action.

2 Choose Actions from the Window menu to open the Actions panel.

3 Click the arrow next to Basic Actions or Actions to expand the group.

4 Double-click the *loadMovie* action to add it to the script.

5 The Parameters pane expands, as shown in Figure 14-2.

6 In the URL window, enter the name of the movie that you want to load. It makes matters simpler if you can have the movie you are loading in the same directory as the base movie. If you are loading the movie from a different directory, make sure to enter the proper path so that Flash can find the movie.

Warning When you upload the finished movies to a Web site, make sure that the movies specified in any *loadMovie* action are in the same directory that you specified in the *loadMovie* actions' URL window. Otherwise, the movie will not load.

7 Enter the level that you want the movie loaded into. Shown in Figure 14-3 is an ActionScript using the *loadMovie* action.

note When you load a movie of a different size, it conforms to the size of the base movie.

FIGURE 14-2

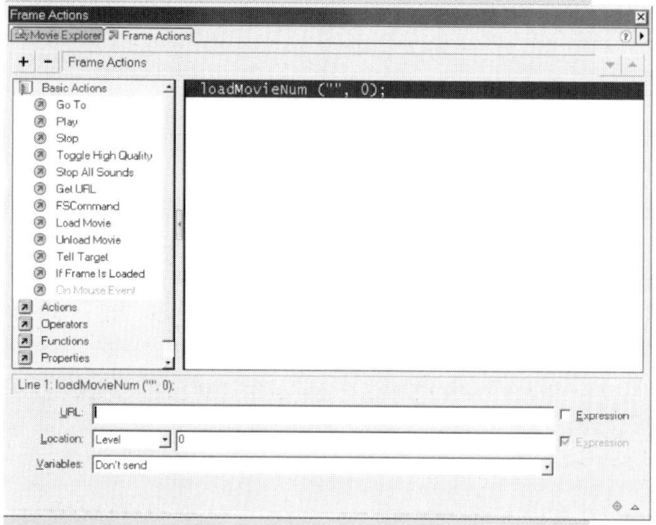

[Frame Actions panel screenshot showing:]

```
loadMovieNum ("", 0);
```

TIP You can use the *loadMovie* action to summon a movie and have it play within a blank area of the Stage. To do this, create the base movie, and leave blank the area of the Stage where you want the other movie to play. Create a second movie the same size and background color as the base movie, and then leave the outer part of the Stage blank, the area where the base movie has buttons or other graphics. Program a button to load the second movie into Level 1, and it will play inside of the base movie.

FIGURE 14-3

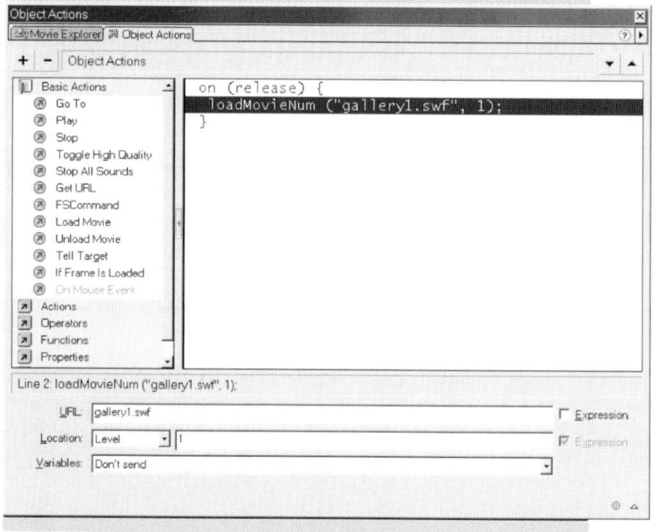

[Object Actions panel screenshot showing:]

```
on (release) {
    loadMovieNum ("gallery1.swf", 1);
}
```

Using the *unloadMovie* Action

You use the *unloadMovie* action to unload a movie that you loaded previously with the *loadMovie* action. If you load a movie in the same level as a previous movie, the *unload-Movie* action is not necessary. Flash replaces the previously loaded movie with the new one. You use the *unloadMovie* action when you are loading a new movie into a different level. If you load a new movie into a higher level without first invoking the *unloadMovie* action, the previously loaded movie is still visible through blank areas of the newly loaded movie. In the majority of instances, you assign the *unloadMovie* action to a button.

To Assign THE *UNLOADMOVIE* ACTION

1 Select the object to which you want to assign the action.

2 Choose Actions from the Window menu to open the Actions panel.

3 Click the arrow to the left of Basic Actions or Actions to expand the group.

4 Double-click the *unloadMovie* action to add it to the script.

5 In the Parameters pane, enter the level of the movie that you want to unload.

Figure 14-4 shows a script that will unload a movie from level 3.

FIGURE 14-4

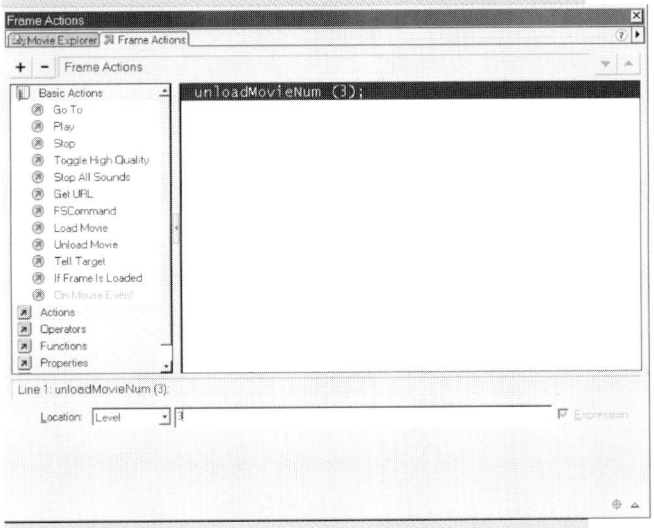

Using the *tellTarget* Action

When you add the *tellTarget* action to a script, you are instructing Flash to follow a path to a named instance of a movie clip or a loaded movie. You can also use the *tellTarget* action to complete an ActionScript that begins within a movie clip, for example a multi-functional button in a movie clip that plays the movie clip and also instructs Flash to go to a specific frame within the main movie.

To Assign THE *TELLTARGET* ACTION TO A SCRIPT

1 Select the object to which you want to apply the action.

2 Choose Actions from the Window menu to open the Actions panel.

continues

continued

3 Click the arrow to the left of the Basic Actions or Actions group, and then double-click *tellTarget* to add it to the ActionScript, as shown in Figure 14-5.

4 Click the Insert a Target Path icon to open the Insert a Target Path dialog box, shown in Figure 14-6.

5 Click a named instance of a movie clip from the list to select it.

6 Assign the action that you want to occur when Flash finds the target.

n°te Occasionally, the Insert a Target Path icon is grayed out even though you have named instances within your movie that Flash can use as a target. If this occurs, click the Expand/Collapse the Parameters Area icon to re-activate the Insert a Target Path icon.

n°te The *tellTarget* action and many other popular actions have been deprecated in Flash 5. The *with* action replaces the *tellTarget* action in future versions of Flash. The *with* action takes the named instance as a target whereas the *tellTarget* action requires a target path and cannot control individual objects. The *tellTarget* action is presented here because many Flash developers are still publishing their work as Flash 4 movies while Internet users are updating their browser plug-ins to the Flash 5 Player.

FIGURE 14-5

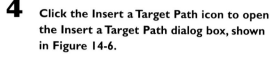

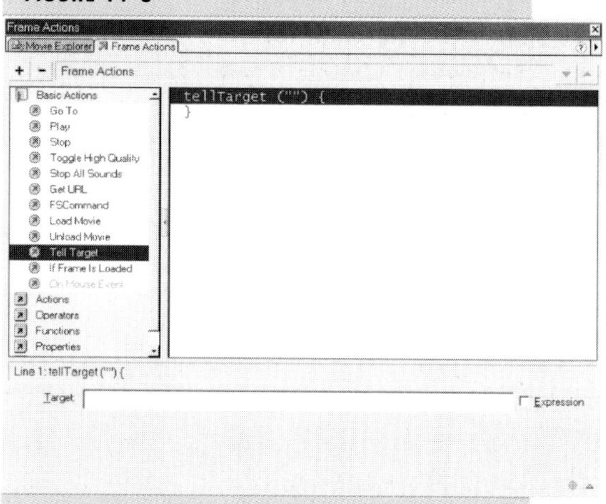

FIGURE 14-6

chapter 14: introduction to ActionScript

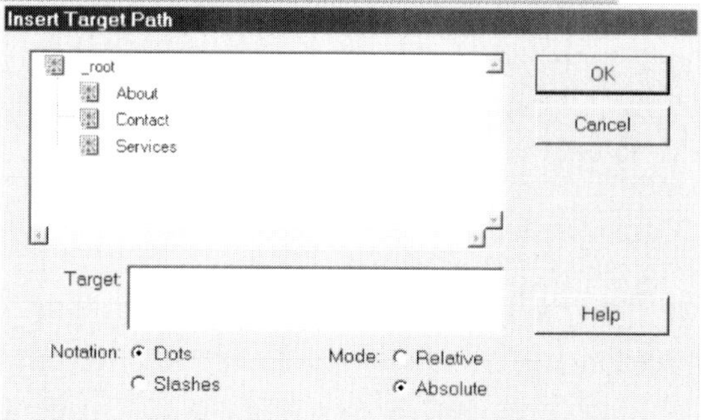

Understanding Target Path Modes

You assign a target path to an action such as *tellTarget* to tell Flash to find a named instance to which Flash applies the next action in the script. You open the Insert a Target Path dialog box by clicking the Insert a Target Path icon at the lower right-hand side of the Actions panel. To assign a target path to an action, you click a named instance in the Insert a Target Path dialog box, and Flash associates the target path to the selected instance with the action. The Insert a Target Path button, found in the Actions panel, is where you select the target path that you want Flash to associate with the action, as shown in Figure 14-7. You have two different modes of target paths to choose from, relative and root. The relative mode refers to the actual movie clip, or in the case of a multi-level movie, the level of the movie on which the target appears. When you choose the root mode, you are instructing Flash to follow a path to the root level, or level 0, of the movie.

A relative path is dependent upon the relationship between a movie clip's Timeline and the target Timeline. When you use a relative path, you can address only a target within the same level of the movie. For instance, you cannot use a relative path in an action on level 0 to target a loaded movie in level 5.

On the other hand, you can use an absolute path to seek out a target on any level of a movie. This is especially useful when you are targeting a movie clip that is part of a movie loaded on a different level. A named instance always has the same absolute path, regardless of whether it is being called from an action in an instance on the same level or from an action on a different level. For example, an instance of a movie clip labeled *Mouse_Cursor* on the main level of the movie always has the following absolute path:

```
_root.Mouse_Cursor
```

FIGURE 14-7

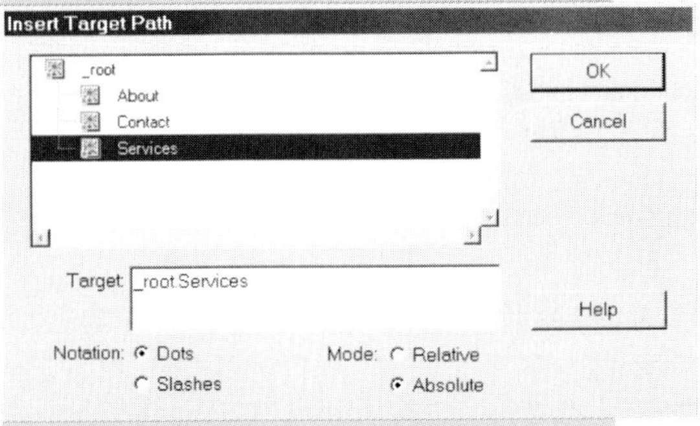

Insert Target Path

- _root
  - About
  - Contact
  - **Services**

OK
Cancel

Target: _root.Services

Help

Notation: ⦿ Dots   Mode: ○ Relative
         ○ Slashes   ⦿ Absolute

Using the *setVariable* Action

A variable is a container that holds information. The actual container (the variable's name) is always the same, but the contents can change as the movie plays. You can use variables to record information input by the user, to record values that change as the movie plays, or to evaluate whether a condition is true or false. You assign a known value to a variable the first time that you define it. If you know which variables you will be using in a movie, you can assign them all in the first frame of the movie. Figure 14-8 shows a variable being declared in the first line of an ActionScript.

In the second line of the ActionScript, the variable changes. A mathematical expression is used to increase the value of the variable by one. The third line of the ActionScript uses the *dowhile* action to repeat the second line of the ActionScript while the variable's value is less than ten.

To Declare A VARIABLE

1 Select the frame where you want to introduce the variable.

2 Choose Actions from the Window menu to open the Actions panel.

3 Click the arrow to the left of Actions to expand the group.

4 Double-click the *setVariable* action. Flash adds the action to the script.

5 In the Parameters pane, enter a name for the variable.

6 Enter a value for the variable. If the variable is a mathematical expression, be sure to click the Expression check box. Figure 14-9 shows a variable with text assigned to it. You can use the variable's text anywhere in a movie by creating a block of Dynamic Text and assigning the same variable to it.

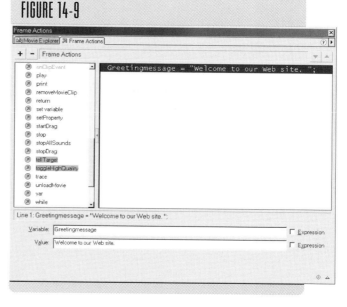

FIGURE 14-8

```
Boxscore = 0;
Boxscore = "Boxscore=Boxscore+1";
do {
} while (Boxscore<10);
```

Line 4: } while (Boxscore<10);

Condition: Boxscore<10

FIGURE 14-9

```
Greetingmessage = "Welcome to our Web site. ";
```

Line 1: Greetingmessage = "Welcome to our Web site. ";

Variable: Greetingmessage
Value: Welcome to our Web site.

Creating Names and Content for Variables

You can enter any name for a variable that you please, but the variable name must begin with a character, not a number. There can be no spaces between characters. If you need to create a separation between two words in a variable's name, separate them with an underscore. Create a variable name that is meaningful to you, something that you will be able to remember when editing your movie. Actual variables can contain any of the following:

Numbers: You choose a number for a variable when you want a variable that can be changed using a mathematical expression. You can use a number variable to score a game. For every correct response, an expression changes the value of the variable.

Boolean: A Boolean variable can be true or false. Flash ActionScript will convert a value that equals "true" to 1 and a value that equals "false" to 0 when appropriate.

String: A string is any variable that is enclosed in quotation marks, for example a name or street address. You use a string variable when you want to display the variable in a block of Dynamic Text.

Null: A null variable is a variable that has been assigned but has no value yet. One use for a null variable is to assign a variable name at the start of a movie and then wait for user input through an Input Text box with the variable name. The user enters a value in the Input Text box, which Flash then assigns to the variable.

Changing a Variable's Value with an Expression

When you create a variable, you assign a value to it. The value can be a text string object, such as a person's name or a block of text created in a word-processing program. It can also be a number that is read by other parts of your movie. You can update the number with a mathematical expression. When you choose to change a variable using a mathematical expression, you select the expression option. Figure 14-10 shows an ActionScript with an expression that raises by one the value of a variable named "score" when *T* is chosen for the variable answer.

FIGURE 14-10

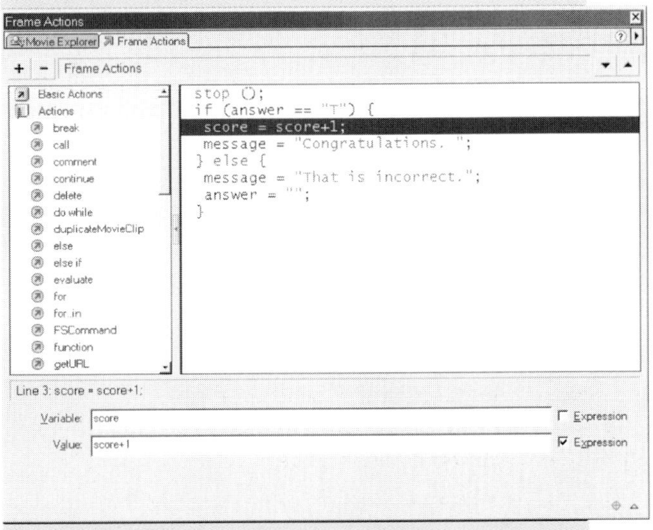

Frame Actions

```
stop ();
if (answer == "T") {
    score = score+1;
    message = "Congratulations. ";
} else {
    message = "That is incorrect.";
    answer = "";
}
```

Line 3: score = score+1;

Variable: score   □ Expression
Value: score+1   ☑ Expression

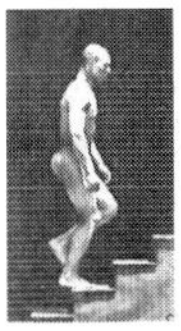

Using *If* Statements

When you need Flash to check whether a condition is true or false, you add the *if* action to a script. If the condition in the statement is true, an action is executed. If the condition in the statement is false, an alternative action is executed. When a condition is not true, the *else* action tells Flash to execute an alternative action. In most cases, you will be evaluating a variable to see if the variable meets a certain condition, for example if an answer to a question in a quiz is true. You can use an *if ... else* statement to evaluate an entered password. If the password is correct, you create an action that admits the user to the Web site. If the password is incorrect, you create an action after the *else* statement that warns the user that they have entered an invalid password and will not be admitted to the site.

To Check A CONDITION IN A SCRIPT

1 Create a keyframe where you want to evaluate the condition.

2 Choose Actions from the Window menu to open the Actions panel.

3 Click the arrow to the left of Actions to expand the group.

4 Double-click the *if* action to add it to the script. Flash adds the action to the script and opens the Condition field in the Parameters pane.

5 Enter the Condition that you want Flash to evaluate for the next action to occur. For example, to have Flash evaluate a variable called "Password" to see if it equals the word "Enter," the condition would read as follows: Password = = "Enter."

6 Double-click the action that you want to occur if the condition is met.

7 Double-click the *else* action to add it to the script.

8 Double-click the action that you want to occur when the condition is not met. Shown in Figure 14-11 is a script that admits a user to a Web site if the password entered is *Bob*. If the wrong password is entered, the movie jumps to a frame labeled "password failed."

FIGURE 14-11

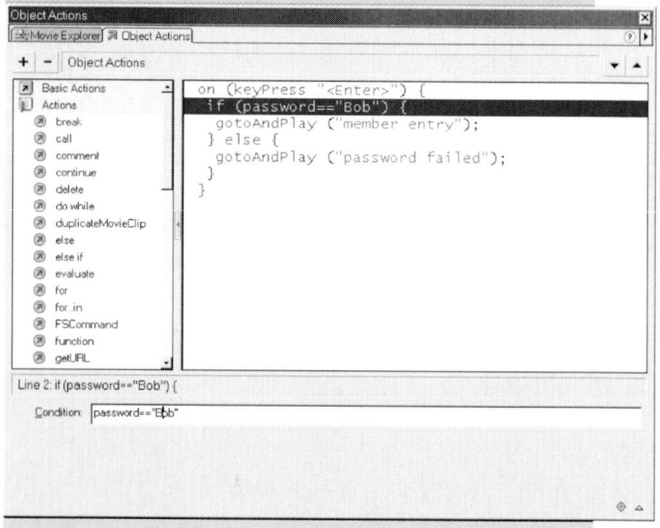

```
on (keyPress "<Enter>") {
    if (password=="Bob") {
        gotoAndPlay ("member entry");
    } else {
        gotoAndPlay ("password failed");
    }
}
```

Line 2: if (password=="Bob") {

Condition: password=="Bob"

Using Operators

When you create an expression, you use operators to determine how Flash evaluates the expression. The type of variables that you use in the expression determines the type of operators that you use. For example, if you use numbers in your expression, you use mathematical operators to evaluate the expression. If you use text variables (also known as string variables), you use operators that test equality, inequality, and other conditions.

Using Mathematical Operators

You use mathematical operators when you want to change or compare the value of a numerical variable. If you attempt to use one of these operators to compare the value of a string, your script will not perform properly.

Flash Mathematical Operators

OPERATOR	FUNCTION
+	Adds two numbers together
-	Subtracts two numbers
/	Divides one number by another
*	Multiplies one number by another

Flash Comparison Operators

OPERATOR	FUNCTION
=	Equal to
>	Is not equal to
<	Less than
<=	Less than or equal to
>	Greater than
>=	Greater than or equal to

Using String Operators

You use string operators to compare two string variables. You can use string operators for many things, such as comparing the expressions in two strings or comparing to see if a string equals a known value input by a user. String operators from Flash 4 have been deprecated in Flash 5; however, they are still fully functional if you want to publish movies in Flash 4 format. Flash 5 string operators are recognized only in version 5 and versions of Flash yet to be created. The following table lists both Flash 4 and Flash 5 string operators.

Flash String Operators

FLASH 4	FLASH 5	FUNCTION
""	""	Indicates that the variable is a string
&	+	Joins two strings (concatenate)
eq	==	Tests for equality
ne	!=	Tests for inequality
gt	>	Greater than
lt	<	Less than
le	<=	Less than or equal to
ge	>=	Greater than or equal to

The "" symbol tells you and Flash that whatever is between the quotation marks is a string of characters. The & (Flash 4) and + operators are for concatenation. You use this operator when you want to append one string onto the end of another string. Shown in Figure 14-12 is an ActionScript using concatenation. When the variable text is displayed in a Dynamic Text box named "text", it reads, "Congratulations. You have mastered level 4." You use the other operators to compare between two strings or to compare variables assigned to strings. These operators evaluate the alphabetical order based on the first character in the string.

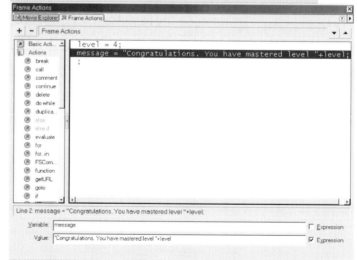

FIGURE 14-12

Flash also has a set of logical operators that you use to evaluate two expressions in a statement. When you use the logical operator && (*and* in Flash 4), you are telling Flash that both expressions must be true for the entire expression to be true. Figure 14-13 shows scripting for evaluating an input user name and password to allow access to a Web site. Both the user name and password must match before the user is allowed access to the site.

n°te To apply multiple operators to a line of script, you need to manually enter the script in Expert mode.

FIGURE 14-13

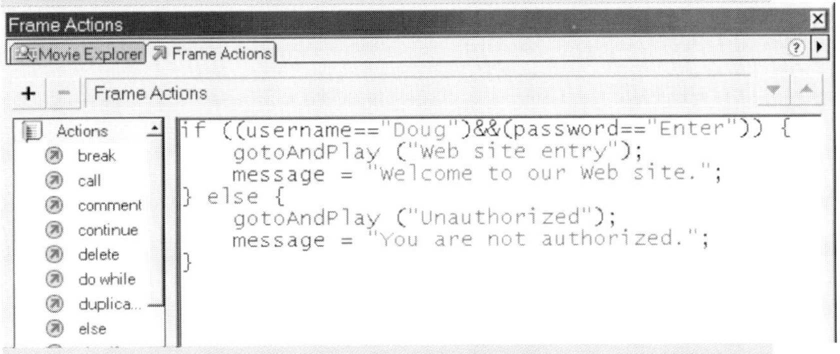

```
Frame Actions                                              ✕
Movie Explorer  Frame Actions                          ?  ▶
+  −   Frame Actions                                    ▼  ▲
Actions      ▲  if ((username=="Doug")&&(password=="Enter")) {
  break           gotoAndPlay ("Web site entry");
  call            message = "Welcome to our Web site.";
  comment    } else {
  continue        gotoAndPlay ("Unauthorized");
  delete          message = "You are not authorized.";
  do while   }
  duplica...
  else
```

When you use the logical operator || (*or* in Flash 4), you are instructing Flash that the entire expression is true if either expression is true. Figure 14-14 demonstrates a script that admits the user to the Web site if either the user name or password matches the user name and password variables in the expression.

FIGURE 14-14

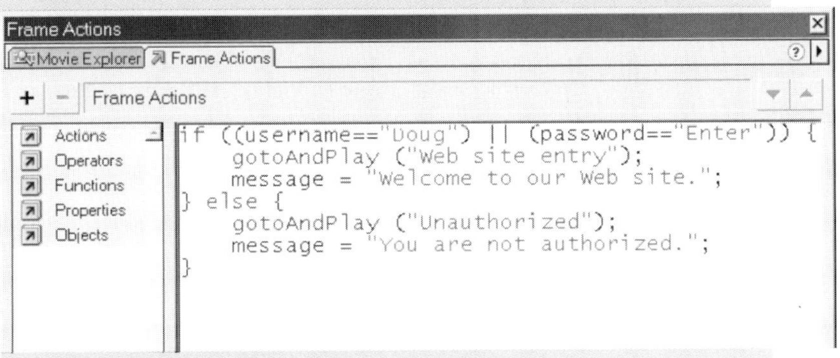

```
Frame Actions                                              ✕
Movie Explorer  Frame Actions                          ?  ▶
+  −   Frame Actions                                    ▼  ▲
Actions      ─  if ((username=="Doug") || (password=="Enter")) {
Operators        gotoAndPlay ("Web site entry");
Functions        message = "Welcome to our Web site.";
Properties   } else {
Objects          gotoAndPlay ("Unauthorized");
                 message = "You are not authorized.";
             }
```

Working with Dynamic Text and Input Text

You use Dynamic Text to add another element of interactivity to your Flash movies. When you use Dynamic Text, you assign a variable to it. As you learned previously, a variable is a placeholder. Therefore, you use Dynamic Text as a placeholder for a value that you have assigned to a variable earlier in your movie, in this case a block of text. You use Input Text to accept user input. You also assign a variable name to Input Text. You can request that the user enter a name, a birth date, a lucky number, or perhaps a password. After the user enters something into the Input Text block, Flash assigns it to the variable, which Flash can then evaluate with an expression or display in another part of the movie, according to the way that you have written the ActionScript for the movie.

To Create A DYNAMIC TEXT BLOCK OR INPUT TEXT BOX

1 Select the Text tool, and then drag onto the Stage to define the size of the Dynamic Text block.

2 Choose Panels from the Window menu, and then choose Text Options to open the Text Options panel.

3 Click the triangle to the right of the Text Type window, and then choose an option, as shown in Figure 14-15:

Select Dynamic Text to create a text box for text that you can update by changing the contents of a variable.

Select Input Text to create a text box that accepts input from a user. You can display user input text in other parts of your movie by assigning the same variable to a Dynamic Text block.

see also For more information on creating text blocks, refer to Chapter 2.

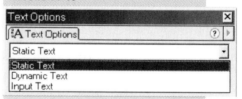

FIGURE 14-15

Adjusting Options for Dynamic Text

After you choose to create a block of Dynamic Text, you can adjust parameters to specify the way that the text appears on the Stage.

To Specify OPTIONS FOR DYNAMIC TEXT

1 Create a block of Dynamic Text as outlined in the preceding steps. After you choose Dynamic Text, the Text Options panel displays Dynamic Text parameters, as shown in Figure 14-16.

2 Choose Panels from the Window menu, and then choose Character to open the Character panel. Choose a font size and color, and then adjust the other text parameters to suit the movie in which the Dynamic Text block is displayed. The parameters that you choose in the Character panel determine how the text will look when it is displayed in the text block.

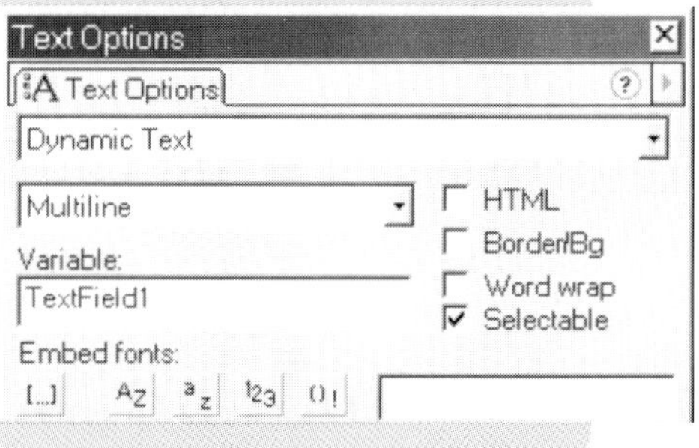

3 In the Text Options panel, click the triangle to the right of the Line Type window, and then choose either Single Line or Multiline. Choose Single Line to display the text as a single line, Multiline to display more than one line of text in the box.

4 If you choose Multiline, the Word Wrap option becomes available. Select it to have the text wrap to a new line when it reaches the end of the text box.

5 The default name for Dynamic Text is Text Field, followed by the next available number. To change the name of the Text field, select the default name, and then enter a name for the text block in the Variable field. You use this name to assign a value to the variable, in this case a block of text that is assigned to the same variable named earlier in the movie.

6 Choose one of the Embed Fonts buttons to embed the font that you selected from the Character panel with the text box. Choose the Include Entire Font Outline button to embed the entire character set. To embed specific characters from the set, enter them in the field to the right of the Embed Fonts buttons.

7 Select HTML to preserve formatting, such as font style, hyperlink, paragraph, and other text parameters, by choosing the appropriate HTML tags in the document in which the Flash movie is embedded.

8 Select Border/BG to display the text box with a border and background.

9 User Selectable is enabled by default. This option allows users to select the text in a Dynamic Text box. If you deselect this option, the text is not selectable.

FIGURE 14-16

Text Options ✕

A Text Options   ? ▶

Dynamic Text   ▼

Multiline   ▼   ☐ HTML
                           ☐ Border/Bg
Variable: ☐ Word wrap
TextField1   ☑ Selectable

Embed fonts:
[...]   Az   ªz   ¹₂₃   0¡

note Always declare the variable before it appears in the movie. It's good practice to declare variables in the first frame of a movie.

Adjusting Options for Input Text

You can also specify parameters for Input Text. The options that you choose will affect how text looks when a user enters it into an Input Text box in your movie.

To Adjust INPUT TEXT PARAMETERS

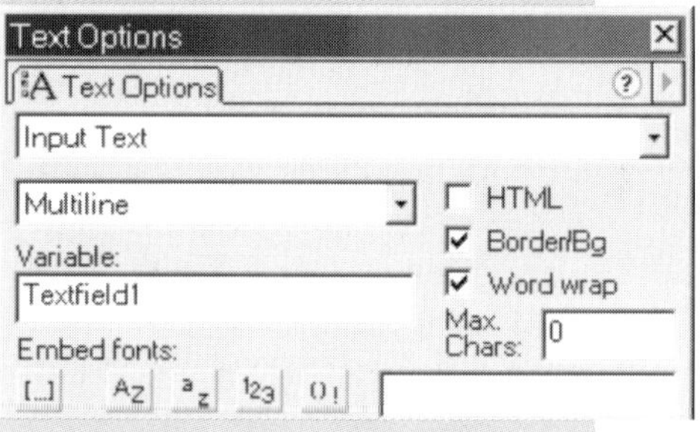

1 Create an Input Text box as outlined previously. After you choose Input Text, the Text Options panel displays Input Text parameters, as shown in Figure 14-17.

2 Choose Panels from the Window menu, and then choose Character to open the Character panel. Choose a font size and color, and then adjust other text parameters. The parameters that you choose in the Character panel determine how the text will look when the user enters it in the text box.

3 In the Text Options panel, click the triangle to the right of the Line Type window, and then choose Single Line, Multiline, or Password. Choose Single Line to display the text as a single line, Multiline to display more than one line of text in the box. If you choose the Password option, text will be displayed as asterisks to protect the user's security when the user enters a password.

4 If you choose Multiline, the Word Wrap option becomes available. Select it to have the text wrap to a new line when it reaches the end of the text box.

5 Enter a name for the text block in the Variable field.

6 Choose one of the Embed Fonts buttons to embed the font that you selected from the Character panel with the text box. Choose the Include Entire Font Outline button to embed the entire character set. To embed specific characters from the set, enter them in the field to the right of the Embed Fonts buttons.

7 In the Maximum Character field, enter a number that represents the maximum number of characters that can be entered in the text block.

FIGURE 14-17

Text Options

- A Text Options ⑦ ▶
- Input Text
- Multiline
- ☐ HTML
- ☑ Border/Bg
- Variable:
- Textfield1
- ☑ Word wrap
- Embed fonts:
- Max. Chars: 0
- [...] Az ªz ¹²₃ 0₁

TIP If the Input Text block is part of a quiz or game that can be played again, assign the variable name for the Input Text box in the frame that the quiz will loop back to when the user restarts the quiz. Assign the variable no value by leaving the Value field blank in the *setVariable* action's Parameters pane. If you neglect to do this, the last value that the user enters will be displayed in the Input Text box when the quiz is reinitialized.

Creating Your First ActionScript

Now that you know the basic components of an ActionScript, it's time to tie everything together and create a working ActionScript. In this case, you create a block of Dynamic Text that is loaded from a text document within the same Web site. A small window displays the text one line at a time. You create a button that scrolls the text forward one line at a time and another that scrolls the text backward one line at a time.

To Create YOUR FIRST ACTIONSCRIPT

1 Create a multi-line document in your word processor. This is the document that will be displayed in the Dynamic Text window. The first line of the document will be text= . Text is the variable. The equal sign is followed by beginning and ending quotation marks. The text that will be displayed in the movie is typed between the quotation marks. Your finished document should resemble Figure 14-18.

2 Save the document as a .txt file, and then name it *text*.

3 Launch Flash, and then create a new document.

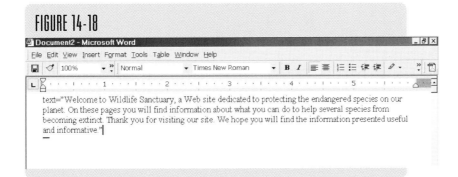

FIGURE 14-18

text="Welcome to Wildlife Sanctuary, a Web site dedicated to protecting the endangered species on our planet. On these pages you will find information about what you can do to help several species from becoming extinct. Thank you for visiting our site. We hope you will find the information presented useful and informative."

4 Select the first frame, and then open the Actions panel by choosing Actions from the Window menu.

5 Click the arrow to the left of the Actions group, and then double-click the *loadVariables* action.

6 In the Parameters pane URL section, enter *text.txt*, the name of the document that you just created.

continues

continued

7 Select the Text tool, and then drag it onto the Stage to create a text block.

8 Choose Panels from the Window menu, and then choose Text Options.

9 Choose Dynamic Text from the Text Type menu.

10 Choose Single Line from the Line Type menu.

11 In the Variable field, enter text. This is the name of the variable in the text block that you created in the word-processing program.

12 Select the Border/BG option. Your Text Options panel should look like Figure 14-19.

13 Close the Text Options panel, choose Panels from the Window menu, and then select Character.

14 Select a font style, size, and color, and then close the panel.

15 Choose Test Movie from the Control menu. If you have more than one line of text displayed in the box, you may need to adjust the size of the text box. In either case, close the Test Movie window to return to movie-editing mode. Now you create the buttons that scroll the text.

16 Create the basic shape for the button with the Rectangle tool. The basic shape should be half as high as the text box.

17 Select the rectangle with the Subselect tool to display the rectangle's points.

note When you are loading variables from a source outside of a Flash movie, make sure that they are in the same directory as the movie and accompanying HTML file. If you do decide to save the variables in a different directory, enter the path in the URL section of the ' Parameters pane so that the Flash Player will know where to locate the file.

FIGURE 14-19

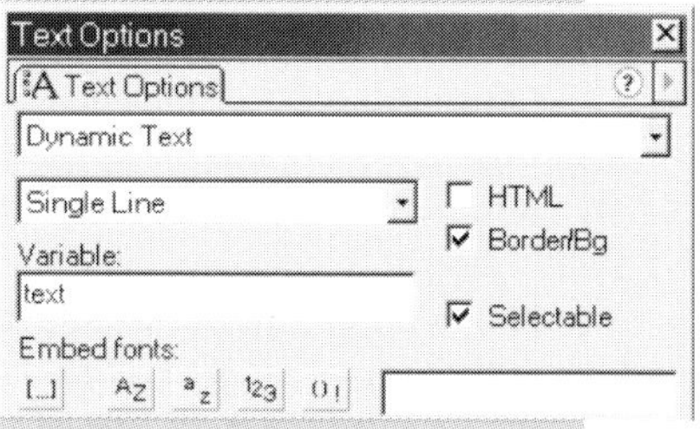

Text Options

A Text Options

Dynamic Text

Single Line | □ HTML
Variable: | ☑ Border/Bg
text
| ☑ Selectable
Embed fonts:
[..] Az ᵃz ¹²₃ 0₁

continues

18 Select the Pen tool, and then click one of the bottom corner points to remove it.

19 To complete the shape, use the Subselect tool to drag the remaining bottom point so that it is centered and below the two points on top of the shape. Your finished button should resemble Figure 14-20. Pleasenote, the button in this figure has beenmagnified.

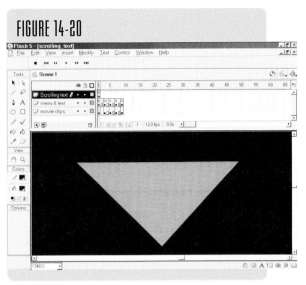

FIGURE 14-20

20 Choose Convert to Symbol from the Insert menu to open the Symbol Properties dialog box. Choose the Button behavior, name the button, and then click OK.

21 To create a duplicate instance of the button symbol, select the symbol, and then while holding down the Alt key (Windows) or the Option key (Macintosh), drag the button above its current position. Release the mouse button, and Flash creates a duplicate instance of the button.

22 Choose Transform from the Modify menu, and then choose Flip Vertical. If necessary, use the Align panel to center the two buttons vertically.

Now comes the fun part: programming the buttons to make the text scroll. To program the buttons, you use the *scroll* function to create two expressions, one that scrolls the text forward one line at a time and another that scrolls the text backward one line at a time.

23 Select the lower button, and then open the Actions panel by choosing Actions from the Window menu.

24 Click the arrow to the left of the Actions label to expand the group, and then double-click *setVariable*. Flash adds the action to the script. Enter *text* in the Variable field of the action's Parameters pane.

25 In the left side of the Actions panel, click the arrow to the left of Functions to expand the group, and then double-click *scroll*. Flash adds the *scroll* function to the variable text.

Adding the *scroll* function to the text variable is what makes the text scroll when the button is clicked. To determine how far a line of text scrolls and in which direction, you need to create an expression.

continued

26 In the Value field, enter this expression: *text.scroll=text.scroll+1*. Select the Expression option by clicking the box to the right of the Value window. This tells Flash that the value you entered is a mathematical expression that will change the variable's value. Shown in Figure 14-21 is the ActionScript for the bottom button.

27 Close the Actions panel, and then select the top button.

28 The script for the top button is identical to that of the bottom button, except for the expression that you enter in the Value field, which is *text.scroll=text.scroll-1*. This expression tells Flash to scroll backward one line when the button is clicked.

29 Choose Test Movie from the Control menu to check the results.

TIP Creating a document to use as a text variable is an excellent way to keep a big block of text updated. Whenever you need to update the text, rather than edit the Flash document, all you need to do is update and reload the text file. The Dynamic Text box automatically accepts the value of the text document because the variable is declared in the first line of the .txt document.

FIGURE 14-21

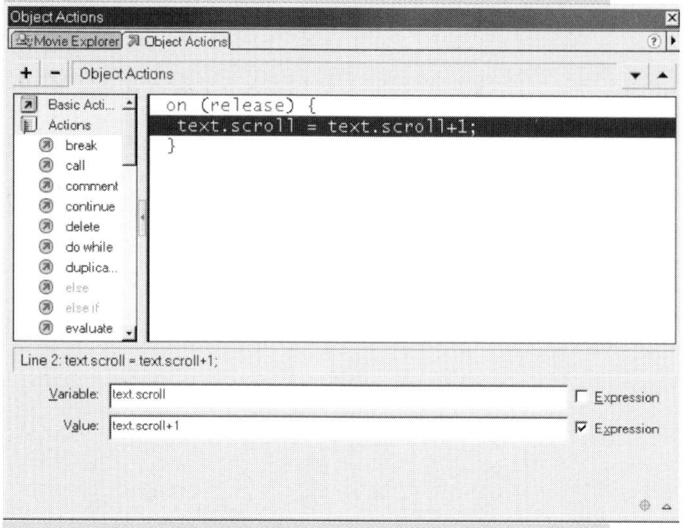

Object Actions

Movie Explorer | Object Actions

+ − | Object Actions

```
Basic Acti...          on (release) {
Actions                    text.scroll = text.scroll+1;
    break              }
    call
    comment
    continue
    delete
    do while
    duplica...
    else
    else if
    evaluate
```

Line 2: text.scroll = text.scroll+1;

Variable: text.scroll   ☐ Expression

Value: text.scroll+1   ☑ Expression

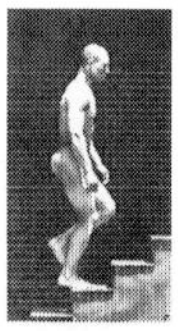

chapter 14: introduction to ActionScript

Publishing Flash Movies

After you meticulously create graphic objects, convert them to symbols, arrange and animate instances of symbols along layers and the Timeline, you then publish the movie as part of a Web site or multi-media presentation. With Flash 5, you have the capability of publishing the movie in one of three ways: in its native .swf format, as a stand-alone movie, or in a format conducive to multi-media presentations. In this chapter, you will learn how to optimize the movie for the smallest possible file size and publish the movie in single or multiple formats.

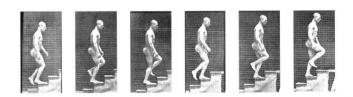

Testing the Movie

Prior to publishing a movie, you need to test it to make sure that it plays properly. Testing a movie provides visual clues to which parts of the movie are not playing properly. You can also test the movie's bandwidth at several popular connection speeds as well as test how the movie streams into the browser.

Using the Test Movie Command

When you invoke the Test Movie command, Flash publishes the movie and previews it with the Flash Player in a separate window. Within the new window are commands that you use to test and debug the movie.

To Test A MOVIE

1 Choose Test Movie from the Control menu.

2 The Exporting Flash Player dialog box appears, the movie is published, and the Flash Player plays it in another window, as shown in Figure 15-1.

After the initial playing of the movie, you can preview it again by clicking the Play button on the Controller or by pressing Enter or Return. You can also use the Controller to rewind the movie to the start or to advance forward or backward a frame at a time. When you are done previewing the movie, close the window to return to movie-editing mode.

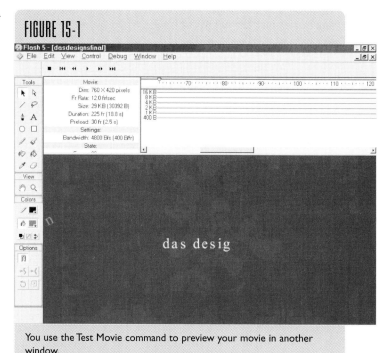

FIGURE 15-1

You use the Test Movie command to preview your movie in another window.

Using the Bandwidth Profiler

You use the Bandwidth Profiler when you want Flash to create a graph that displays your movie frame by frame. The Bandwidth Profiler displays the size of each frame of your movie in kilobytes. The Bandwidth Profiler presents you with visual clues as to which frames in your movie may halt the movie's play while streaming into a viewer's browser.

To Use THE BANDWIDTH PROFILER

1 Choose Test Movie from the Control menu. Flash exports the movie and plays it in another window.

2 After the movie has played, choose Bandwidth Profiler from the View menu. Flash creates a frame-by-frame graph of your movie, displaying each frame's size in kilobytes, as shown in Figure 15-2.

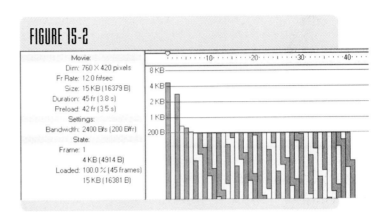

FIGURE 15-2

In Figure 15-2, the window to the left of the graph displays information about your movie. In the Settings section, Flash displays the current bandwidth settings that you selected to test the movie with. In the State section, Flash displays information about each frame as the movie plays. The shape of the graph varies, depending upon whether you choose the Frame By Frame Graph view or the Streaming Graph view.

Using the Frame by Frame Graph View

When you choose to view the Bandwidth Profiler using the Frame by Frame Graph view, Flash displays the size in kilobytes of each frame, as shown in Figure 15-3. Notice the red bandwith line that runs parallel to the base of the graph. If any frames appear above the red line, Flash may halt the movie until the frame is fully loaded. For example, if you have a large movie clip loading on a keyframe, the movie clip's size may exceed the bandwidth of a user's connection. If this occurs, the Bandwidth Profiler displays the movie clip's frame above the red line. When a frame exceeds a connection's bandwidth, Flash halts the movie while the movie clip streams into the user's browser. Not only is this jar-

ring to the viewer, but it can also throw other elements in your movie out of synch, for example a sound loop that has already downloaded, has begun playing, and is scheduled to halt after two loops. The sound loop could potentially finish playing before the movie clip downloads.

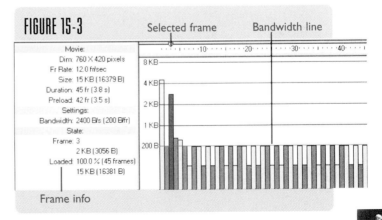

FIGURE 15-3

Selected frame   Bandwidth line

Frame info

261

To Display THE BANDWIDTH PROFILER WITH A FRAME BY FRAME GRAPH VIEW

1 Open the Bandwidth Profiler as outlined in the preceding steps.

2 Choose Frame by Frame Graph from the View menu. Flash displays the Bandwidth Profiler as a Frame by Frame graph, as shown previously in Figure 15-3.

3 To display information about a particular frame, click its bar on the graph. Flash displays the information in the window to the left of the graph.

Using the Streaming Graph View

You use the Streaming Graph to display the frames that will cause delays in downloading. Frames are displayed in alternating colors of light and dark gray. The height of the frame designates its size in kilobytes, which can be found by looking at the legend on the left side of the graph.

To Display THE BANDWIDTH PROFILER IN STREAMING GRAPH VIEW

1 Open the Bandwidth Profiler as outlined previously.

2 Choose Streaming Graph from the View menu. Flash displays the Bandwidth Profiler as a streaming graph, as shown in Figure 15-4. To better understand the differences between the two options, compare this figure with Figure 15-3.

3 To display information about a particular frame, click its bar on the graph. Flash displays the information in the window to the left of the graph.

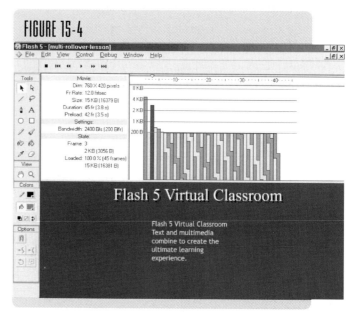

FIGURE 15-4

Changing Download Settings

When you use the Bandwidth Profiler, you can change download speeds to get an accurate reflection of the potential wait time your viewing audience will experience while your movie downloads. If the majority of your viewing audience accesses the Internet with a slower connection, the Bandwidth Profiler lets you know if you need to create a preload loop that the viewer watches while the movie downloads.

To Change DOWNLOAD SETTINGS

1 Display the Bandwidth Profiler as outlined previously.

2 Select the Steaming Graph or Frame by Frame view as outlined in the preceding steps.

3 Choose Debug and then choose a setting from the menu shown in Figure 15-5.

FIGURE 15-5

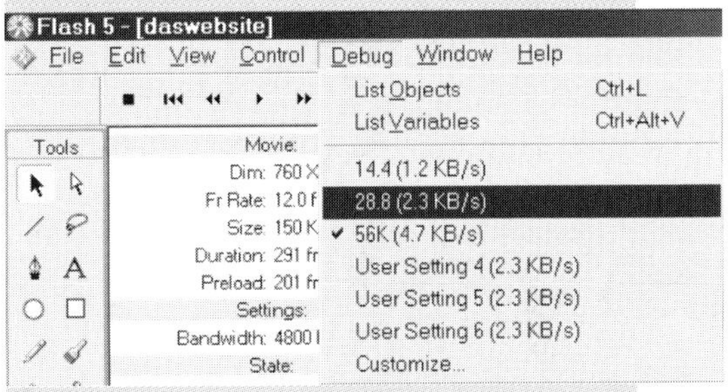

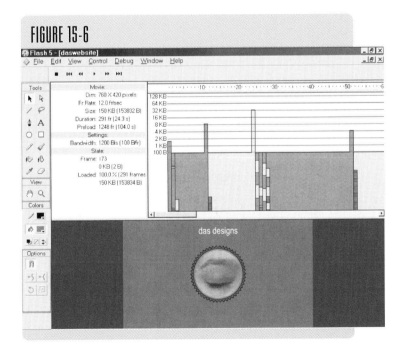

Flash displays the Bandwidth Profiler with the chosen setting. Figure 15-6 shows a Frame by Frame graph with a download setting of 14.4 kbps.

FIGURE 15-6

Using the Show Streaming Command

When you invoke the Show Streaming command, Flash displays a green bar in the Time-line on the top of the Bandwidth Profiler. The bar moves, giving you a representation in real time of how the movie will stream into a user's browser. The speed of the bar changes depending upon the download setting that you choose from the Debug menu. When you preview a movie with the Show Streaming command, pay attention to where the frame indicator is in reference to the green bar. If the frame indicator catches up with the green bar and stops, when the movie is published and uploaded to the Internet, the Flash Player halts the movie and waits for more frames to download before playing again.

To Simulate STREAMING WITH THE BANDWIDTH PROFILER

1 Open the Bandwidth Profiler as outlined previously.

2 Choose Debug, and then choose a download speed.

3 Choose Show Streaming from the View menu. Flash displays a moving green bar in the Profiler's Timeline indicating the movie's download progress, as shown in Figure 15-7.

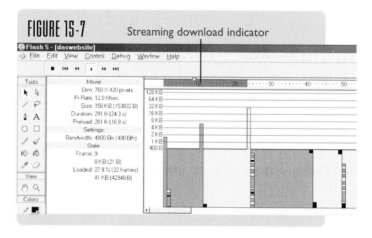

FIGURE 15-7 Streaming download indicator

Using the Movie Explorer

You use the Movie Explorer, as shown in Figure 15-8, to view all of the components of your movie as a visual outline. You can choose which components of your movie are displayed in the Movie Explorer. You can also use the Explorer to navigate within your movie.

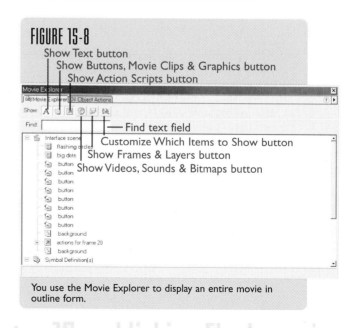

FIGURE 15-8
Show Text button
Show Buttons, Movie Clips & Graphics button
Show Action Scripts button

Find text field
Customize Which Items to Show button
Show Frames & Layers button
Show Videos, Sounds & Bitmaps button

You use the Movie Explorer to display an entire movie in outline form.

To Access THE MOVIE EXPLORER

 Choose Movie Explorer from the Window menu. Alternately, click the Movie Explorer button on the Launcher bar.

In its default mode, the Movie Explorer displays text objects, buttons, movie clips, graphics, and ActionScripts. To display or hide particular objects in your movie, click one of the buttons shown previously in Figure 15-8.

To Customize WHICH ITEMS THE MOVIE EXPLORER DISPLAYS

1 Click the Customize Which Items to Show button to display the Movie Explorer Setting dialog box, shown in Figure 15-9.

2 Select the items that you want the Movie Explorer to display.

3 Click OK to apply the settings.

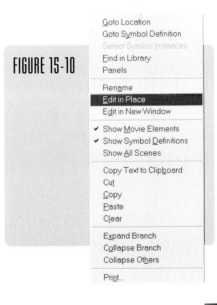

FIGURE 15-9

To Find AN ITEM USING THE MOVIE EXPLORER

 Type a name in the Find text field. The Movie Explorer displays all instances of the item used in the movie.

Once you select an object in the Movie Explorer, you can perform a number of functions on it by selecting a command from the Movie Explorer's Options menu.

To Access THE OPTIONS MENU

 **Click the triangle at the top right corner of the Movie Explorer window, to open the Options menu shown in Figure 15-10.**

You can use the Options menu in several ways: to navigate to a symbol instance's or a frame's location; to rename a selected object; to edit a selected object; to cut, copy, or paste a selected object; or to expand or collapse a branch in the Movie Explorer. You can also expand a branch by clicking the + icon to the left of a branch or collapse it by clicking a - icon to the left of a branch in the Movie Explorer window.

FIGURE 15-10

Optimizing Your Flash Movies

The file size of your Flash movie is important, especially if you are publishing it for use on the Internet. When you create a movie for a Web page, your goal is to create the smallest file size possible. Here are a few ways to optimize your movies:

Convert any graphic that you are using more than once into a graphic symbol.

Convert any animation that you are using more than once into a movie clip symbol.

Nest a symbol within a symbol when you already have a symbol that resembles an object needed for a new symbol. Remember that you can always resize an instance of a symbol or apply an effect to it to change the way that it looks.

Use tweened animations instead of frame-by-frame animations whenever possible. Frame-by-frame animations are always larger than their tweened counterparts.

When possible, export all sounds in the MP3 format.

Avoid extensive use of bitmap images, especially when creating animations.

Before publishing the movie, open the document Library, click the triangle in the upper-right corner of the window, and then choose the Select Unused Items command from the menu. Delete the unused items so that Flash does not publish them with the movie.

Minimize the number of fonts that you use in your movie.

Minimize the use of special strokes, such as dotted or dashed lines. Solid lines use the least amount of memory.

Minimize the use of gradients. They're lovely to look at but create larger files.

Minimize the use of Alpha transparency. It can slow down the playback of your movies.

Publishing Your Flash Movie

After you meticulously craft objects for a movie, animate the objects, assign actions to the objects and frames, you publish the movie. Flash's default publishing mode is its native .swf format, which Flash can simultaneously embed in an HTML document for use on the Internet. You can also choose to have Flash publish the movie in one of its other formats for use in a Web page, as part of a multimedia production, or as a stand-alone executable movie.

Adjusting Publishing Settings

If you accept the default publishing settings, Flash publishes the movie as a.swf file and embeds the movie in an HTML document. You can modify the default settings for the Flash format and HTML format. You can also simultaneously publish the movie in other formats for which you can specify the settings.

To Adjust PUBLISHING SETTINGS

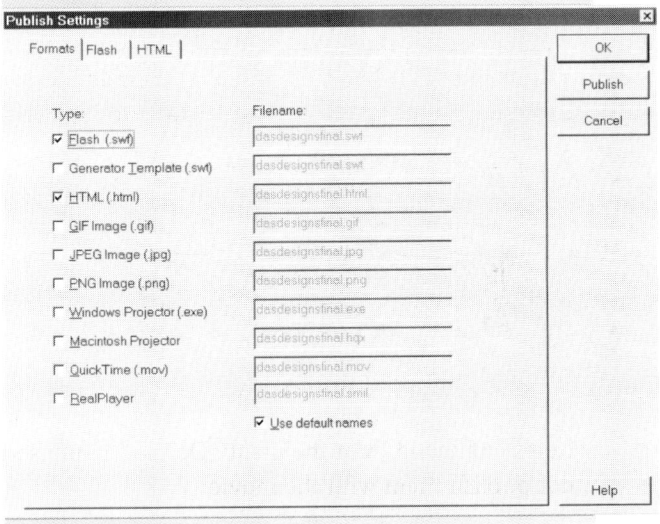

1 Choose Publish Settings from the File menu. Flash displays the Publish Settings dialog box, shown in Figure 15-11.

2 From the Formats tab, select one or more of the following:

Flash: Choose this option to have Flash publish the movie in its native .swf format.

Generator template: Choose this option to have Flash publish the movie as a Generator template.

HTML: Choose this option to have Flash embed the .swf file within an HTML document.

GIF image: Choose this format to have Flash publish the movie as an animated **GIF** file. If you choose this format, note that Flash interactivity and sounds are not supported when you publish the movie in the **GIF** format. The **GIF** format is also limited to 8 bit (256) colors, which may not be suitable if your movie has bitmap images in it.

JPEG image: Choose this format to have Flash publish a single frame of your movie as a compressed 24-bit bitmap image. This format is useful for creating a single frame of a movie as a proof for a client. Flash creates an image of the frame on which the playhead is stopped when you invoke the Publish command.

PNG image: Choose this format to have Flash publish a single frame of your movie. The **PNG** format is cross-platform and supports transparency.

FIGURE 15-11

Publish Settings

Formats | Flash | HTML |

OK
Publish
Cancel

Type:
☑ Flash (.swf)
☐ Generator Template (.swf)
☑ HTML (.html)
☐ GIF Image (.gif)
☐ JPEG Image (.jpg)
☐ PNG Image (.png)
☐ Windows Projector (.exe)
☐ Macintosh Projector
☐ QuickTime (.mov)
☐ RealPlayer

Filename:
dasdesignsfinal.swf
dasdesignsfinal.swf
dasdesignsfinal.html
dasdesignsfinal.gif
dasdesignsfinal.jpg
dasdesignsfinal.png
dasdesignsfinal.exe
dasdesignsfinal.hqx
dasdesignsfinal.mov
dasdesignsfinal.smil

☑ Use default names

Help

continues

267

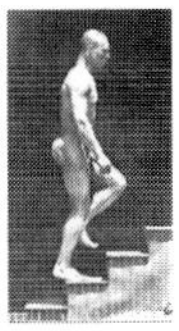

continued

Windows Projector: When you choose this format, Flash publishes the movie with a stand-alone projector that can be viewed with a Windows operating system. The movie can be viewed by executing the file. This format supports all features of Flash. You can use this format to use a Flash movie as part of a multimedia production. Flash movies published as projector files also make great animated greeting cards.

Macintosh Projector: Choose this format to have Flash publish the movie with a stand-alone projector that can be viewed with a Macintosh operating system.

QuickTime: Choose this setting to have Flash publish the movie in the popular QuickTime format that can be viewed on Apple's QuickTime player. Movies published in this format retain most of their interactivity and other advanced features.

RealPlayer: Choose this format to have Flash publish three files: a .swf file, an .rm file for Real Audio, and an. smil file. The. smil file links the Flash .swf file and the Real Audio file, playing them in the RealPlayer. If you publish a Flash movie without streaming sound, Flash creates only the. smil and .swf files. To publish a movie in RealPlayer format, you must publish the Flash movie in Flash 4 or earlier format.

3 After you select the formats that you want Flash to publish the movie in, a tab appears for each chosen format, as shown in Figure 15-12.

4 Adjust the publishing settings for a chosen format by clicking its tab and adjusting the format's available parameters.

5 To assign a unique name to your movie, deselect the Use Default Name option. When this option is unchecked, a Filename field opens to the right of each format's name. Enter a name in the Filename field, and Flash publishes the movie using the input filename and the format's extension.

FIGURE 15-12

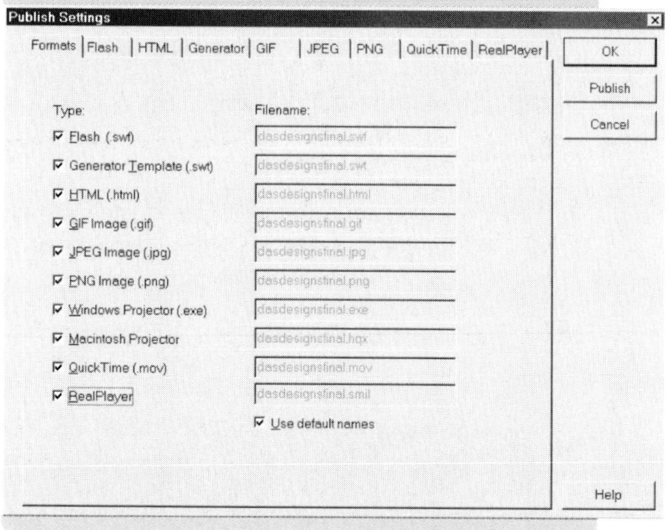

Publish Settings

Formats | Flash | HTML | Generator | GIF | JPEG | PNG | QuickTime | RealPlayer |

OK
Publish
Cancel

Type:

☑ Flash (.swf)
☑ Generator Template (.swt)
☑ HTML (.html)
☑ GIF Image (.gif)
☑ JPEG Image (.jpg)
☑ PNG Image (.png)
☑ Windows Projector (.exe)
☑ Macintosh Projector
☑ QuickTime (.mov)
☑ RealPlayer

Filename:

dasdesignsfinal.swf
dasdesignsfinal.swt
dasdesignsfinal.html
dasdesignsfinal.gif
dasdesignsfinal.jpg
dasdesignsfinal.png
dasdesignsfinal.exe
dasdesignsfinal.hqx
dasdesignsfinal.mov
dasdesignsfinal.smil

☑ Use default names

Help

Adjusting Format Settings

Each format has different settings that you can apply to modify the movie that Flash publishes. In the following sections, you will learn to modify the settings for publishing the movie in native Flash format, in Flash format embedded in an HTML document, in Windows projector format, and in Macintosh projector format. The HTML format was chosen because most Flash productions end up on the Internet. The remaining formats were chosen because they are the most popular and retain all of Flash's interactivity. You are urged to experiment with publishing your movies in the other formats if you have a need for them in your work.

Adjusting HTML Settings

The majority of Flash movies find their way to the Internet. To have Flash embed the published movie in an HTML document for use on the Internet, you need to choose the HTML format. When you choose the Publish Settings command, Flash automatically chooses the Flash and HTML formats by default.

To Embed A FLASH MOVIE IN AN HTML DOCUMENT

1 Choose Publish Settings from the File menu to open the Publish Settings dialog box. Flash chooses the Flash and HTML formats by default.

2 Click the HTML tab to open the HTML Settings section, shown in Figure 15-13.

FIGURE 15-13

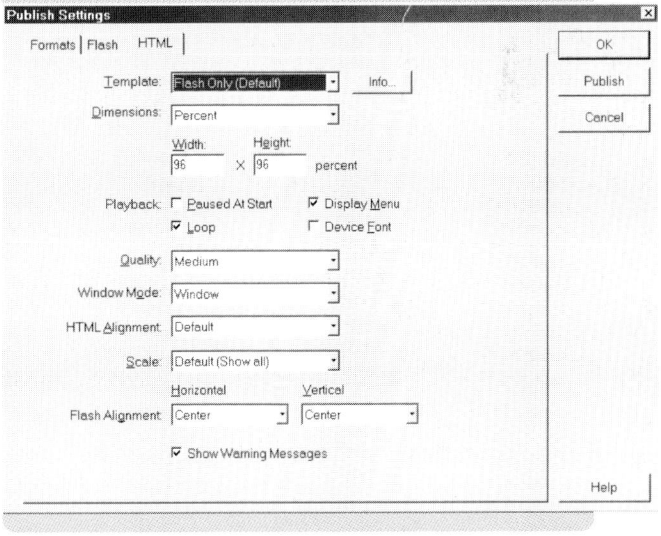

Publish Settings

Formats | Flash | HTML

Template: Flash Only (Default) Info...

Dimensions: Percent

Width: 96   Height: 96   percent

Playback: ☐ Paused At Start   ☑ Display Menu
☑ Loop   ☐ Device Font

Quality: Medium

Window Mode: Window

HTML Alignment: Default

Scale: Default (Show all)

Horizontal   Vertical
Flash Alignment: Center   Center

☑ Show Warning Messages

OK
Publish
Cancel

Help

continues

269

continued

3 In the Template section, accept the default setting to publish a Flash movie. Alternately, click the triangle to the right of the window, and then choose one of the templates from the drop-down menu shown in Figure 15-14. The templates on the menu are in the Flash 5/HTML folder on your hard drive. The templates other than default contain more advanced features, such as browser detection. Select a template from the menu, and then click the Info button to have Flash display a description of what the template does.

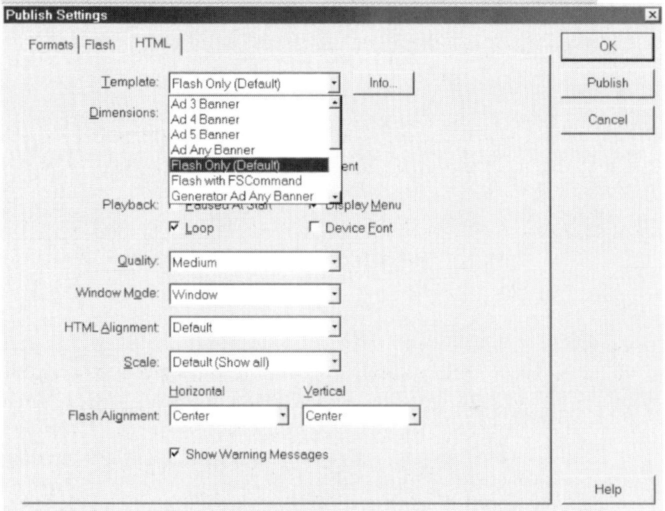

4 In the Dimensions section, accept the default Match Movie option. To publish the movie at a different size than you specified with the Modify Movie command, click the triangle to the right of the window, and then choose from the following:

Pixels: You choose this option when you want to specify the exact size of the movie as it will appear in the user's browser.

Percent: You choose this option when you want to specify what percentage of a user's browser the movie will fill.

5 If you opted to change the movie size, enter a value for Width and Height in the Dimensions section.

Warning If you increase the size of a Flash movie containing bitmap images, the images will be distorted because bitmap images are resolution dependent and therefore will not display properly when the Flash Player resizes the movie.

continues

FIGURE 15-14

TIP If you've chosen the Match Movie option and set the size for 100 percent of a targeted browser desktop size, use the settings referenced in the table to match a Flash movie size with desktop size. If you don't choose to match a specific browser and want your movie to fill as much of the user's browser as possible without a scroll bar appearing, choose the Percent option in the Dimensions section, and then enter a value of 96 for both Width and Height.

Match Movie Settings

TARGETED DESKTOP SIZE	FLASH MOVIE SIZE
640 x 480	600 x 300
800 x 600	760 x 420
1024 x 768	955 x 600

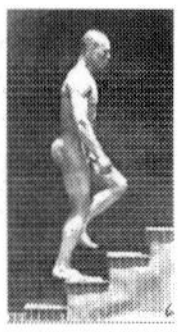

continued

6 In the Playback section, choose one or more of the following options:

Paused at Start: Choose this option if you want the movie to start playing after the viewer clicks a button in the movie or selects Play from the Flash 5 shortcut menu.

Select Display Menu to have the Flash Player display a shortcut menu when the user right-clicks (Windows) or Control-clicks (Macintosh).

Select Display Device Fonts (Windows only) to substitute an aliased system font for fonts not installed on the user's system. This option affects only Static text.

7 In the Quality section, click the triangle to the right of the window, and then choose an option from the menu. This setting determines how much antialiasing is applied to each frame. The default setting of High gives you the best image quality. If your movie is going to be accessed by users with slow connections to the Internet, choose a lower setting. When you choose a lower setting, image quality suffers, but download times are quicker.

8 In the Window Mode section, you choose settings that affect the Windows version of Internet Explorer 4.0 with the Flash Active X Control. Click the triangle to the right of the window, and then choose one of the following:

Opaque Windowless: This option prevents other elements behind an embedded Flash movie on a static HTML page from showing through.

Transparent Windowless: This option shows the background of the HTML page through transparent areas of your Flash movie. This option may slow down your animations.

9 In the HTML alignment section, there are several menu options for aligning your Flash movie within a browser. Unfortunately, these options aren't working properly in this version of Flash. Top left is the browser's default alignment, and Flash's HTML alignment does not overwrite this. To align your movie within a browser, use an HTML editor.

10 In the Scale section, click the triangle to the right of the window, and then choose one of the following from the menu:

Default: Choose this option and when the movie is published, the Flash Player displays the movie in the specified area while maintaining the movie's aspect ratio. When you choose this option, a border may appear on each side of the window.

No Borders: Choose this option and the Flash Player will display the movie with no borders, maintaining the aspect ratio and cropping if necessary.

Exact Fit: Choose this option and the Flash Player will display the movie in the specified area. The movie's aspect ratio will be changed if necessary to accommodate the window, resulting in distortion of the graphics in your movie.

continues

continued

11 In the Flash Alignment section, click the triangle to the right of the Vertical and Horizontal windows, and then choose an option from the menu. This setting determines where the Flash Player places the movie within the movie window.

12 Select the Show Warning Messages option and Flash displays a warning message if tag settings conflict.

13 Click OK to save the settings.

Adjusting Flash Settings

When you choose to publish your movie in Flash format, you can specify how Flash publishes the movie. You can specify the load order of layers within a frame and your movie's password to prevent prying eyes opening the downloaded production in Flash.

To Adjust FLASH SETTINGS

1 Choose Publish Settings from the File menu. The Publish Settings dialog box appears, and then Flash displays the Formats, Flash, and HTML tabs by default.

2 Click the Flash tab. The Flash Settings tab opens, as shown in Figure 15-15.

3 In the Load Order section, click the triangle to the right of the window, and then choose either Bottom Up or Top Down. This setting determines how the Flash Player loads a frame's layers into a browser when a user is accessing the movie through the Internet.

4 In the Options section, select any or all of the following:

> Generate Size Report: Choose this option and Flash generates a report (in .txt format) listing the items used in the movie as well as the size in bytes of each frame.

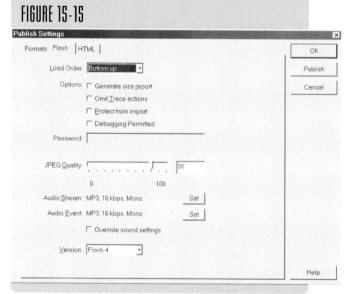

FIGURE 15-15

TiP If you have multiple layers in your movie and your viewing audience is accessing the Internet with slow connection speeds, choose the Load Order option that displays the most important content of a frame first. Alternately, create a preloader that plays while enough frames download so that the movie plays without interruption.

continues

continued

Omit Trace Actions: Choose this option and Flash ignores the Trace action in a movie, which prevents comments from being displayed in the Output window.

Protect From Import: Choose this option to prevent viewers from importing your published Flash movie into the Flash program and converting it to a movie. When you choose this option, the Password window is activated. If you choose to enter a password and the published movie is imported into Flash, the Password dialog box appears. The movie will be successfully imported if the proper password is entered. If the wrong password is entered, Flash accepts three incorrect passwords before a dialog box appears, saying that the author has protected the file and it cannot be imported. If the password option is not selected, Flash displays the warning anytime someone attempts to import the published movie into Flash.

Debugging Permitted: Choose this option and Flash actives the Debugger when the movie is played, allowing you to debug a Flash movie from within a Web browser. This option also activates the Password window.

5 If you choose the Protect From Import or Debugging Permitted option, you can enter a password in the text field. If this option is selected, you and others must enter the correct password to successfully import or debug the published movie.

6 In the JPEG area, drag the slider to determine how bitmaps in your movie are displayed when the movie is played back in a user's browser. When you choose lower settings, Flash applies more compression to the bitmaps. This results in smaller file sizes with a loss of image quality. Choose higher settings and Flash applies less compression. Your bitmap images will look better, but the file size of the published movie will be larger.

7 To adjust output settings for streaming sounds in your movie, click the Set button to the right of the Audio Stream setting, and the Sound Settings dialog box appears. Select the desired settings for export, and then click OK.

8 To adjust the output settings for event sounds in your movie, click the Set button to the right of the Audio Event section to open the Sound Settings dialog box. Select the desired output settings, and then click OK.

see aLso For more information on Flash's sound formats and adjusting sound settings, refer to Chapter 13.

9 Select the Override Sound Settings option and Flash overrides settings applied to individual sounds using the Sound Properties dialog box and produces a movie with higher fidelity sound for local use (the Windows Projector and Macintosh Projector) and lower fidelity for the Web.

10 In the Flash section, click the triangle to the right of the window, and then choose which version of Flash you want the movie to be published in. Note that not all of the actions and interactivity in Flash 5 are supported in earlier versions of Flash.

11 Click OK to save the settings.

273

Publishing Movies in Projector Formats

When you choose to publish a movie in Windows Projector or Macintosh Projector format, Flash creates a stand-alone executable file that can be played in the user's computer. When you choose the Windows Projector format, Flash publishes the movie with the Flash Player for playback in a computer with a Windows operating system. If you choose the Macintosh Projector format, Flash publishes the movie with the Flash Player, and the movie can be played back in a computer with the Macintosh operating system.

To Publish YOUR FLASH MOVIE AS A STAND-ALONE EXECUTABLE FILE

1 Choose Publish Settings from the File menu to open the Publish Settings dialog box.

2 To publish the movie in Windows Projector format, choose Windows Projector. The Windows Projector format has no adjustable parameters. Flash publishes the movie according to the settings that you specified when you opened the Flash tab in the Publish Settings dialog box.

3 To publish the movie in Macintosh Projector format, choose Macintosh Projector. The Macintosh Projector format has no adjustable parameters. Flash publishes the movie with the settings that you specified when you opened the Flash tab in the Publish Settings dialog box.

4 Click OK to save the settings.

Previewing the Publication

In earlier chapters, you learned to use the Test Movie command to preview the movie with the Flash Player. After adjusting your publishing settings, you can preview the movie in each of the chosen formats. When you choose to preview a publication, Flash publishes it and creates a preview in the applicable format within your operating system's default Web browser.

To Preview YOUR MOVIE IN ALL CHOSEN PUBLICATION FORMATS

1 Choose Publish Preview from the File menu. Flash displays a submenu, as shown in Figure 15-16. Selected formats will be active; others will be grayed out.

2 Select one of the formats from the submenu to preview the movie. Flash publishes the document in the selected format and opens it in the default Web browser.

FIGURE 15-16

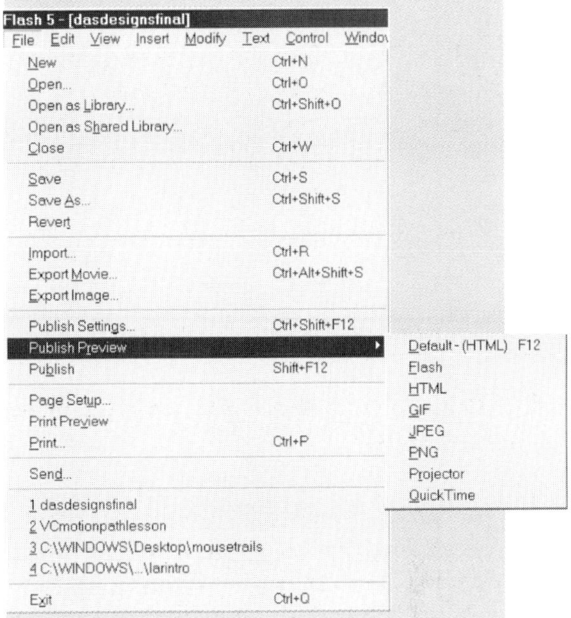

Flash 5 - [dasdesignsfinal]		
File Edit View Insert Modify Text Control Window		

New	Ctrl+N
Open...	Ctrl+O
Open as Library...	Ctrl+Shift+O
Open as Shared Library...	
Close	Ctrl+W
Save	Ctrl+S
Save As...	Ctrl+Shift+S
Revert	
Import...	Ctrl+R
Export Movie...	Ctrl+Alt+Shift+S
Export Image...	
Publish Settings...	Ctrl+Shift+F12
Publish Preview	▶
Publish	Shift+F12
Page Setup...	
Print Preview	
Print...	Ctrl+P
Send...	
1 dasdesignsfinal	
2 VCmotionpathlesson	
3 C:\WINDOWS\Desktop\mousetrails	
4 C:\WINDOWS\...\larintro	
Exit	Ctrl+Q

Publish Preview submenu:
- Default - (HTML) F12
- Flash
- HTML
- GIF
- JPEG
- PNG
- Projector
- QuickTime

Publishing the Movie

If you preview the movie in the selected formats and all is to your liking, you use the Publish command to have Flash publish the movie. When Flash publishes the movie, separate files are created for all selected formats.

To Publish YOUR FLASH MOVIE

 Choose Publish from the File menu. Alternately, click the Publish button after adjusting the publish settings for the movie with the Publish Settings command.

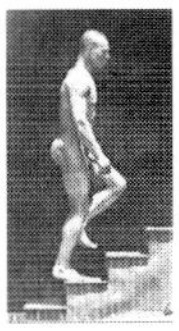

INDEX

d

index

f

9

m

P

index

293